C000179898

LEADERS

PROFILES IN
COURAGE AND
BRAVERY IN
WAR AND PEACE
1917–2020

LEADERS

Profiles in Courage and Bravery in War and Peace 1917–2020

Robin Knight

*This book is dedicated to
my parents who sent me to
The Nautical College, Pangbourne.*

Uniform
an imprint of Unicorn Publishing Group
5 Newburgh Street, London
WIF 7RG
www.unicornpublishing.org

All rights reserved. No part of this publication may be reproduced,
stored in or introduced into a retrieval system, or transmitted, in
any form or by any means (electronic, mechanical, photocopying,
recording or otherwise), without the prior written permission of the
copyright holder and the above publisher of this book.

Every effort has been made to trace copyright holders and to obtain
their permission for the use of copyrighted material. The publisher
apologises for any errors or omissions and would be grateful to be
notified of any corrections that should be incorporated in future
reprints or editions of this book.

© Copyright 2021 by Robin Knight

This edition first published by Uniform, 2021

All images from authors' collection unless otherwise credited.

Contemporary photographs: Birger Stichelbaut.

A catalogue record for this book is available from the British Library.

ISBN 978–1–913491–62-8

Designed by Matthew Wilson
Print Production managed by Jellyfish Solutions

CONTENTS

FOREWORD

*F*ortiter ac Fideliter, or 'bravely and faithfully,' is a superb motto, and in the lives of Old Pangbournians recorded here, Robin Knight compellingly and inspiringly explores how this motto has been translated into action by generations of OPs.

Regarding bravery, as examples in this book show, this takes many forms. There is bravery of the berserker kind, when the red mist of anger drives an individual to leave their own place of safety to charge the enemy or to save another life. There is bravery when a person, knowing the dangers, repeatedly runs the same risks, like a bomber pilot flying recurring sorties over enemy territory at night, or a sailor on Atlantic convoys in World War 2 when to the ever-present danger of the violence of the enemy may be added the dangers of the sea.

There is another bravery – the bravery of the unit, the aircrew or the ship's company when through teamwork and leadership it achieves some difficult or daring task, though perhaps only the actual leader may be recognised with an award. Some individuals evidently are able to make bravery a life style, while for others being brave is a matter of opportunity, often unwanted and uninvited, when, to paraphrase Shakespeare, bravery is thrust upon them and they reacted instinctively well. There are numerous examples of all these different kinds of bravery in the pages which follow.

What is truly remarkable is that a single school, The Nautical College, Pangbourne (as it was then), founded a little over a century ago for one purpose, to prepare boys to become officers in the Merchant Navy, should have produced so many exceptional people in so many walks of life. They include – at least – the winners of two George Crosses, two George Medals, thirty one Distinguished Service Orders, ninety-one Distinguished Service Crosses, seventeen Military Crosses, and eighteen Distinguished Flying Crosses, not to mention many lesser awards and uncounted Mentions in Despatches. More astonishing still is that for most of its history the College's roll has been only a little over a couple of hundred pupils. Clearly, the early leaders of Pangbourne established a distinct and enduring ethos.

Many of the first cadets in the 1920s and 1930s reached positions in the Second World War where they could show the qualities with which they had been imbued at Pangbourne. However, as Robin Knight shows the reader, this was not some accident of timing or the incident of war. In the post-war years, OPs have continued to be true to their motto and to show the same qualities, *Fortiter ac Fideliter*, in the police and in sports and in day-to-day life as well as in later wars.

From the beginning, the College's inspiration, the far-sighted Sir Philip Devitt, wanted the cadets to have a well-rounded education. But he could not have known how strongly or how well *Fortiter ac Fideliter* would become embodied in the soul of the College. Pangbourne College remains a place where the individual matters and where the Headmaster can boast that first and foremost, Pangbourne is a 'people place,' committed to the personal development of its pupils.

The boys and girls of today's Pangbourne will do well to look to their predecessors' record and to follow their example.

Captain Peter Hore RN

I

WHAT IS COURAGE?

Defining courage has puzzled humanity throughout history. All too easily one person's courage is, to others, a matter of routine or "doing one's duty." Circumstances vary so greatly. So do perspectives. In Western society we might coalesce around a definition that relates to an individual's achievements and character. In societies deriving their values from Confucian ethics, the meaning is more likely to include putting other's interests before one's own in difficult circumstances.

Few, if any, of the people featured in this book would have considered themselves heroic. Such individuals rarely do. Many of them flourished in wartime but most were not belligerent or aggressive by nature. Some seem to have attracted trouble wherever they were; equally fearless men went through the entire six years of the 1939–45 conflict far from the action. Luck always plays a huge part in demonstrating courage. So does free will and obligation. Awards are a hit-and-miss way of separating the wheat from the chaff, being subjective and often dependent on marginal calls made by people far from the battlefront. One OP featured in this book received a DSC for, he alleged, saving the money on board an aircraft carrier when it sank, while another was Mentioned in Despatches for, he wrote, "superintending the installation of bomb-proof latrines in Normandy 50 miles behind the advancing British front line."

Yet courage is recognised universally. The root of the word 'courage' is *cor* – a Latin term for heart. There is moral courage of the sort displayed by someone who speaks their mind regardless of the consequences or, on another level, by a submarine commander who has the inner strength to order his vessel to be scuttled rather than be captured by the enemy. There is 'cold courage' – knowing the dangers, but repeatedly confronting them over a prolonged period. Typically, this is epitomised in a letter received at the Nautical College during World War 2: "I have spent most of the war in destroyers and cruisers. My last ship 'bought it' off the Italian coast in January and as a result I got myself a bit bent and am now minus my left leg. Luckily, however, I lost it below the knee and with any luck I'm hoping to be back at sea in the New Year." He was. This remarkable individual, David Ramsay (26–28), lost his leg when hit by an aerial torpedo in 1943. He remained in the Royal Navy until 1957, played squash and always was a hard man to beat.

Courage tends, too, to entail some sort of cause, and here the definitional boundaries begin to blur. A sense of duty or a well-defined patriotism are not, in themselves, sufficient. In war, the belief that one is fighting for a just cause may be the difference between courage and bravery; many British and French, German and American men and women were brave in various ways in World War 1 without any clear understanding for what they were fighting. Matters seemed more black-and-white in World War 2 when the enemies were fascism and German and Japanese territorial ambitions. Only retrospectively did the justifications extend to take in genocide as the scale of Nazi atrocities against Jews and Japanese against Allied prisoners-of-war and subjugated peoples became known. More nuanced confrontation, such as the global ideological struggle epitomised by the Cold War, or the British-Argentinian conflict over the Falkland Islands, rarely unite in the same way while still throwing up many examples of courage and bravery.

Fear is involved too. "Fear is a reaction. Courage is a decision," remarked Winston Churchill. On another occasion he claimed: "Courage is the first of human qualities because it is the quality that guarantees all others." Courage, in this sense, can be defined as weighing up a situation and deciding to act – in other words, it is a mindful, premeditated action. Given this, realising that risking one's own life to save another is hopeless, and failing to act, may be as morally brave as acting pointlessly and losing one's life. Yet, as a rule, bravery lacks the element of fear because it is spontaneous – acting before thinking. There is impulsive bravery of the sort recorded elsewhere in this book by an 84-year-old man diving in to the sea to save a drowning teenager – an instant decision to engage with a real threat that days later led to the man's heart attack and death. Or the decision by the first on the scene to pull a man from a burning car. Or the off-the-cuff choice of a youth to dive into a harbour to save a floundering swimmer or to edge along a cliff to rescue a friend in peril. "Every brave person is brave in his own way" concluded Vasily Grossman, the Russian war correspondent and novelist who witnessed more bravery than most on the Eastern Front in the Soviet Union's "Great Patriotic War," paraphrasing Tolstoy in *Anna Karenina*.

"Courage and bravery – just another pair of English words that can be found side by side in a Thesaurus entry," goes one rather blunt characterisation. "To most, these two words are mere synonyms that express fearlessness, dauntlessness, intrepidity, boldness; the quality of mind or spirit that enables a person to face difficulty and danger." Yet to those perhaps more intellectually inclined, courage and bravery are notably different words. Bravery, goes one explanation, "is the ability to confront pain, danger, or attempts at intimidation without any feeling of fear." In contrast, courage "is the result of a deep understanding of the matter; a courageous person understands what they are getting themselves into and who or what they are doing it for." Submariners, to give an example, went out on war patrols month after month in World War 2 knowing that the odds of survival were worsening each time they left port. Extraordinary courage and endurance and determination were needed to achieve success.

Definitions of courage and bravery can vary hugely depending on culture and time and place. The very meaning of the word 'hero' has changed down the centuries. In Greek times, the word *heros* meant 'protector' or 'defender.' Today, footballers are called 'heroes' and 'anti-heroes' have as much literary or entertainment cachet as 'heroes.' David Twiston Davies, who wrote obituaries for *The Daily Telegraph* for many years and compiled three books of military obituaries, reflected on this ambivalence in an essay he wrote in 2003: "Exactly what motivates soldiers to risk their lives is a mystery that only deepens if probed. The lure of adventure, the thrill of danger, the thirst for success play a part. There is also the camaraderie of military life and that feeling of loyalty which still draws the Queen's men from the farthest ends of the earth." Or to put it another way, as a species, human beings always walk a fine line between the heroic and foolhardy.

In reality, heroism applies equally to acts of courage and bravery. Comparisons are odious – yet it should be admitted that heroism is easier to recognise than either courage or bravery. Writing and researching a book like this, drives home that point. The men who repeatedly took part in the ordeal of the Arctic convoys in the Second World War – "the worst journey in the world" according to Winston Churchill – seem indescribably heroic to a modern generation. Then, the toughest enemy was the life-threatening weather and the huge, freezing seas. During the ten days the journeys took British and American sailors to and from Russia in winter, ships might accumulate 150 tons of ice. Eyelids froze over, anyone who fell overboard died of exposure within minutes. Conditions on board were never less than brutal – and all this is without mentioning the ever-present threat of attack from enemy submarines and aircraft. Not surprisingly, the so-called three

'Ts' – tiredness, tension and terror – took a huge toll. Equally, the actions of the exhausted Army officer who realised he could no longer move through the jungle, ordered his company to go on without him and accepted a lonely fate can only be described as heroic. So, too, the will-power of men who repeatedly piloted outnumbered or outgunned aircraft into aerial battle knowing full well how slim their chances of survival were. "Never give up; never despair – that was the message of VE-Day," Queen Elizabeth II remarked in 2020.

There is another form of courage that should be respected – one that involves confronting and overcoming inner fears, or, as has been said, sometimes, simply putting one foot in front of another. Charlie Mackesy, the author/illustrator, has the boy asking the horse in his best-selling book *The Boy, the Mole, the Fox and the Horse*: 'What's the bravest thing you've ever said?' 'Help' replies the horse. Eleanor Roosevelt, the indomitable campaigning spouse of President Franklin Delano Roosevelt, once identified this type of courage: "Courage is more exhilarating than fear and, in the long run, it is easier. We do not have to become heroes overnight – just a step at a time, meeting each challenge as it comes, seeing that it's not as dreadful as it appeared, discovering we have the strength to stare it down."

What links these displays of courage is something else – the optimism of the human spirit. One reason for a book like this is to capture and preserve tales of epic human behaviour. As the years pass, it is all too easy to forget the sacrifices which otherwise 'ordinary' generations of men and women who went before us made – and how such lives were changed for ever, or lost, or blighted, as a result. Moreover, it is not only in wars that courage and bravery are shown. Some individuals have extraordinary natural abilities that set them apart which is why sports heroes are included in this book; at certain peaceful times and in certain places, sporting "gods" come to epitomise a national awakening such as the cricketer Don Bradman's impact on Australian society in the 1930s, or the footballer Pelé's role in Brazil in the 1960–70s, or the ice-hockey player Wayne Gretzky's importance to the growth of a proud Canadian national identity. Scientists can become heroes, too, although usually in retrospect – think Marie Curie or Albert Einstein or Alan Turing or Rosalind Franklin. Now, in the wake of the greatest pandemic the world has seen in a century, it is epidemiologists and health care workers with their dedicated combinations of skill, stamina and stoicism in the face of death, who, like organ donors before them, have joined the ranks of heroes and been enshrined by a prevailing mood.

Discovering stories that illustrate courage and bravery is far from straightforward. When the wartime singer Vera Lynn died in 2020, she was mourned as "a powerful totem of our national identity" – a person who epitomised an extraordinary generation and helped a whole nation to pull in the same direction. "The sheer scale of their endurance, their fortitude, their sacrifice and the dangers to which they (those living from 1939–45) were exposed is something few not alive at the time can even begin to comprehend," reckoned one columnist on Dame Vera's death. "Queen in all but Name" headlined an obituary in *The Economist* magazine. Vera Lynn never saw herself as heroic, just a person with some natural abilities who was able to capture a mood and make use of her talents in the national cause.

As often as not, heroes are anonymous, modest, self-effacing, do not seek the limelight and wish to be overlooked. Many are. Who remembers now the name of the Army Sergeant who defused scores of bombs in Afghanistan and lost his life doing so, or the names of the firemen who entered the burning Twin Towers in New York after the 9/11 attack, or the immigrant who climbed up the outside of a Parisian apartment block to save a child, or the civil servant who used a narwhal tusk to confront a terrorist on London Bridge? Captain Sir Tom Moore, the centenarian who became an unexpected hero of the Covid-19 pandemic in England when he raised £33 million single-handed for NHS Charities Together, may one day fall in to this category although his wonderful determination not to be beaten by circumstances will remain an inspiration. Yet the collective memory is short – and when it comes to armed conflict, the desire to move on once the fighting ends, and not to dwell on the past, can be overwhelming.

Over the years, too, the concepts of courage and bravery evolve. Today it is outmoded to talk about, let alone to praise, Britain's colonial or military past. The country's role in slave-trading is considered more "relevant" by identity historians than its global role in spreading literacy, democracy and law-based government. Yet once, not so long ago, the British Empire was the stuff of Boy's Own legends, with Kiplingesque tales of heroism from Sudan to India in the cause of King and Country in distant, mysterious lands, instantly being devoured by successive generations. It is said that harnessing the past to serve the political or cultural present is a dangerous game. In these more sceptical times, stories of derring-do on behalf of British interests are as rare as hens' teeth. Life has become more cynical and shaded.

Another unfashionable element that resonates through this book is the notion of duty – to one's friends, to one's unit, to one's ship or regiment or squadron, to one's Service and ultimately to one's country. By the 21st century, such concepts had become deeply dated. But as the military historian Max Hastings has observed, "To that (wartime) generation the idea of duty was very real." Many of those featured in this book were far from jingoistic or one-dimensional characters. Most acted as they did in a time of acute national danger to save and to serve their country. Yet many wished, too, to encourage the emergence of a "new Britain" after the hostilities. Indeed, the longer the 1939–45 war dragged on, the more the desire for change grew among British forces in the field after two appallingly costly conflicts in 30 years. Old-fashioned courage and bravery and a sense of duty continued to be demonstrated. But the context was shifting. It always does.

The true nature of courage is to confront and overcome fear as World War 2 pilots and bomber crews had to on every scramble. Missions that ran into several hours required something even more demanding: sustained courage," an Air Marshall argued in a letter to *The Times* in 2021. Some 25 centuries earlier, Plato had claimed that "courage is a kind of salvation." Today, if the alternative is juxtaposed – timidity, fearfulness, even cowardice – there seems little argument. The destroyer captain who realises he needs a rest in wartime and declines another dangerous mission surely is every bit as courageous as the person who continues fighting when unfit to do so and possibly jeopardises the lives of others? Yet until it becomes necessary to demonstrate bravery or courage or leadership, no one can be certain how he or she will react in the heat of war. Or how they will respond when faced with life-or-death choices in peacetime.

Nor is it straightforward to define what constitutes leadership or makes a good leader. Asked once to identify the attributes that were needed to achieve flag rank in the Royal Navy, the former First Sea Lord, Admiral Sir Jonathon Band, picked out three – career ambition; brain power ("a useable intellect" as he put it) and a degree of ruthlessness in decision-making linked to an aura or presence. "At, or near, the top in most walks of life," he said, "sooner or later you have to display some harsher qualities and be able to make unpleasant decisions." Then he added a fourth requirement – luck, which relates to timing, being in the right place at the right time and having the right qualifications.

Originally, this book was titled *Fortiter ac Fideliter* – the motto of Pangbourne College, a small school in southern England, founded in 1917, and the link that connects all those mentioned. At best, it is a tenuous relationship. Character and temperament, it is true, become clearer in adolescence and are only refined at the edges in later life. Some of those featured in these pages did credit the school with developing aspects of their character, or skills, that aided them when they were called upon to act. The great majority did not. Far more important, it was the context of the times that shaped these individuals. Without war, or danger or challenge or simple opportunity, most of these Old Pangbournians would not be regarded by other generations as particularly courageous at all. Time and place were everything – as was the nature of their response.

War, indeed, is rarely the primary motivation for courage or bravery. "War settles nothing," once wrote Field Marshall Lord Bramall, one of Britain's most distinguished recent commanders. "It may have its moments, it may bring out the best in some people. But apart from the suffering it causes in human and economic terms, it usually creates more problems than it solves." Many of our subjects knew this full well as their letters written at the time underline. This book is not a glorification of war. Instead, it is meant to bear witness to gallant individuals and to rescue their stories from the mists of time. *Fortiter ac Fideliter* – bravely and faithfully – has been the motto of the College at Pangbourne since 1922. Its originator defined the maxim loosely as 'Act always with courage and show yourself worthy of trust.' It seems an apt summation of this book.

2

TWO GEORGE CROSSES, TWO GEORGE MEDALS

— ◉ —

Four contrasting Old Pangbournians won four of the highest British awards for courage during the 1939–45 World War. Two of them left the Nautical College to serve in the Merchant Navy in the Blue Funnel line. One came to Pangbourne for a year intending to go to sea and changed his mind. The fourth decided a career at sea was not for him, trained as a doctor but went to sea in the RNVR during the war.

Two remained involved with the sea all their lives while the others led more sedentary existences as a solicitor and a doctor. Two earned their award for defusing bombs – that most dangerous of skills, especially in wartime when new enemy devices were constantly emerging and bombs and mines often had to be made safe in extraordinary circumstances. In each case there was an immediate commitment to take action regardless of the great personal danger involved. By any definition, this was bravery in action. Comprehending what motivated the four is complex. One of the leading authorities on bravery wrote once that "There is no rhyme or reason to it…Who can say whether it takes more courage to attack an angry bull elephant with a spear than to disarm a very sensitive mine?"[1] The question is, perhaps, better left unanswered.

John Gregson (37–40) is an unlikely hero. The most modest, disarming of men, he spent seventeen happy years after the Second World War in a blissful corner of far-away New Zealand working as a conscientious harbour pilot in the Bay of Plenty escorting vessels of every size through the peaceful waters around Tauranga,

---

1 Brig. Sir John Smythe "The George Cross"

today the largest port in the country. It was typical of the man. He never wanted to do anything else in his life but to be involved in some way with the sea and ships. He never sought fame or fortune or publicity. He went to sea as a callow 16-year-old and remained at sea well into his sixties. Throughout his long life he downplayed his bravery in World War 2 sometimes remarking, tongue-in-cheek and with a charming, humorous smile on his angular face, that he had received a medal for throwing someone into the sea. Yet, deep down, he was proud of the recognition his outstanding display of bravery as a young man in 1942 had given to the sailors of the Merchant Navy. Only on one occasion late in life he did feel personally flattered when invited, in 2006, to fly half way round the world to take part in what turned out to be a memorable anniversary service at Westminster Abbey attended by most of the living Victoria Cross and George Cross/Albert Medal holders.

Although Gregson was born in Bombay (now Mumbai) in 1924 where his father worked as an architect, John and his elder sister Elizabeth were sent back to England in 1926 to live with his grandmother in Hull. Here, perhaps, his love of the sea began to emerge and in 1937, aged 13, he arrived at the Nautical College, Pangbourne. He was always bound for the Merchant Navy but, like most of his generation at the NCP, the onset of war two years after he arrived aroused a strong desire to be involved as soon as possible. In Gregson's case, this meant the moment he was old enough to sign an apprenticeship with a shipping line. Aged 16, this is what he did early in 1940, becoming an employee of the Blue Funnel Line, a strong supporter of the College at the time. Part of the Alfred Holt company, Blue Funnel's mostly medium-sized ships carried general cargo and a few passengers all over the world. In the First World War, the line had lost 16 ships. In World War 2 it was to lose 30.

Initially, Gregson sailed mostly to the Far East. As the war intensified in 1941–42, he found himself in the thick of the action in a succession of perilous Atlantic convoys. Serving on mv *Dolius* (all Blue Funnel ships were named from Greek legend or history), he was in the vessel when it was bombed in the Firth of Forth in April 1941 but survived unscathed. After some marginally less eventful months on another Blue Funnel ship, mv *Alcinous,* he joined the 7,585 tons general cargo vessel mv *Mentor* in 1942 and was promptly torpedoed in May 1942. The ship sank off Florida and he spent four days in a lifeboat before being rescued by a nearby Blue Funnel vessel.

John Gregson as an MN officer.

On return to England Gregson was assigned to the mv *Deucalion*. Built in 1930, *Deucalion* was a 7,740 tons cargo carrier with a top speed of 14 knots. It had been bombed for the first time at the end of 1940 while in dock in Liverpool and again the following year whilst on a return trip from Malta to Gibraltar. In August 1942 it was included in what became the most famous Malta relief convoy of the war, codenamed Operation Pedestal. By that stage the island of Malta was on its last legs having endured relentless, hugely destructive bombing by the German and Italian air forces for the previous two years. Supplies and ammunition were so low by mid-1942 that food rations had been cut to starvation level and anti-aircraft fire was restricted to a core minimum.

To relieve the island a convoy of 14 merchant vessels and an escort of up to 35 Royal Navy ships including two battleships and three aircraft carriers assembled off Gibraltar to "make a dash for Malta through the Straits of Sicily" in the words of Gregson's obituary in *The Times*. Two days out of Gibraltar *Deucalion* was disabled by a direct hit from a Junkers 88 aircraft by a bomb that passed through one hold and out through the side of the ship before exploding. Badly damaged and slowed to eight knots, *Deucalion* had to be left to its fate by the rest of the convoy. Accompanied by a lone destroyer, HMS *Bramham*, it was ordered to try a southerly inshore route to Malta through the Tunisian narrows and shoals. It "was not to escape" recorded *The Times*. Attacked and hit twice by torpedo bombers, *Deucalion's* cargo of aviation fuel in Hold 6 exploded, flames spread rapidly and the captain gave the order to abandon ship.

Gregson survived the bomb attack without a scratch but one of his fellow officers, another apprentice manning an anti-aircraft gun, was not so fortunate and was trapped beneath a life raft. With a third apprentice, Gregson overturned the raft to free the man but discovered that his shipmate was so badly injured he could do nothing for himself. With flames enveloping the area and the ship sinking rapidly, Gregson realised he had no choice but to drop his injured colleague overboard. This he did, following him immediately into the Mediterranean. At the NCP Gregson had been rated a "strong swimmer" which was just as well. Once in the water, he located his comrade, supported him and looked around for help. No one else was nearby. So he set out to tow his by now unconscious companion to the *Bramham*, 600 yards away. He succeeded – an "astonishing haul" according to a report of the incident.

It was not for another eight months that Gregson's selfless action was recognised. Long before then, five of the 14 merchant vessels in Operation Pedestal had reached Malta – just enough to lift the siege of the island. One of the ships that got there, the American-built tanker *Ohio*, was damaged badly and had to be towed in to the

Grand Harbour by the escorting destroyers. *Bramham* was on her port side with Gregson, in his words, "assisting with the towing." Undeterred by this episode, he was soon back at sea with Blue Funnel, sailing in ss *Rhesus* in Atlantic convoys until March 1943 and earning his 2nd Mate's Certificate within four months. A few weeks before that it was announced that John Gregson had been awarded the Albert Medal for Gallantry in Saving Life – at the time the highest possible award for civilian bravery at sea. He was also awarded the Lloyds War Medal for Bravery. Whilst in London in 1943 he was able to attend his investiture at Buckingham Palace.

From mid-1943 to the end of the war Gregson served in ships owned by the Liverpool-based, Cunard-owned Brocklebank Line – ss *Mahout*, ss *Matheran* and ss *Mayfair*. Most of these years proved stressful but not fatal, involving repeat dangerous voyages in convoys to Africa, India and finally the Far East in support of the Burma campaign. He ended the war, aged just 21, with an array of medals including the Albert Medal, the Atlantic Star, the Africa Star, the Burma Star and the War Medal 1939–45. In 1971 the Albert Medal was replaced by the George Cross. Gregson, "in a manner typical of the man" in the words of *The Times*, chose not to exchange his medal although he was always happy to represent holders of the Albert Medal at reunions of the Victoria Cross/George Cross Association.

After the war, having obtained his Master's Certificate in 1949, John Gregson joined the Orient Line and was sailing to Australia in 1952 in ss *Oracades* when he met his wife-to-be, Mary. A year later he emigrated to New Zealand, married soon after and began a new seagoing career with the Union Steam Ship Company, part of the Shell Group. He died on Christmas Day 2016, aged 91. "My whole life has been either at sea or connected with shipping such as piloting or marine surveying and I do not regret any of it," he had written to the Old Pangbournian Society a few years earlier. He meant it.

———

If Gregson's George Cross was, in one sense, predictable for an Old Pangbournian employed in the merchant marine in wartime, that awarded to **Jack Easton (20–21)** in 1940 was as improbable as Beethoven playing golf. Born in 1906 in Maidenhead, he attended the Nautical College for a year in 1920 before changing his mind about a career at sea and leaving for Brighton College. After Brighton he qualified as a solicitor in his grandfather's London-based law firm William Easton & Sons.

A keen yachtsman, Easton volunteered for the Royal Naval Volunteer Reserve (RNVR) on the outbreak of war in 1939 and received officer training at HMS *King Alfred*, an RNVR shore-based facility located in a leisure centre in Hove. One day in the spring of 1940 the raw recruits were called on to dispose of or defuse 40 mines and he was "pushed forward." Evidently, he did well. After basic training he volunteered for HMS *Vernon,* the torpedo and mining school. By October 1940, now a Temporary Sub-Lieutenant aged 34, he was working in London attached to the Land Disposal Section of the RNVR.

Jack Easton.

One day, as The Blitz intensified, Easton was summoned to Clifton Street, Shoreditch where a huge mine had landed but failed to explode. Accompanied by Able Seaman Bennett Southwell, he walked through rapidly-emptying streets to the place where the bomb – a German Type C magnetic device containing 1,000lb of explosive, almost nine feet long – had crashed through the roof of a house. It was hanging suspended by its parachute lines through a hole in the ceiling about six inches off the floor in a darkened room. Immediately, Easton knew it was too risky to try to move the device and it would have to be dismantled at once. He began work, with Southwell standing outside the window of the room, handing him the tools he needed.

Within a minute the bomb slipped. Easton heard the whirr of its mechanism and knew he had precisely twelve seconds to get clear. Shouting to Southwell to run, both men fled in different directions. Easton forced open the door of the room in which he had been working and managed to throw himself into a surface air raid shelter opposite the house. Southwell got as far as a nearby road when the bomb exploded. Easton was knocked unconscious and buried under rubble in the shelter, his back and skull fractured, his pelvis and legs broken. Southwell was decapitated. Six streets of houses close by were destroyed and it was six weeks before Southwell's body could be recovered. Both men were awarded the George Cross in January 1941 "for great gallantry and undaunted devotion to duty." Easton, still recovering in hospital, heard the announcement on the radio on the 6:00pm BBC news. Hospital staff, who had been told by the Admiralty what was coming, had hidden three cases of champagne under Easton's bed. "The celebrations went on long into the evening" according to an account of the incident in a book titled *George Cross Heroes.*

Easton spent a year in plaster before returning to duty at the end of 1941. In 1950 he wrote vividly about the Shoreditch incident – his 17th bomb disposal assignment – in a publication called *Wavy Navy.* Describing how he walked down "the drab street" to the damaged house, he captured the overwhelming danger and loneliness of bomb disposal work. "I had the feeling that a vast audience was watching the way I walked. It had been the last scene for several men I knew, though such morbid thoughts were absent that day. I was looking for the house described." He went on to explain how the bomb slipped from its 'moorings' and how he escaped from the building. "On such work one had to plan ahead…I had no time to use distance for safety, and ran across the roadway to a surface air raid shelter opposite where I was. I flung myself on its far side, its bulk between me and the house I had just left. I flung myself tight against it, face down to the ground. I heard no explosion…I was not blinded by the flash that comes split seconds before an explosion, but that was all I experienced. I do not know what time passed before I became conscious. When I did, I knew I was buried deep beneath bricks and mortar and was being suffocated. My head was between my legs and I guessed my back was broken but could not move an inch. I was held, imbedded. Men dug me out. To this day I do not know how long I spent in my grave. Most of the time I was unconscious. The conscious moments were of horror and utter helplessness. Being buried alive is certainly a good example of a living hell."

This was not Easton only brush with death. Another of his exploits before the Shoreditch bomb had been to defuse a parachute mine that fell through the roof of the Russell Hotel in central London. The owner of the hotel was so relieved that his business had been saved that he wrote Easton a cheque for £140 (about £6,000 today) and announced that Easton and his family could have Sunday lunch at the hotel free for life. On recounting the story to his commanding officer, Easton was ordered to refuse the money and the lunch offer; he had merely been doing his duty, it was pointed out.

Late in 1941 and back on duty, Jack Easton was appointed to HMS *Britannia II*, a trawler base at Dartmouth. Soon after he began a succession of sea commands in armed trawlers and minesweepers. During the D-Day landings he led a motor minesweeper flotilla. A seaborne mine exploded under his ship HM *MMS 22* but again he survived. After the war he returned to the family law firm, continuing to work into the 1970s. During this time, he became legal adviser to the VC and GC Association. He died in November 1994, aged 88. "Whenever he walked into a house or a room or a gathering of any kind, laughter and happiness walked with him," his godson said in a Tribute at his cremation service.

———————

A similarly unlikely route into wartime bomb disposal work and subsequent national recognition was taken by **Martin Johnson** (25–28). He had left the Nautical College for a career in the Merchant Navy with Blue Funnel in 1928. Born in South Africa in 1911, the son of a clergyman, he had arrived at the NCP from Christ's Hospital school in 1925, played rugby for the 1st XV and became a cadet captain (prefect) in the 4th Illawarra intake. Following some years at sea, he moved ashore in the mid-1930s and began selling second-hand cars before finding his true vocation working with young delinquents for the Prison and Borstal Commission, unkindly known to some as the 'theatre of hooligans'" according to a contemporary newspaper report. Called up as an RNR officer in 1941, he served with the Department of Torpedoes and Mines Investigation Section for the next three years.

Martin Johnson.

Early on in this period Johnson was summoned to the Vickers shipyard in Barrow-in-Furness for what proved to be a unique challenge in the 1939–45 period – to make safe four 500lb torpedoes packed with TNT in the only German submarine to be captured intact, brought to the UK and converted into an RN vessel during the Second World War. It was August 1941, and *U-570* and her inexperienced crew on their first operation had surrendered to an RAF Lockheed Hudson reconnaissance/bomber aircraft belonging to Coastal Command having been depth-charged, machine-gunned and apparently disabled south of Iceland. The vessel was one of 500 similar Kriegsmarine submarines and, potentially, a magnificent prize with clear propaganda value. But it had been badly damaged in its disastrous encounter with the RAF and its four live electric torpedoes, each with 500lbs of explosive in it, could not be extracted because the bow plates were crushed in on top of the torpedo tubes.

Johnson, a Lieutenant, followed by his boss Lt. Cdr F. Ashe Lincoln RNVR, arrived at the yard on a dismal Sunday morning with mist and rain enveloping the facility and workers in the dockyard, not surprisingly, refusing to use their blow torches anywhere near the crippled submarine. The vessel itself was marooned at the bottom of a dry dock overlooked by a wooden stage. None of its machinery was working. Neither officer had dismantled a German torpedo although Johnson had been trained to do so. He began by asking one of the workers how to use an oxyacetylene cutter. At this point a younger man standing by stepped forward and agreed to cut through the outer casing. All three were uncomfortably aware that a single spark could set off an explosion. The preliminary task was completed safely and the steel casing cut. The welder, his face "pallid and streaked with grime", according to Lincoln, was thanked profusely. "Always try to help the Navy, sir" he responded.

The two officers moved alone to the remotest part of the yard. Here, Johnson set to work opening the so-called magnetic "pistols" – ingenious gadgets that comprised primers, detonators and strikers and were capable of producing a lethal explosion. Using a screwdriver that kept slipping to force the primers apart, the detonators were made safe. "It had been the longest, wettest Sunday in my recollection" Lincoln wrote feelingly afterwards. Skill, and some luck, not to mention ice-cool nerves and considerable courage, had been on the two men's side. Two weeks later, when a German torpedo of the same type as the one removed in the Vickers yard came ashore in Dutch Guiana (now Suriname), the Royal Dutch Navy asked the RN for guidance. Detailed instructions were sent, but the pistol blew up and seven people were killed.

Johnson's George Medal "for gallantry and undaunted devotion to duty" was gazetted in December 1942. The award had only been instituted a couple of years earlier and is specifically designated for bravery "not in the face of the enemy." Ashe Lincoln, a leading QC after the war, recalled: "The question of danger did not bother Johnson personally... but he was most anxious that nothing should be done to damage the submarine." Nor was it. *U-570* became HMS *Graph,* carried out three wartime patrols with a Royal Navy crew and was the only submarine to see active service on both sides during the war. In October 1942 it went to sea under the command of an Old Pangbournian, **Peter Marriott (29–32)**, and attacked and seemingly crippled the German submarine *U-333* in the Bay of Biscay. Marriott was awarded the DSO for his "great courage, skill and determination in a successful submarine patrol." In 1944 *Graph* had to be withdrawn from service due to maintenance problems.

Martin Johnson remained in the RNVR reaching the rank of Lt. Commander. In 1944 he transferred from the mine disposal unit to become an instructor at a school run by the RN for juvenile offenders on the Wirral known as Akbar – "the spiritual descendant of HMS *Akbar*, a reformatory ship for boys moored in the Mersey from 1862 onwards" according to *The Daily Telegraph*. In 1950 he became captain of the school and held the post until 1956 when the facility was closed by the government. As compensation he was offered the role of senior instructor at the National Nautical School in Portishead, near Bristol, remaining there for 18 years until he retired in 1974. "My father looked back fondly to his time at Pangbourne and proudly wore his OP tie," his son Johnny informed the OP Society on his father's death in 2004 aged 93. "He encouraged and supported his family through all life's adventures, swapping stories through his Woodbine smoke. His house rang with the laughter of friends. He loved poetry, Greek dancing, ballet, sea shanties and boogie woogie. His tangible enthusiasm and love of life were matched by his humour and his faith and touched all who knew him. During his last days he told me he believed he had done his duty and had had a wonderful run. He was at peace."

Less is known about the other George Medal recipient. **Philip Raymond Charles Evans** (31–34) was born in Edinburgh, the son of a Welsh doctor and a French mother. He arrived at the Nautical College in 1931 as a 14-year-old, remaining for three years and leaving from the Fifth Form for "Civil Life" as *The Log* put it. He had decided to follow in his father's footsteps, and entered Guy's Hospital, qualifying in 1942. The same year he joined the Royal Navy as a temporary surgeon lieutenant RNVR.

In 1943 Evans was serving in HMS *Wivern,* an aging destroyer based in Gibraltar and deployed on Mediterranean escort duty. On February 22 it came to the aid of a Canadian corvette HMCS *Weyburn* which had struck a mine and was sinking stern first off Cape Espartel with the loss of her commanding officer and 12 crew. As *Wivern* was rescuing survivors, 20 depth charges from the disappearing *Weyburn* detonated, severely damaging *Wivern.* A press report at the time stated: "Evans was helping survivors aboard the destroyer when the corvette sank and an under-water explosion snapped both his legs below the knee. He was carried round the decks and the wardroom for 14 hours examining and directing the treatment of the wounded" and even amputating a wounded man's leg before being stretchered off to hospital himself. For his courageous devotion to duty, Evans was awarded the George Medal.

Philip Evans was to suffer from his wounds for the rest of his life. In hospital, where he was sketched by one of the Admiralty's official war artists, William Dring, he developed a chronic infection (recurrent osteomyelitis) in both his ankle bones which led to him being invalided out of the Navy and one of his legs being amputated below the knee. He rarely complained of his fate. Post-war, he worked for three years as a medical registrar at Guy's Hospital, qualifying as a research doctor and member of the Royal College of Physicians (RCP). In the early 1950s he moved to North Wales and became a consultant physician in the Wrexham Group of Hospitals until his retirement in 1979. He died in 1984.

An obituary written by a colleague and published by the RCP stated: "Evans' temperament was mercurial which was not perhaps surprising in view of his mixed French and Welsh blood. He could be devastatingly comic on occasion and full of gaiety. But, at times, he suffered from periods of depression, though this was known only to his close friends. He bore the burden of recurrent foot infection for many years with little complaint, even though it meant that nearly every form of sport and active recreation was denied him. At one time he was a keen yachtsman; and he always enjoyed the gastronomic delights of France on his regular visits to the family house in the Haute Loire. Kindly, shrewd and wholly lacking in conceit, Evans was much loved as a physician and well deserved the devotion and regard he received from a wide circle of friends."

3

"A NEW KIND OF SAILOR":
THE DESTROYER
COMMANDERS

— ◉ —

By the outbreak of the Second World War in 1939 many of the Old
Pangbournians who had been at the Nautical College in the 1920s and the
1930s and entered the Royal Navy were in their late-twenties or early thirties
– qualified and eager to captain a ship. The result was an abundance of OP
destroyer and submarine commanders during the war, many of whom survived
and fought throughout the conflict and became respected and decorated
Captains or Commanders in the process.

Both destroyers and submarines had played a significant, but lesser, role in the
First World War. During the 1939–45 conflict they assumed real importance in
the global conflict at sea, as battleships and cruisers began to be overtaken by
technological advances and waned in importance, whereas aircraft carriers and
air capability at sea, in particular, evolved rapidly – and protecting merchant ship
convoys became crucial to the UK's survival. In this chapter, the emphasis is on
destroyers and their commanders. A subsequent chapter will focus on submarines.
At the beginning of the conflict, the Royal Navy had about 180 destroyers in
commission. Of these, 110 were designated as fleet destroyers and 70 were convoy
escort destroyers. The former, epitomised by the 'D' class which began to be built
in 1928–29, were around 1,400 tons, had a top speed of 36 knots and a range of
nearly 6,000 miles. They were equipped with 4.7-inch guns, some anti-aircraft
guns, eight torpedo tubes and depth charges and a crew of about 145 men. The
latter, such as the 'Hunt' class which was built between 1939–43, were smaller –

around 1,000 tons with a top speed of 27 knots and crews of 160 – and equipped with more depth charges but fewer guns and no torpedoes. Their primary role was to protect convoys against enemy submarine and air attacks.

During the 1930s fleet destroyers evolved. By 1939 the newest weighed in at 1,900 tons, had a range of 5,800 nautical miles, carried a crew of 190 and was far more heavily armed than its escort cousin. Mostly, these destroyers were regarded as key elements in anti-submarine warfare and the flank protection of major warships such as battleships and cruisers. Vessels of both types could be used, too, to attack enemy naval and merchant ships, deliver shore bombardments and act as troop and supply transports. A rapid build-up of the destroyer force began in 1936–37 but not until 1943 did the Royal Navy begin to feel that it had enough of these ships, and the right mix, to wage the sort of aggressive war at sea that might speed the path to victory.

Events were to show that the human side of this expansion mattered every bit as much as the material. The essence of destroyer command, be it of a fleet or escort vessel, then or now, is aggression – to seek out the enemy and attack. Commanding such exposed, relatively lightly armed, cramped little ships was not for the faint-hearted. Strong leadership and constant crew training proved to be crucial. By the early 1940s as many as eight out of ten of the men on board a majority of destroyers had never been to sea before, let alone served in a frontline ship under attack. Split second decision-making, and nerves of steel, became core requirements for the successful destroyer captain. Many ambitious, want-to-be commanders fell by the wayside under the intense pressure of battle and fatigue, and drop-outs were commonplace. A total of 389 British, Australian and Canadian destroyers took part in the conflict. About 153 of these ships – around 40 per cent – were sunk or damaged beyond repair by enemy action. Some 11,000 destroyer-crew lost their lives. It was a hazardous, often brutal existence. "Life in destroyers of the Royal Navy was hard, made worse by their operational theatres," wrote M.J. Whitley in *Destroyers of World War Two* – and it was hardest of all for their commanders.

Perhaps the most revealing account of the pressures exerted on a 1939–45 destroyer captain ever published is that by Lt. Commander **Roger Hill (23–27)** who went into the R.N. direct from Pangbourne and was awarded a DSO and DSC during the war as well as being Mentioned in Despatches. In his candid memoir, *Destroyer Captain*, published two decades after the end of the fighting, he observed self-disparagingly: "The captain of a destroyer in World War 2 was a think-box into which radar, radio and sight reports were fed, and out of which were triggered response orders some of which were considered decisions and some wild guesses. Mine were lucky." He was damning himself with faint praise yet, in his own eyes, Hill always was the outsider struggling to prove himself and never part of the naval "family." As he put it: "I leaned over backwards to avoid the least impression of flattery." Mostly going his own slightly rebellious way, and occasionally questioning orders, while always longing for recognition and promotion, over the years he must have rubbed dozens of stuffy naval noses out of joint. But his crews backed him to the hilt, regarding him as a 'lucky' skipper, and many of his more far-sighted superiors recognised his outstanding flair, bravery and fighting abilities.

Admiral of the Fleet Sir Philip Vian – not exactly a man over-fond of praising subordinates – once wrote of Hill that his "intrepidity and resource seemed to have no limit." This was certainly true of his record in the crucial 1942–44 period. Ultimately, the war made Roger Hill but it broke him too. Subsequently, he found it hard to settle down to peacetime realities, his unhappy first marriage dissolved and he was unable to find a job. "The English post-war world had no use for damaged destroyer captains," he observed with some bitterness 20 years after 1945. So, in the mid-1960s with his second wife and two young children, he emigrated to New Zealand, became a dock labourer at a wharf in Nelson on the South Island (it was during this period that he composed his memoir) before teaching navigation in Nelson and farming nearby.

Hill's first taste of destroyer life had occurred in 1935–37 in HMS *Electra* when the ship was put on a war footing in Alexandria and the Mediterranean for more than two years following the Italian invasion of Abyssinia and the outbreak of the Spanish civil war. His commander gave his opinion that Hill "needed the discipline of a big ship," so he was moved to the battleship HMS *Hood*. He duly hated big ship life, engineered a transfer to the cruiser HMS *Penelope* and found himself leading naval shore patrols in Palestine to help the British Army suppress an Arab revolt. Even when the Second World War began his goal of a "small command" seemed elusive. First, he was posted as a Lieutenant to an armed minesweeping trawler for five months and afterwards to a converted Admiralty yacht, the sloop HMS *Enchantress*, for a grim, slogging year of transatlantic convoy duty. At last, at the end of 1941 and still a Lieutenant after 14 years in the R.N., he was unexpectedly promoted to Lt. Commander and given a command – a new destroyer called HMS *Ledbury*, at the time being fitted out in Southampton. "It had been a long wait," he recalled with feeling.

It was as captain of *Ledbury* that Hill made his name as one of the Royal Navy's boldest and most imaginative destroyer commanders – in effect, the start of what his obituary in the *Daily Telegraph* was to describe in 2001 as "his exemplary service" during the Second World War. In *Ledbury* he was to take part in three Arctic convoys, play a leading role in Operation Pedestal to Malta, support the Allied landings at Anzio in Italy and the D-Day landings in France, and be congratulated personally by the prime minister, Winston Churchill, in a rare and much coveted 'Well done' signal.

Ledbury was a typical 'Hunt' class destroyer weighing in at 1,050 tons. It was armed with three twin 4-inch standard naval anti-aircraft/dual-purpose guns (known colloquially as 'Pip', 'Squeak' and 'Wilfred' by the crew), a four-barrelled anti-aircraft pom-pom gun, two anti-aircraft Oerlikon guns and 110 depth charges. Its top speed was 25 knots, it had a theoretical range of 3,600 nautical miles and a crew of 164 men. Three months after commissioning, *Ledbury* was given its first active assignment escorting ships taking part in perilous supply convoys to the Soviet Union – "a naval operation that was strategically and tactically unsound" in Hill's characteristically robust assessment. "The political requirement (to aid Stalin) was predominant."

These convoys, usually consisting of 20–30 merchant ships plus a dozen escorting RN vessels – had to get from Scotland or Iceland north of Bear Island (400 kms north of the German-occupied Norwegian coast) to Archangel or Murmansk without the benefit of air cover or any friendly nearby bases. In contrast, the Germans could call on adjacent airfields, submarine bases and safe anchorages for their largest surface ships such as the battleship *Tirpitz*. Arctic pack ice usually prevented the convoys steering very far north. Along the favoured route through the Barents Sea conditions were dreadful in winter as high winds whipped up the water which broke over the bows of the destroyers and froze, covering the decks with ice a foot thick. Clothes worn on the bridge often had to be chipped off below deck, there could be no rescue for anyone who fell into the sea and the longer trips lasted the more crews were prone to strange neuroses. Three 'T's' – Tiredness, Tension and Terror – became as much a danger to the men as the enemy. Winston Churchill unblinkingly described the passage as "the worst journey in the world." One hundred ships were sunk on these convoys between 1941–45, 3,000 men lost their lives but four million tons of supplies were delivered to the USSR. For decades after, Moscow ignored this Allied contribution, but in 2014 attitudes softened and the Russian ambassador in London wrote to all veterans of the convoys still alive stating: "Your deeds will continue to serve as the supreme expression of bravery and a high point in human spirit."

Each convoy – designated PQ if Russia-bound or QP for empty convoys returning to the UK – had to be protected by one or two battleships or aircraft carriers and a destroyer screen. The first two convoys Hill escorted, PQ15 and PQ16, proved relatively uneventful. *Ledbury's* job was to accompany fleet tankers for the first week or so of the convoys, on the second occasion leaving the convoy to steam on to Russia just as a German bombing attack was beginning – "We felt like children being sent to bed after tea and not allowed to play grown-up games," Hill observed in his book. His third, the infamous PQ17 convoy in June/July 1942 – was to leave a lasting scar on Hill's psyche. This time *Ledbury* was to escort the merchant ships all the way to Archangel, refuelling *en route*.

Convoy PQ17 turned out to be the largest to Russia to that date consisting of 34 freighters carrying enough weaponry for an army of 50,000 including 500 crated aircraft and 300 tanks, shielded by 21 British and American navy vessels including six destroyers. Northeast of Iceland, the ships were spotted by German aircraft. By the start of July, they were being shadowed by packs of German submarines; one day Hill saw seven on the surface. The next day, July 4, 26 Heinkel HE 111s attacked. "They came at us like a cavalry charge and came so hard and fast they could not turn away," Hill remembered. The attack was beaten off. In *Ledbury*, jubilation quickly turned to sour despondency. The convoy at its very moment of success had received the first of three confusing orders from the Admiralty in London to 'scatter.'

This was a decision taken by the senior officer in the Royal Navy, Admiral of the Fleet Sir Dudley Pound, who feared that the *Tirpitz* and her two heavy battle cruiser companions were steaming out to destroy every vessel in the Allied convoy. It proved not to be the case. A terrible error of judgement had occurred. Only gradually was the depressing order understood in *Ledbury* – "We were abandoning the convoy and running away," Hill wrote unsparingly in *Destroyer Captain*. "I can never forget how they (merchant ships' crews) cheered us as we moved out at full speed to the attack" when the Heinkels had come in. "It has haunted me ever since that we left them to be destroyed." More than 40 years later, in an interview in 1996, Hill was still appalled. "It was really terrible. Even now I have never got over it. It was simply awful." Altogether, 23 of the merchant ships in the now-unescorted and highly vulnerable convoy were sunk, 190 men on them lost their lives and untold tons of vital military equipment sank into a freezing, watery grave.

On the way back to Scotland, *Ledbury* got lost in fog and icebergs and Hill toyed with the idea

Roger Hill.

of turning around and returning to the convoy. "But discipline is strong and our orders were clear." And *Ledbury* was short of fuel. Days after, the ship made it back to Scapa Flow where the admiral in charge of destroyers summoned Hill and the other destroyer captains to his cabin to demand to know why they had left the convoy. One of them replied quietly that they had received an order, turned on his heel and filed out pursued by his angry colleagues – so averting an "explosion." Next day Hill cleared the lower deck, congratulated the whole ship on its performance (three enemy planes had been shot down by *Ledbury)* and said that he thought the Admiralty had made "a complete balzup (sic)." Soon after Hill was dealing with incidents onshore as several of his crew got into fights with Americans who accused the British of cowardice. His commanding officer on PQ17, Captain Jack Broome reckoned: "After PQ17 he (Hill) had little faith in the shore staff who directed operations at sea. He was part rebel: in another age he would have made an excellent – if humane – pirate."

Disagreements with by-the-book shore staff do, indeed, crop up throughout Hill's career – one reason, perhaps, that it took him so long to advance in the rule-bound Royal Navy. On this occasion, he was given no time to ponder. Within three weeks "after the usual unsatisfactory leave," *Ledbury* was ordered to accompany a convoy to Gibraltar at the end of July and there to join a vital convoy to Malta – WS21S, known as Operation Pedestal and the most famous convoy of the war. "At least ten Old Pangbournians are thought to have taken part." Carrying vital supplies, it represented the last chance for the besieged island which was close to running out of fuel, food and ammunition. Surrender, after months of intense, unrelenting Axis bombing, was reckoned to be less than a month away. In early August, 13 merchant ships and, crucially, an American-built but British-crewed oil tanker called *Ohio,* set out. To protect the group, the RN assembled an unprecedented array of vessels – two battleships, three aircraft carriers, seven cruisers, seven submarines and 32 destroyers – by far the largest escort force ever. Very quickly, it was spotted.

For the next six days the convoy was subjected to relentless, near-continuous attack by German and Italian aircraft, submarines and E-boats (fast attack craft). Within two days the convoy was depleted badly and short of air cover after the sinking of one aircraft carrier, the damaging of another and the withdrawal of both battleships. Emotions ran high. Throughout the war, the question of whether or not to rescue enemy personnel from the sea caused trouble, on both sides. In the midst of this life-and-death battle Hill spotted a parachute coming down near *Ledbury*. In an interview, reprinted in *Lost Voice of the Royal Navy*, he described what happened next. "I thought 'Blimey, that might be Red Leader' (an FAA pilot) so I rushed over to pick him up. I hung over the side and said to my first lieutenant 'What is he, Jimmy?' and he said, 'A fucking Hun, sir. Three more parachutes coming down to starboard.' 'Let them go to hell,' I replied. That evening our troubles really started." An all-night attack by wave after wave of Ju88 dive-bombers and torpedo aircraft ensued. Hill responded by taking *Ledbury* to the head of the column to find a better place to fire back. "For a few desperate moments we were the only protection for the merchant ships."

Not long after, the steering gear on *Ohio* was hit by a torpedo and the tanker swerved away from the convoy. Hill was ordered to get it back in line. After hours of inspired but highly dangerous improvisation, he succeeded. Of this testing day and night, he wrote: "What do you think? ... Before you sail, waking in the dark in your cabin and alone, you are scared stiff. And after it (a battle) is all over, you have, probably, a bad reaction. But during it, with all the things to attend to on the bridge, all your young men around you and dependent on you...you never think anything will happen to you." Nearing Malta, in Hill's words, *Ledbury* came under the "mother and father of an attack" by Ju88s. Close by *Ledbury*, the freighter *Waimarama* carrying petrol cans and explosives blew up after being hit by a stick of bombs. The flames blazed hundreds of feet in the air and the sea was on fire as far as the eye could see. *Ledbury* sailed through the inferno to rescue 44 men from *Waimarama* as yet another German torpedo plane attacked. Such was the intensity of the blaze that Hill, leaning over the side of the destroyer to help pluck individuals from the sea with ropes, held on to his beard for fear of it catching fire.

By now acutely short of fuel, 30 miles behind the convoy but less than a hundred miles from Malta's Grand Harbour, *Ledbury* hurried back to join what was left of the convoy. When it got there, another day and night of aerial bombardment was endured; *Ohio*, disabled and still drifting left, had to be towed and prodded along at two knots by three destroyers including *Ledbury*. Nine Ju87s attacked but finally the Grand Harbour loomed and a tug miraculously appeared to take over. By that stage the doctor on board *Ledbury* was handing out Benzedrine pills to the dog-tired crew, including Hill. Thousands of cheering men and women on the island turned out to greet the incoming vessels. "The sense of achievement, the relief of having brought her *(Ohio)* there after so much striving, to have no casualties amongst my own people and, perhaps above all, the knowledge that the ship *(Ledbury)* would be secured and I could sleep and sleep" overwhelmed Hill. Awarded an immediate DSO, he expected to be promoted to Commander "in due course." It was not to be.

By this stage, on his own admission, Hill was "irritable and inconsiderate and prone to irrational outbursts." From Malta, *Ledbury* was ordered back to its home port of Portsmouth to be repaired. On the way, Hill had a row in Gibraltar with a Staff officer who had failed to make arrangements for *Ledbury's* wounded to be disembarked. In Portsmouth he was told by "a gentleman in a dirty overall suit with a cigarette out of his mouth" that the ship must go to Hull. "This seemed to be to be the last straw," he remembered. Putting on his blue uniform and not stopping to think, he barged in to the Commander-in-Chief's cabin. The Admiral heard him out sympathetically. The Chief of Staff was not so well disposed and bawled him out, calling him "a young puppy…Who the hell do think you are going over my head?" Next morning, *Ledbury* sailed for Hull. Hill had made matters worse by putting in a claim for salvage of the *Ohio*; eventually he received £19. 18s. 4d.

Since *Ledbury* left Malta, Hill had been in what he called "a bad state of nerves." He realized that after seven years' service on a continuous war footing in a variety of ships and circumstances, he had to leave *Ledbury* and take a rest. "I think it was the most bitter and difficult decision that I ever made. There is no ship like your first command," he wrote, tellingly, in his memoir. Whether the break did any good is moot. After another unhappy leave at home near Reading and a short recuperative spell as an instructor at a shore-based training establishment, he was appointed to command a new home-based destroyer *Grenville* – bigger and faster than *Ledbury*, armed with eight torpedoes. *Grenville,* it turned out, had been assigned to night-time blockade-enforcing duties in the English Channel and the Bay of Biscay, sailing from a base in Plymouth. Several dangerous actions occurred in mid-1943 including a "close fight" with five German destroyers, a scary encounter with a new type of controlled bomb, the sinking of a submarine which *Grenville* detected edging through the Bay of Biscay and numerous high-risk night-time patrols deep in enemy waters. For his success in sinking the U-boat, Hill was awarded a DSC. Still, there was no promotion. A Lt. Commander he remained.

At this point, *Grenville* was now sent to the Mediterranean. Hill, though, was cracking up, existing on sleeping pills and whisky and becoming increasingly superstitious. "The only real rest a destroyer captain received was when his ship was sunk or destroyed," he recalled. Biting the bullet, in December 1943 he requested ten days' leave in Gibraltar. It made no difference. Re-joining *Grenville* he patrolled the Adriatic and took part in the Anzio Landings. The following February he was moved to command another destroyer, *Jervis,* which had had 25 feet of its bow blown off at Anzio by a glider bomb. In *Jervis* Hill was to take part in D-Day – one of 45 destroyers involved – covering assault ships, bombarding targets and protecting the flanks of invading troops. He was Mentioned in Despatches. It was very hard-earned recognition.

For the destroyers, the Allied invasion of Europe proved to be anything but straightforward. At first all went well from a naval point of view. But soon after the landings German aircraft appeared and began dropping a new type of mine into the sea and around the invasion fleet. Much damage was sustained, and in one ten-day period in early July 118 mines exploded close to *Jervis*, each one potentially lethal. Meantime, the longer *Jervis* was required to trundle back and forth across the Channel collecting fuel and ammunition, the more trouble there was on board as crew members collapsed in exhaustion. Soon after, *Jervis* was detached to join an American-led naval force patrolling between Cherbourg and the Channel Islands. On August 18, 1944 Roger Hill's war effectively came to an end when *Jervis* led the capture of an isolated, rocky islet called Roches d'Oeuvres. At this point the ship's turbine engines had had enough. A long refit in Belfast then took place. Roger Hill, too, was at the end of his tether and it was months before he recovered his strength. The Admiralty had received no reports on him from his immediate superior in his four years as a commanding officer, while Vian's assessment may not have reached London. Hill was given the recuperative command of a shore-based naval air station. One day, travelling in an ambulance, he was involved in a traffic accident and suffered a serious head injury. After six months in hospital, he was invalided out of the Royal Navy at the end of July 1946.

When he wrote his memoir *Destroyer Captain* in the mid-1960s Hill did it mainly for his "own relief" and for the benefit of his six children. He made few references to his own bravery or pugnacity or abilities – rather the opposite if anything. Instead, he straightforwardly and "without hindsight" tried "to show what our young men can achieve and endure in wartime." The average age in *Grenville* was twenty-four. Fewer than one in five had been to sea before. Hill rose to the challenge and proved to be an inspired captain of his ships, respected, trusted and admired by all who sailed with him, if not by so many of his superiors.

Aubrey St. Clair Ford.

After his death in 2001 in New Zealand, his ashes were scattered in the sea off Malta

One destroyer captain who, perhaps, squared this circle rather better than Hill was **Aubrey St. Clair Ford (17–18)**, one of the original entrants to the Nautical College in 1917 and the teenage offspring of a real "naval family." Four St. Clair Fords have gone to Pangbourne and many more have served in the Royal Navy. Aubrey's brother Drummond was killed at sea in 1942 when

Traveller, the submarine he was commanding, was sunk in the Mediterranean (see Chapter 10). Retiring from the RN with the rank of Captain, Aubrey's naval career lasted 37 years. During this period, he was awarded the DSO twice and was Mentioned in Despatches four times including twice during the 1950–53 Korean war when he commanded the light cruiser *Belfast*. After the Second World War he became the 6th Baronet of Ember Court.

St. Clair Ford's 1939–45 war was defined by his three years from 1939–42 commanding a destroyer called *Kipling* – "a famous and gallant little ship" according to Admiral Sir Philip Vian. In particular, three memorable events stand out – rescuing Lord Louis Mountbatten from the sea in May 1941 after Mountbatten's ship, *Kelly*, was sunk by a German Stuka aircraft off Crete; single-handedly running down a U-boat, *U-75*, off Mersa Matruh; and being sent on what amounted to a suicide mission in May 1942, with three other destroyers and no air cover, to intercept a large and better-armed Italian convoy conveying troops, weapons and supplies to north Africa.

After the war a Lieutenant in *Kipling*, N.B. Robinson, who served throughout with St. Clair Ford, gave a lecture about the destroyer. In it, he described how, off Crete, St. Clair Ford "wriggled his ship through more than 40 air attacks (47 to be precise, lasting three hours) at times almost disappearing under columns of water" to rescue survivors from *Kelly* and a sister destroyer *Kashmir*. "Every time *Kipling* slowed or stopped to pick up survivors, she was a sitting target for the dive bombers" noted Ewart Brookes in his book *Destroyer*. This was "the finest performance *Kipling* ever put up" according to Robinson. Mountbatten was duly grateful and never forgot his rescue. *Kipling's* return to port after the battle was delayed by damage to the hull and she was presumed lost. When the ship belatedly limped in to Alexandria, crammed to the gunwales with 285 survivors from *Kelly* and *Kashmir*, "the whole Mediterranean fleet lined decks and shouted and bellowed themselves hoarse as the hero of the hour nosed its way in to the harbour." St. Clair Ford was awarded a DSO "for inspiring leadership and great skill in handling his ship."

A year on, at dusk one evening off Benghazi in Libya, there was to be no escape. German aircraft sighted the four-destroyer British force very quickly. Although the ships tried to escape, reversed course and "tore on at 30 knots praying for darkness…before dark we were found by two waves of 31 German Ju88 bombers based on Crete" in Robinson's words. The aircraft attacked in relays and *Kipling* was hit by three bombs and after ten minutes heeled over and broke in half. Two of the other destroyers were hit and sunk as well. The fourth, *Jervis*, picked up

650 survivors from the three ships including St. Clair Ford and 220 others from *Kipling's* 250-strong crew after they had spent four hours in the water. The ship's company's "fine bearing and behaviour in the water whilst being picked up spoke eloquently of the spirit with which they were imbued and reflected great credit on him" (St. Clair Ford) stated the Citation for this Mention in Despatches.

By that final moment *Kipling*, and St. Clair Ford, had taken part in almost non-stop action for three years starting with a bombardment of an airfield at Stavanger in Norway in April 1940. That autumn, *Kipling* was part of the destroyer raid on Cherbourg in 1940 intended to destroy German invasion barges. This was followed in July 1941 by repeat runs under sustained enemy air attack to supply the besieged Allied garrison at Tobruk, taking part in both the first and second Battles of Sirte with the Italian navy in December 1941 and March 1942, and the isolation and sinking of *U-75* off Mersa Matruh, Egypt at the end of 1941 – Winston Churchill sent a personal 'Well done" message to St. Clair Ford on that occasion and another DSO resulted. *Kipling*, moreover, is credited with destroying at least half a dozen Axis Ju88s bombers whilst on convoy escort duties to Malta where the ship's company sometimes had to sleep in caves onshore to avoid the ceaseless Axis air attacks.

St. Clair Ford – "a round and jolly man with a high colour in his face, so that he was widely known by a nickname 'Aubrey Strawberry'" according to a colleague – in retirement wrote a 90-page account of his war which is preserved in barely-readable microfilm in the Imperial War Museum. It is notably modest in tone, but realistic and occasionally dramatic. St. Clair Ford always had a strong bond to his ship – "extremely handsome and practical" – and soon after taking command made contact with the Kipling Society and instituted a "very potent Kipling Cocktail" in the wardroom. "We were all terribly shaken" by the loss of *Kelly* and *Kashmir*, he wrote, and it was *Kipling's* "stupendous good fortune" to make it back to Alexandria with five large gashes in her hull and her "sharp stem" six feet under water. On the sinking of *U-75*, he recalled, in particular, the submarine's "gallant commander (Helmuth Ringelmann) standing on the top of the conning tower after his crew had got on the casing of the upper deck and, still under heavy fire from *Kipling's* guns, calling for three cheers for *U-75* before ordering 'Abandon Ship.' Just after this, Ringelmann was killed by *Kipling's* gunfire."

As for *Kipling's* denouement on May 11, 1942, St Clair Ford makes it clear, without being overly critical, that the plan to attack an enemy convoy moving to Benghazi was always risky in the extreme. In the event, the RN destroyers never had a chance, being attacked repeatedly by waves of Ju88s bombers over several hours' duration. When *Kipling* was hit, St. Clair Ford wrote that he had time to call for three cheers for the ship before he "slipped into the water," joined other survivors 40 yards behind the stern of his sinking vessel and watched as it plunged vertically to the ocean bed. He was then picked up by *Jervis*. "This is the story of one particular ship," he adds at the end of his account, "but it is also, in all its detail, the story of most destroyers in war time."

'Bill' W.A.F. Hawkins (21–25), too, saw much action during the Second World War and was awarded the DSO, OBE and DSC and Bar. Aged 31 when he took command of the destroyer *Sardonyx* in 1939, he served throughout the conflict, retiring from the RN as a Captain in 1958. At the end of 1939 he took command of *Winchelsea*, one of the World War One hold-over destroyers still in naval service. In the thick of the evacuation at Dunkirk, Hawkins made seven trips to the beaches and rescued more than 2,000 soldiers despite relentless attacks by enemy dive bombers. He received his first DSC. At the end of 1940 and early in 1941, in terrible weather, *Winchelsea* rescued 130 men from four British merchant ships sunk in three German submarine attacks on Atlantic convoys as well as towing a damaged ship, *Leeds Castle*, 1,000 miles back to harbour in what the *Daily Telegraph* described as "an epic feat of seamanship." Hawkins received the OBE in recognition.

Through 1942 he commanded a new destroyer, *Partridge*, in the Mediterranean. That June he was part of 'Operation Harpoon,' a screening convoy codenamed WS19Z to Malta. After a ferocious encounter with a larger Italian force, *Partridge* survived thanks to her captain's "violent manoeuvring" and reached Gibraltar. Hawkins acquired both a nickname, 'Hardover Hawkins,' and a DSO. Six months on, *Partridge* was on an anti-submarine sweep southwest of Oran, Algeria, when she was torpedoed, broke in half and sank in a few moments. Thirty-eight men out of the 211-strong crew lost their lives but Hawkins was one of those picked up by another RN destroyer after two hours in the water. The loss of his ship, stated an obituary in 1989, was "an emotional blow from which he never really recovered."

True or not, in 1943 he was given temporary command of the cruiser *Belfast*, today a museum ship moored on the Thames in London. At the end of that year, *Belfast* was part of a nine-ship flotilla despatched by the Admiralty to intercept the German battlecruiser *Scharnhorst* and its five protecting destroyers which had left a base in northern Norway

W.A.F. 'Bill' Hawkins.

35

to attack an Allied Arctic convoy. Quickly ordered to scurry back to base once British intentions became clear, *Scharnhorst* was radar-detected by *Belfast*. After an eight-hour cat-and-mouse chase, battle was joined in near-darkness at 5:00pm. Nearly three hours went by before *Scharnhorst*, crippled by accurate gunfire and torpedoes, ground to a halt. *Belfast* was ordered to finish her off with torpedoes but before it could do so the battlecruiser exploded and sank, killing nearly 2,000 German sailors. Hawkins was awarded a bar to his DSC. He ended his war in a fifth destroyer, *Whirlwind*, as part of the British Pacific Fleet and participated in several bombardments of Japanese-held oil refineries in Sumatra.

Jack Bitmead (33–36) fits into a different mould – a man who unhesitatingly rose to the occasion in a life-or-death situation, at a very young age. At Pangbourne, which he left for the Royal Navy in 1936, he had excelled in most areas and showed real leadership potential, being Chief of Hesperus division in his final year and runner-up for the King's Gold Medal. In the Navy he always seemed marked out

Jack Bitmead.

for high rank. Promoted to Lieutenant in 1940, he had first shown outstanding bravery when serving in the destroyer *Broke* as navigating officer. *Broke* had been diverted to Brittany that June to help evacuate some 215,000 Allied troops trapped in north western France after the Dunkirk evacuation. The ship's initial role was to support the demolition of harbour installations at Brest by French forces and to get them out afterwards. This achieved, *Broke* sailed south and helped to rescue more than 20,000 Polish Free Forces troops trapped in St. Nazaire. Bitmead played a leading role in the evacuation and was awarded the Polish Krzyz Walecznych (Cross of Valour).

By 1942 he was First Lieutenant in a destroyer, *Forester*, on the brutal Arctic convoy run. On the morning of May 2 *Forester*, escorting a cruiser called *Edinburgh* conveying Soviet gold bullion westward to the Allies in payment for war supplies – was back in Murmansk. *Edinburgh* had been torpedoed three days before, badly damaged and separated from a homeward-bound convoy. As low cloud and snow squalls swept across the gloomy northern sky that morning, three German destroyers appeared and attacked the slow-moving RN ships. Badly outgunned, *Forester* steered straight towards the enemy. She was quickly hit by two shells that plunged through the hull, killing the captain and nine officers and crew. Aged 23, Bitmead was left in command.

When Bitmead took over, *Forester* lay stopped, only two miles from the enemy. Fearing the Germans would board his ship, he ordered all confidential documents be thrown overboard. This led to a moment of unintended levity when Bitmead, according to the *Daily Telegraph*, asked why tombola tickets were floating on the starboard side of the ship only to realise that they were pages of a code book which had burst open. Shortly after, two German torpedoes raced towards *Forester* and *Foresight,* the other Allied destroyer in the vicinity. They missed but went on to hit the crippled *Edinburgh* amidships. Meantime *Forester's* engineers performed heroics and Bitmead was able to steer the ship back towards *Edinburgh*, making smoke as he went and firing fiercely at the Germans from the ship's after turrets. During the exchange of fire, a German destroyer was sunk and another badly damaged. Taking no risks, both sides withdrew. *Edinburgh,* however, was hit by another torpedo a few hours after and sank; "Stalin's gold" was only salvaged in the 1980s.

Forester limped back to Murmansk where she was patched up for the ten-day return to Scapa Flow as part of an escort for another damaged RN ship, the cruiser *Trinidad.* Bitmead kept the command. This convoy was attacked repeatedly by the Luftwaffe and soon *Trinidad* caught fire. Bitmead immediately manoeuvred *Forester* alongside *Trinidad* and took off 30 casualties as flames licked the side of his ship, small arms ammunition exploded everywhere and a German bomber aircraft roared in for another attack. *Forester* survived and got home safely. As seen by the Navy, in the words of Bitmead's commanding Admiral in a letter he sent: "It was a magnificent show and a great victory." By way of recognition, Jack Bitmead was awarded an immediate DSO "for outstanding services in the face of relentless enemy attacks" together with two years' seniority. He remains one of the youngest naval officers ever to win a DSO.

The rest of Bitmead's wartime naval career was something of an anti-climax involving an offbeat submarine training experience, which he found "interestingly unpleasant," promotion to Lt. Commander, and command of a Hunt-class destroyer *Meynell* escorting convoys in the Channel and North Sea. He remained in the Navy until 1967, skippering three more destroyers and a frigate, was promoted to Captain but never achieved flag rank. In retirement, he grew strawberries and asparagus at a pick-your-own farm in East Lothian in Scotland. At his funeral in 2010 a one-time colleague described him as "quiet, kind and calm but nevertheless demanding high standards in everything…A magnificent leader, highly efficient in his professional skills… An extraordinarily fine and kind person who taught me and many others how to be a naval officer."

George Crowley.

Another much respected destroyer commander was **George Crowley** (30–33) who rose to become a Rear Admiral and was awarded a CB and DSC and Bar during a 35-year naval career as well as being Mentioned in Despatches. In the national press he was described as "one of the most effective sea officers of the Second World War which he spent almost entirely in destroyers." When the conflict broke out, he was navigating officer in the destroyer *Kashmir*. Two months into the war he took part in the sinking of the German submarine *U-35* east of the Shetlands – one of the first U-boats to be destroyed. *Kashmir* and two other destroyers were commanded by Lord Louis Mountbatten who took the rare and risky step of rescuing the crew of the German submarine. All 43 hands on board survived and spent the rest of the war in captivity.

In 1941, after service in three other destroyers including a French ship, Crowley was posted to the Australian-manned destroyer *Nestor* where several of the crew were under arrest for near-mutiny. He was instrumental in turning morale around, and *Nestor* took part in the hunt for the German battleship *Bismarck* in May. After numerous narrow escapes in various actions, in June 1942, as part of Operation Vigorous (protecting an 11-ship Allied convoy carrying supplies to Malta), *Nestor* had to be scuttled off Crete having been hit by bombs from an Italian aircraft. Crowley and almost all the crew survived and he was immediately posted to another Australian destroyer *Norman*. In *Norman* he took part in the successful capture of Madagascar from the Vichy French. For his service in both Australian ships he was awarded the DSC.

Crowley's first command, aged 27, was a 1918-vintage destroyer *Walpole* late in 1943. Mostly, *Walpole* escorted convoys in the North Sea. In June 1944 it took part in the D-Day landings. His second DSC came after a successful action against 24 German E-boats in the Scheldt estuary at the end of that year. The Citation to his medal recognised his "gallantry, skill and leadership... *Walpole* has had several encounters with E-boats during the last five months and in every case Lt. Commander Crowley has handled and fought his ship with marked ability." Early in 1945 *Walpole* hit a mine off Flushing in the Netherlands and had to be broken up. Soon after, Crowley was given command of *Tenacious*, a T-class destroyer, and sent to the Far East. Here the ship joined the 3rd US Pacific fleet, took part in the assault on Truk in the Caroline Islands and the bombardment of Japan and was part of the fleet in Sagami Bay that witnessed the surrender of the Japanese. Still in the South China Sea at the start of January, Crowley rescued six Australian air force crew who had ditched their DC3 aircraft after both engines failed. For this George Crowley was Mentioned in Despatches. He went on to become Director General Naval Personnel Services. Retiring in 1969 he was appointed Bursar of Corpus Christi college at Oxford University. He died in 1999. An eye infection that he picked up in the Far East caused him to go blind in his later years.

George Forman (24–27) is unique among this group in being awarded three DSCs during the Second World War – one each in 1942, 1943 and 1944 in addition to being Mentioned in Despatches twice, in 1941 and 1943. He served with distinction in no less than five destroyers – *Kingston, Middleton, Airedale, Lookout* and *Garth,* commanding the last three. Post-war, as a Commodore RN, he was seconded to become the first head of the independent Ghanaian Navy. He received a CB in 1962. Throughout his career he was famous for his *sang froid.* On one occasion, when his ship was being bombed, he was seen by his crew reclining in a deck-chair on the bridge smoking a cigarette and quietly giving orders to his quartermaster – and on his head was a panama hat. Morale on this ship, needless to say, was "very big."

George Forman.

In *Kingston* Forman was Mentioned in Despatches for his role in the Allied withdrawal from Greece. This was quickly supplemented by a DSC as the Allies evacuated Crete in May 1941 when *Kingston* rescued more than 500 survivors from three RN ships sunk by German airstrikes. In *Airedale*, Forman's first command, he had several narrow escapes. In May 1942 the ship was part of the same destroyer flotilla as *Kipling* (above) but not with *Kipling* when she was sunk. The following month in Operation Vigorous – a convoy from Alexandria to Malta that had to sail through the so-called 'Bomb Alley' between Crete and Cyrenaica – *Airedale* was hit by two bombs and near-missed by three. Forty-five of her crew were killed. The ship had to be scuttled, but Forman was among the 133 survivors.

That August he was back in charge of another destroyer, *Lookout.* In *Lookout* Forman was to win two DSCs, be Mentioned in Despatches and be promoted to Commander. As part of Operation Corkscrew – the Allied assault on the Italian island of Pantelleria in June 1943, prior to the Allied invasion of Sicily – *Lookout* was part of a large RN destroyer force. During this action, the ship achieved the "distinction" of being the most heavily-bombed destroyer to survive the war when, at dusk one evening, it was spotted by German aircraft. Only "violent evasive actions by Forman averted disaster as she found herself alone, outgunned and under assault by a flight of Luftwaffe bombers. Forman received his second DSC. His second MiD came soon after during *Lookout's* involvement in the Allied landings in Sicily the following month. Then, while present at the Allied landings at Salerno, *Lookout* was hit by an Axis glider bomb but survived. Forman was awarded his third DSC for leadership and saving his ship which had to limp back to Malta for repairs. Early in 1944 he was posted to another Hunt class destroyer, *Garth,* and in June took part in the D-Day landings. At the end of October, *Garth* gave crucial gunfire support during the legendary assault by the Canadian infantry brigade on the island of Walcheren in the Scheldt estuary close to the key port of Antwerp.

Robert 'Jumbo' Jenks (25–27), the son of a former Lord Mayor of London, was another who had a very lively war. A Lt. Commander for most of the conflict, he was awarded a DSC for his role commanding the destroyer *Quail* in the Salerno landings in 1943. He was also Mentioned in Despatches after captaining the 'Hunt' class destroyer *Atherstone* in the so-called New Year 42 operation and received a second MiD in February 1942 for his leadership when the 15th Destroyer Flotilla beat off a German air attack, and a Croix de Guerre and third MiD for his role in the commando raid on St. Nazaire in May 1942. Ahead of that raid, Jenks was one of five commanders shown aerial photos taken days before the raid by a lone RAF reconnaissance Spitfire. This revealed several large merchant ships. "What a prize! All of us were full of excited anticipation over these beautiful pictures" he is quoted as saying in a book about the raid, *Into The Jaws of Death.* But the select group was also shocked to spot five high-speed Kriegsmarine surface ships, similar to British Hunt-class destroyers, anchored in the Normandie Dock area. *Atherstone's* main contribution occurred when, together with another destroyer, it attacked *U-593* and forced the submarine to stay submerged for hours, so preventing it from interfering with the operation against the Normandie docks. Another role was to rescue any commando survivors. Jenks was, wrote Commander Robert Ryder VC, commanding officer of the raid who travelled to and from St. Nazaire in *Atherstone,* "of the very greatest assistance."

John Burfield (31–34) captained the F-class destroyer, *Faulknor,* and a frigate, *Byron,* in the 1944–45 period. But it was from 1939–42, as First Lieutenant for four years in the H-class destroyer *Havok* – one of the best-known British warships of the Second World War with eleven battle honours to her name – that Burfield came of age as a combative, creative and resilient young naval officer. His war had commenced in April 1940 when he was *Havock's* Boarding Officer as the ship took part in the Royal Navy raid on Narvik harbour in northern Norway during which two enemy destroyers were sunk. In retirement he recalled vividly the speed at which *Havock* left the area after the boarding party he was leading discovered that a German transport, which the British flotilla had set fire to, was carrying ammunition and was about to explode.

John Burfield.

The perilous Narvik operation set a pattern. *Havock* was transferred to the Mediterranean Fleet soon after, and Burfield was to be Mentioned in Despatches twice in the next 12 months as one engagement with the enemy succeeded another. In a fierce battle with the Italian Navy off Cape Spada, *Havock* rescued more than 500 sailors from a sinking Italian cruiser. In October it surprised an Italian submarine, *Berillo,* on the surface and forced it to scuttle before rescuing the crew. Another Mention in Despatches for Burfield resulted. By March 1941 *Havock* was screening Allied battleships and cruisers during the Battle of Cape Matapan. In what turned out to be a decisive Allied naval victory, it sank an Italian destroyer. Burfield was awarded a DSC. Repeat operations in the Mediterranean developed that year as *Havock* assisted the Allied evacuation from Crete in May, ran ammunition and troops several times into the besieged fortress of Tobruk in north Africa and escorted numerous perilous convoys to Malta.

In March 1942 *Havock* took part in the Second Battle of Sirte, helping to protect another Malta-bound convoy successfully. Burfield, by now the First Lieutenant on board, was again Mentioned in Despatches. Damaged in this action, *Havock* – described at the time by the *Daily Mirror* as "Britain's No. 2 destroyer in the war" – was on its way from Malta to Gibraltar for repairs when a navigational error led it too close to the Tunisian coast and the vessel ran into a sandbank. Before long, the entire ship's company, including Burfield, had been interned by the Vichy French authorities at Laghouat, a "Beau Geste" style fort 150 miles from the coast on the edge of the Sahara Desert. Conditions here were tough, medical supplies non-existent and there was never enough food or water. The only diversion was trying to escape through three rows of barbed wire. Burfield did so three times, was caught on each occasion and spent 90 days in solitary confinement. The captain of *Havock* was eventually court-martialled, reprimanded for hazarding his vessel and never given another command. Like his crew and most destroyer commanders, he had been sleep-deprived and exhausted at the time his ship ran aground. In an account Burfield wrote of his time in *Havock* and in captivity, and in evidence he gave at the court martial, it seems clear that he had a strained relationship with his commanding officer, blaming him for not asking him to take control of navigation through the dangerous waters off Tunisia.

Freed after seven months when the Vichy French in north Africa switched sides following Operation Torch and the American landings in Algeria, John Burfield soon returned to the fray in *Faulknor*, known as "the hardest working destroyer" in the Royal Navy. In 1944 *Faulknor* was part of the D-Day naval force providing gunfire support off Juno beach. At one stage the ship became a glorified ferry, conveying General Bernard Montgomery to France the day after the invasion and taking the First and Second Sea Lords, the Naval Secretary and the Lord Privy Seal (Lord Beaverbrook) on day trips to view the assault area. At the end of 1944 Burfield, still a Lieutenant, received his first command – an American-built Lend Lease frigate called *Byron*. In *Byron* he took part in the sinking of two German U-boats, *U-722* and *U-1001*, in March and April 1945, winning a bar to his DSC for his role in the latter action off southwest Ireland. Resigning from the Navy in 1959, he joined the oil company BP and ran the company's aircraft refuelling operation in Europe for some years before retiring to the south coast and spending "many happy years" re-building and sailing an 1875 Bristol pilot cutter. He died in 1998.

Other Old Pangbournians who captained destroyers with distinction during the Second World War include **Robert Woodward (29–32)** who was once towed successfully across the North Sea with a live German bomb in his ship's engine room and commanded several ships including *Scout* and *Whitshed*; **John Aitken (31–35)** who won the DSC in *Bulldog* when the destroyer attacked *U-110* and seized its codebooks and minefield charts before the submarine sank. He was also Mentioned in Despatches for "distinguished services" on the Murmansk convoy run; **James Wilford (19–21)** who took part in the 1941 commando raid on the Lofoten Islands and went on to command *Chelsea* and *Volunteer*, in the latter escorting the 1st US Division to the beaches of Normandy in 1944; and **Arthur Rowell (22–25)**. In *Walker*, Rowell took part in six convoys to and from Murmansk in 1943–44, surviving unscathed and being Mentioned in Despatches twice. **David Ramsay (26–28)** won a DSC and lost a leg at Anzio in 1944 after *Spartan*, the destroyer he was captaining, was hit by an aerial torpedo and sank. Before that, he had survived the sinking of the destroyer *Wessex* in 1940. **Jack Keir (34–37)** served in *Boadicea* 1941–43, taking part in convoy duty in the North Atlantic, two convoys to Russia and the Allied landings in North Africa when he was Mentioned in Despatches. Given command of the frigate *Spey* at the start of 1944, he sank two U-boats in the Western Approaches off southwest Ireland in March and was awarded the DSC. In 1966 he was one of 200 veterans to receive a medal from the Soviet Union in commemoration of the Arctic convoys. **Peter MacIver (19–21)** captained three ships from 1940–45 – *Periwinkle* (a corvette), *Georgetown* (a destroyer) and *Hargood* (a frigate). In *Periwinkle*, together with another RN vessel, he "depth-charged *U-147* to destruction" on June 2, 1942 northwest of Ireland after the German

Peter MacIver.

submarine had sunk a merchant vessel in a convoy *Periwinkle* was escorting – an action for which he received a DSO, a rare honour for a Lt RNR at the time.

It might be said that each of these destroyer commanders was simply doing his duty and deserved no special recognition or awards. Moreover, while the destroyer attrition rate was very high – a total of 57 RN destroyers were sunk by enemy action between 1939–45 in the Mediterranean alone – all the men in this chapter, if not their ships, did survive the six-year conflict. Yet few spoke publicly about their wartime experiences, none glamourized their role or regarded themselves as anything special and, unlike Battle of Britain pilots, they were never lionised by the British public. Indeed, dozens of books have been written about World War 2 destroyers, but none about their captains. Two films – the 1942 Noel Coward/ David Lean hit *In Which We Serve,* and *The Cruel Sea* which came out in 1953 and was based on a best-selling 1951 book by Lt. Commander Nicholas Monsarrat RNVR – did at least highlight their contribution.

Three generations after the 1939–45 conflict what stands out today is the loneliness and strain of wartime destroyer command – and the guts needed to return to the fray time and again. In the heat of continuous battle, who knows how a person will react? Many young lives rested on split-second, often instinctive, decisions taken by the captain of a ship. The hardship of war at sea, particularly in winter in the bleak north Atlantic and on the Arctic run, the round-the-clock threat of possibly fatal attack from the skies or the oceans' depths, the threadbare conditions on board a destroyer with few rest or recreational facilities and no chance of communication with home, and the repetitive nature of convoy operations often for years at a time, all piled on the pressure. In addition, some destroyer commanders seemed to steer into trouble far more often than others; as Roger Hill observed wryly in his memoir, after he left *Ledbury* the ship had a largely uneventful war. Hill, on the other hand, ran the gauntlet wherever he served – and actually thrived on encounters with the enemy, until his nerves gave out.

One day, Hill was alone on the bridge of *Grenville* in the Bay of Biscay during the summer of 1943. Out of a clear sky, sixteen German Dornier 217s carrying a hitherto unknown type of munition that tracked its target on hitting the water and could turn in circles, came at the ship at 400 mph. Hill, speeding along at 32 knots, zig-zagged *Grenville* frantically from side to side, dodging one bomb after another and firing up at the attackers. "Those were the most taut and exciting minutes that can possibly be imagined... Suddenly it was over. The planes had gone, the guns ceased fire and we wiped our foreheads. "Pass the word to Charley for hot tea on the bridge," a relieved captain ordered. Roger Hill lived to fight another day – and, like so many destroyer commanders, helped to win a war.

4

THE SUBMARINERS: BRAVE PIRATES OF THE DEEP

— ◉ —

On March 3 1943 the First Lord of the Admiralty, A.V. Alexander, made a lengthy statement in the House of Commons about the progress of the war at sea. During it he said: "The House might like me to put on record the names of a few commanding officers of submarines who have operated in the North African campaign and who, between them, have sunk a very large number indeed of enemy supply ships and their escorts. Here are the names." Two of the nine submariners highlighted were Old Pangbournians. Two years on, in February 1945, Alexander visited the Nautical College. In a short speech he stated: "We have appreciated to the fullest possible extent the contribution which the College has made in providing officers for the Royal Navy and, more especially, the Merchant Navy…The College has every reason to be proud of the record of those who have passed through it into the Services…Your Honours List grows and grows."

The exploits of OP submariners were, indeed, spectacular. A number lost their lives including three commanding officers – Frank Gibbs, Michael Willmott and Drummond St. Clair Ford. At least two RN submarines during the war are known to have been officered entirely by OPs, while OPs often succeeded each other in command or served together or served under one another. Something about life and battle beneath the waves evidently appealed to the Pangbourne Spirit – the opportunity to display initiative at sea; early command of one's own boat; the chance to get to know a crew; the prospect it offered to take the fight directly to the enemy; the concentration and endurance and cunning and sea skills needed to stalk an elusive prey; even perhaps some of the danger and hardships involved.

Life on a Second World War submarine certainly was not for the timorous. The boats suffered from many mechanical defects. Plans changed with dizzying frequency. Only the captain really knew what was going on – for most of the 40–60 men on board, where they were heading and what they were aiming to achieve was a mystery. Better not to know went the prevailing mantra of the ordinary seaman. More to the point, one repetitive meal a day was the norm, fresh bread would quickly develop mould from the damp conditions and food poisoning was rife. Water was only for drinking, not washing. Men slept where they could and never shaved or undressed on patrol. Smoking was banned inside the submarine but rum sometimes was issued neat.

During daylight hours, a submarine would usually remain submerged and there was a lot of sitting around waiting for something to happen. To men in submarines, the sea is full of noise, no more so than in wartime. Some is recognisable, such as an engine. Others, like the curious 'North Sea grunt,' heard in both world wars is more mysterious and probably caused by dolphins or porpoises. When a vessel did surface in complete darkness – its most vulnerable moment – the men would take it in turns to climb up to the conning tower to get some fresh air. Pastimes inside the 16-foot-wide steel hull – slightly wider than a London underground train – varied from cards to chess, carving and board games. Discipline on board was less formal than the Navy norm, as was dress. Somewhere inside the boat an argument might be going on to pass the time. Then a target is spotted, diving stations are ordered and each man jumps to his post. Tensions rise, absolute silence prevails. Maybe torpedoes are fired. Soon after, depth charges might rain down on the attacking submarine 60–70 feet or more beneath the waves, as a deadly cat-and-mouse chase begins. Mechanical breakdowns were all-too common. In the Mediterranean, with Allied air superiority constantly challenged, nerves could quickly become shredded. Here war patrols lasted two to three weeks and a crew would expect to return to port dirty, smelly and exhausted yet glad, once again, to be safely on dry land. After a too-short rest, they would do it all again. In the circumstances, under such fraught conditions, the toll was bound to be heavy; from 1940–45 a total of 45 RN submarines were lost in the Mediterranean. As Vice Admiral Max Horton, the outstanding Flag Office Submarines 1940–42, put it bluntly: "There is no room for mistakes in submarines. You are either alive or dead."

What sustained submariners is hard to pin down – the typical officer was not particularly introspective or emotional or religious although many were patriotic and, as the war wore on, increasingly determined to destroy the fascist menace once and for all. Mutual trust among a crew was vital. In his fine memoir *One of Our Submarines,* Edward Young, an RNVR officer who captained a submarine, reflects from time to time on his motives. At first, he simply wished to learn celestial navigation. Having volunteered, he tried "to convince myself that I was doing the right, the heroic thing." But it was too late to back out – "I should never have the courage to retract." By the time, after five adventurous years, he steered his submarine safely into Portsmouth harbour from the Pacific in April 1945, it was simply the feeling that he had brought his ship and crew home in one piece – "It was a most satisfactory feeling." Nothing heroic.

Yet for Royal Navy submariners, eight of whom won the Victoria Cross for their exploits during the Second World War, their memory of the fighting differed markedly from that of other combatants, and their casualties were correspondingly greater. German and British submarine losses both underline the difference. Each country began World War 2 with about 55 submarines. The Germans built 1,156 more during the war and lost 784 (65%) including 28,000 U-boat crew. The British built about 250 submarines and lost 79 (26%), six out of ten in the Mediterranean. One in three British submariners, or about 4,000 men, were killed in action – "a heavy price to pay" in the words of the official history of the war at sea.

From the outset, protecting trade routes and the import of vital raw materials was key to the British effort. In the early years of the conflict, with naval clashes concentrated off Norway, in the North Sea, around the entrance to the Baltic and in the Atlantic, RN submarine losses were heavy with few offsetting gains. As German warships and merchant ships, if not the U-boats, were bottled up by an Allied naval blockade of German and French-held ports, Axis target opportunities in the Atlantic dried up. At this point the British submarine focus turned decisively south.

Two basic types of boats constituted the backbone of the Royal Navy's force – large patrol submarines epitomised by the T-class with its range of 9,000 miles and powerful weaponry including 16 torpedoes; and medium-sized patrol submarines such as the U-class. Cheap, easy to build, and manoeuvrable, these carried ten torpedoes and were suited to conditions in the Mediterranean. For much of this period, the Germans had command of the skies from nearby airfields whilst the relatively shallow depths in the Mediterranean forced Allied submarines through a small number of risky 'choke points' that the Italians mined heavily. Should a submarine strike a mine, its chances of survival were about zero. If it was depth charged by air or by a destroyer and hit, few of the crew had much realistic chance of escape either. And if spotted on the surface, it was vulnerable to ramming, would always be outgunned and normally had to surrender.

Throughout the Mediterranean campaign, five war patrols were "about par" for an RN submarine before it was sunk or damaged beyond repair. It was in the Mediterranean, though, that RN submarine commanders actually came into their own and played a significant role during a three-year struggle for dominance with Italian and German naval ships and aircraft. Initially, the fight was to maintain supplies to the besieged island of Malta. In time, as the battle on land edged the Allied way, it became a struggle for control of supply routes to Axis forces in North Africa. This, too, tended to see Allied naval forces on the back foot until the relief of Malta and the victorious battle of El Alamein in late-1942. Subsequently, the focus switched to support Allied land campaigns to liberate Italy and Greece and the islands of the Aegean.

Typical of the older breed of submarine commander was **Mervyn Wingfield** (24–25). He had joined the Submarine Service in 1933 and served most of the

Mervyn Wingfield.

Second World War in submarines – one of the few RN officers to do so and survive. Along the way he was awarded the DSO, DSC and Bar and Mentioned in Despatches. His eventful war included colliding with a British trawler and sinking in the North Sea, wintering in the Arctic, taking part in the St. Nazaire raid, being the first RN submarine commander to sink a Japanese submarine, and getting stuck in the mud in the Malacca Straits whilst being depth charged by a chasing Japanese ship.

Long after the war Wingfield wrote a lively memoir, *Wingfield at War*, published first in 1983 and again in 2016. An often frank, self-deprecating tale reflecting Wingfield's deceptively laid-back personality, it is full of tongue-in-cheek humour and shows the author robustly unimpressed by naval tradition – a typical trait of submariners of the time. "Nobody pretended to do much work" he writes of a submarine he served in before war broke out. When the fighting began, Wingfield started his war nonchalantly with "a couple of games of golf" at Penang golf club and took his dinner jacket and golf clubs on patrol out of Colombo, to Mauritius and the Seychelles in late-1939. He sailed for Malta at the start of 1940 and "the real war began."

Wingfield's first command was *H 43* – built in 1917 and "quite unfit" for World War 2. In it he stalked a U-boat for the first time in the Heligoland Bight at the end of 1940. In *H43*, too, he experienced the first of four occasions when he was bombed by aircraft of his own side. "I always disappeared fast – to safety, at a depth of 100 feet!" Early in 1941 he took command of a new U-class submarine, *Umpire*. Belying his relaxed reputation, Edward Young, one of his young officers, describes Wingfield as looking "older and sterner than he was." Two days after taking the submarine to sea for the first time, at midnight off Cromer in Norfolk, *Umpire* was run down by an armed RN trawler. "He barely had time to shout 'You bloody bastard! You've sunk a British submarine!', his obituary recounted, before being swept into the sea. He was kept afloat by a kapok-lined Burberry given him by his wife, remaining in the water for 40 minutes before he was rescued, unconscious and frozen. Out of 31 men on board, only nine survived.

By way of compensation, after two months he was given command of *Sturgeon*, "a cranky boat prone to break surface after firing a full salvo of six torpedoes." In 1942 it nearly sank, having suddenly dropped to 250 feet in rough sea before Wingfield could stabilize it. For a time, *Sturgeon* was based in Polyarnoe in northern Russia. Here its torpedoes froze in their tubes and became immobile; relying on ingenuity, Wingfield submerged to clear mounds of ice off the foredeck and thaw out the torpedo tubes. Whilst in the far North, he sank two German merchant ships, one by penetrating Trondheim fjord for 22 hours at 100 ft depth to avoid minefields while seeking the German battleship *Tirpitz*. When he finally surfaced, batteries exhausted, the air inside the boat was so foul that a cigarette would not burn. He was awarded the DSO "for courage and skill" and the formidable Max Horton sent him a congratulatory signal "on a fine submarine feat…better luck next time." Soon after, *Sturgeon* was sent south to act as a navigational marker for commandos taking part in the St. Nazaire raid. To do so, he navigated through 450 miles of enemy-controlled ocean to a precise spot off the French coast – "the nautical equivalent of finding a needle in a haystack" according to one report. On arrival, he cooperated with a fellow OP, **Robin Jenks (25–27)**, captain of the destroyer *Atherstone*. Jenks, who had a "stentorian" voice, alarmed Wingfield at dawn before the raid by using his loud hailer to shout across "Good morning Mervyn" at a time when strict silence was the order of the day.

Command of the new-build T-class submarine *Taurus* followed in the autumn of 1942. Wingfield always prided himself on his gunnery and his crews nicknamed him 'Dillinger.' One day in late 1942, practising firing in Loch Long in Scotland, he ordered the gun crew to fire at a ruined cottage on the shore and destroyed the Duke of Argyll's precious wood store. This earned an official reprimand. "Like many another submarine captain at this time, I was beginning to get a little too big for my boots. After all, we had a high scarcity value and could get away with almost anything" he wrote in his memoir. Moved to Algiers in March 1943 at a time when the RN had only ten submarines left in the Mediterranean, he was awarded a DSC for three war patrols which included sinking at least ten merchant ships, among them a Spanish vessel trying to beat the blockade off Toulon, landing agents behind enemy lines and rescuing Allied escapees. Once, he brazenly entered a port in the northern Aegean on the surface and began to fire at ships in the harbour. A squadron of Bulgarian cavalry wearing breast plates and carrying lances opened fire with machine guns strapped to the horses' backsides. *Taurus* quickly retreated. Normally, after a successful patrol, Wingfield would take a day's holiday from the war, entering in the log 'Continued patrol, nothing sighted.' On this occasion the coxswain brought him a large glass of rum, saying "Complaints about the rum, sir. You'd better taste this."

Taurus was sent next to the Far East. After several abortive patrols which left Wingfield "under a cloud," he experienced his "finest hour" as a submarine commander at the end of 1943 when informed that a Japanese submarine, *134*, and its escort were approaching Penang. A salvo of six torpedoes hit *134* amidships and one sank it instantly. *Taurus* was pursued relentlessly by a Japanese submarine chaser and a bomber aircraft as it slid away. Having grounded the submarine, depth charges by the enemy caused some damage so Wingfield brought *Taurus* to the surface. The submarine's gun crew promptly silenced the chaser's guns and disabled its engines with accurate fire before the bomber reappeared and moved in for the kill. Wingfield sounded the diving warning with 15 people still on deck and firing. "In a matter of seconds, we were under water with every man safe inside," wrote his First Lieut. **Derek Godfrey (36–39)**. Another DSC followed. *Taurus* moved on to land Gurkha soldiers on an Andaman island on a recce mission. A Mention in Despatches ensued.

Tongue-in-cheek and self-aware throughout his book, Wingfield records his decorations without comment but does add that "some extraordinary decisions" were made by a department called 'Honours & Awards' during the war. These included, he wrote, a DSO to a destroyer captain "while he was in hospital with appendicitis." Mervyn Wingfield's active war came to an end with two desk jobs. His time at sea in submarines, he remarked, was "the most important of my life and left deep impressions. Fear is something I became well acquainted with during the war years. I believe most people feel fear to about the same extent. But the trained man doesn't show it and doesn't let it influence his actions. In retirement, he arranged mortgages for yacht owners, delivered yachts, hosted some memorable lunches and, as a Second Officer, made several voyages in merchant vessels. Life, he always felt, was for living.

That was certainly a view shared by **Ian McGeoch (28–31)**, one of the outstanding young submariners highlighted in parliament by A.V. Alexander. McGeoch, too, wrote a post-war memoir about his "odyssey" in wartime submarines *An Affair of Chances*. The title came from a saying attributed to Thucydides – "Consider the vast influence of accident in war before you are engaged in it. As it continues, it generally becomes an affair

Ian McGeoch.

of chances." Given his first command aged 28 in *P228* (subsequently renamed *Splendid*), in six crowded months "as a daring naval commander (McGeoch) cut a swath through enemy shipping in the Mediterranean" in the words of an obituary in *The Guardian* in 2007. During five war patrols from October 1942 to April 1943 he sank 14 ships including two destroyers and, on each patrol, sank at least two vessels – more than any other Allied submarine in the period. A DSO awarded early in 1943 cited his "outstanding zeal and efficiency and daring…His coolness and skill in handling his submarine enabled him to avoid damage during subsequent depth-charge attacks… (He displayed) leadership and daring (and) a very high standard of fighting efficiency."

On his first war patrol in *Splendid* McGeoch managed to sink an Italian destroyer with the last of his 13 torpedoes – a dozen had missed their target – and sink a damaged enemy merchant ship with gunfire before evading a double torpedo attack. He described this patrol as "exhilarating." On other patrols he landed agents covertly behind enemy lines, sank more anti-submarine vessels and destroyed a 10,000-ton tanker for which he was awarded a DSC in April 1943. On his fifth patrol at the end of that month his luck ran out. South of Capri *Splendid* was depth-charged and sunk by a German destroyer. In the action McGeoch lost the sight in one eye and was taken prisoner after realising that the situation was hopeless and ordering 'Abandon Ship." As a result of this order, 27 of the 45-man crew survived. "It took great moral courage to take the decision to abandon ship and thus save the lives of the majority of his crew," wrote Admiral of the Fleet Sir Terence Lewin in a Foreword to McGeoch's book.

Having made sure no one else was alive on the submarine and that it would sink, McGeoch was the last man to escape. Hauled out of the water by a German delivering the classic line "For you ze vor iss ofer," McGeoch thought to himself 'No it bloody well isn't." He declined assistance, despite his wounded eye, until he had assured himself that his surviving crew were being helped. McGeoch's direct superior, Captain G.B.H. Fawkes, subsequently termed him a "brilliant and fearless officer." Rear Admiral Claud Barry, commander of RN Submarines in 1943, cabled: "Lt. McGeoch is a gallant, determined and most outstanding officer. His temporary loss to the Submarine Branch is profoundly regretted by all in it" – a sentiment echoed by the Commander-in-Chief Mediterranean Admiral A.B. Cunningham. Lewin, a junior destroyer officer during the Second World War, added: "The difference in our experiences is profound. While we slipped out of our forward base to catch the enemy at night, and were often back in harbour at dawn before the Luftwaffe was active, the submarines patrolled for weeks at a time, playing the waiting game in conditions that favoured the submarine hunters. At that time (1942–43) our success rate was meagre (whereas) throughout the whole of the war in the Mediterranean our submarines made a major contribution to the Allied armies' ultimate victory in North Africa by strangling the enemy's supply line – but at a price."

McGeoch was true to himself and soon escaped from captivity in Italy (for which he was Mentioned in Despatches), reached neutral Switzerland and spent six months there scheming to return to England through occupied France which, in time, he did. Post-war, he became one of the Navy's most celebrated and cerebral officers rising to the rank of Vice Admiral and being knighted in 1969. His memoir is particularly notable for the observations it includes about wartime submarine combat. Fighting a submarine successfully, he believed, was largely a matter of experience with many missed targets along the way. Missing targets, he admitted, had a negative impact on crew morale particularly if this followed days of silently stalking a vessel. Having been outpaced on the surface by two German U-boats, he wished British submarines were faster. He added that the longer patrols went on, the more defects developed in *Splendid* – a very common complaint. Commanding a submarine to maximum effect, he reckoned, was "often a collective activity" with other officers necessarily advising the captain on some aspect of tactics or speeds or escape routes. "It is impossible," he wrote "to recapture the ineffable bliss of being back in harbour after two or three weeks of physical discomfort, imminent danger and continuous concentration." Yet within days he always wanted to get away from "the bantering small talk of the mess (on a depot ship) and, above all, the need to be in uniform."

The second OP mentioned in the House of Commons by A.V. Alexander was Lt **Peter Harrison** (27–30) who was awarded the DSO and two DSCs during the war. It was while captain of *Ultimatum,* a U-class submarine which he commanded from the builders' yard at Barrow in July 1941, that Harrison's reputation was forged over the course of 15 nerve-racking war patrols in the Mediterranean during 13 months to late-1942. That he survived more than 100 depth-charges by enemy ships unscathed amazed his peers, on one occasion being straddled by three Italian destroyers and having to dive to 270 feet – *Ultimatum's* maximum depth – and stay there for many hours to escape. That he sank an Italian submarine and two Italian surface ships in this period, put a German U-boat out of action and survived Operation Pedestal – the ferociously-attacked convoy sent by the Allies to relieve the island of Malta in August 1942 which Axis forces assailed with 150 bombers and 80 torpedo aircraft – makes his achievements especially noteworthy.

Returning to London in October 1942, Harrison was summoned to meet Admiral Horton to describe his experiences first-hand – a rare honour. Towards the end of the war, he undertook risky patrols off the Japanese-defended Dutch East Indies (Indonesia) in the submarine *Tiptoe* during which he sank a number of enemy coasters. *Tiptoe* was to appear in a post-war film called *Morning Departure* starring John Mills and proved to be the last T-class submarine afloat, not being scrapped until 1979. Harrison's first DSC had been awarded during his stint as First Lt. in *Tetrach* in 1940 following four combative and operationally active patrols in the North Sea. The award citation states that it was "For bravery and determination during arduous and successful patrols." Given his first command in *Ultimatum*, his DSO was recognition for torpedoing one of the best Italian submarines, *Ammiraglio Millo*, in mid-March 1942 off the Calabrian coast. *Ammiraglio Millo* had been returning from a patrol off Malta. *Ultimatum* managed to rescue 14 of her 57-strong crew and Harrison changed course to land the men in Malta. The Italian commander, who survived the sinking, became one of Harrison's friends after the war. The citation simply refers to his "courage and skill in successful patrols in HM submarines." His second DSC came after *Ultimatum's* essentially defensive role during Operation Pedestal.

One OP who captained no less than six submarines between 1942–45 – *H28, H44, H33, Utmost, Sturgeon* and *Spirit* – and served in three others, taking part in at least a dozen war patrols, was **Anthony 'Tim' Langridge (29–32)**. He had entered the Royal Navy in 1933 and in 1939 joined *Narwhal* of the 5th Submarine Flotilla. He was in the boat in February 1940, while escorting a convoy to Norway, when *Narwhal* was instrumental in forcing a U-boat to surface and scuttle. Shortly after,

Tim Langridge.

Narwhal was sunk but Langridge was in hospital having suffered an appendicitis. Described by one of his captains as a "thoroughly capable and zealous submarine First Lieutenant," he was given his first command in *H44* in early 1942. That April he became captain of *Utmost* and did three war patrols in the Mediterranean as part of the 10th Submarine Flotilla including taking a "patrol position" off Sicily during Operation Pedestal to relieve the island of Malta.

Langridge won his DSC as commander of *Spirit* having been sent to the Far East early in 1944. The citation highlighted his "outstanding courage, efficiency and daring." Four active patrols saw repeated run-ins with bellicose Japanese vessels off Ceylon (Sri Lanka) and Siam (Thailand) and in the Java and South China Seas. At least six Japanese coastal tankers and junks were sunk during these incursions and *Spirit* had several highly dangerous gunfire exchanges with shore batteries, one of which involved a hasty dive to escape when an enemy aircraft suddenly appeared. On another occasion the submarine by chance picked up three grateful RAF aircrew from a ditched Barracuda bomber.

Langridge's ninth war patrol in March 1945 in *Spirit* – by now in dire need of repairs – almost proved to be her last. Having sunk a coaster with a crew of 40 Japanese sailors in the South China Sea, *Spirit* stopped to rescue the survivors. A dangerous delay followed since only two of the Japanese seamen were prepared to be taken on board. Soon after, still on the surface, Langridge ran into a well-armed Japanese escort vessel. Diving immediately, *Spirit* was caught on an uncharted pinnacle of coral. For hours the crew maintained total silence as the enemy searched relentlessly above. Managing to slip away undetected, the submarine had another close shave when an RAF aircraft mistook *Spirit* for an enemy boat and fired on her (eliciting an apology from the pilot). In the resulting confusion, a member of the ship's company fell into the sea. Knowing the man could not swim, Langridge dived in himself and undertook the rescue confident, he explained, that his second-in-command would not dive the submarine without him.

Langridge came through the war unscathed and remained in the Navy for 13 years before launching a post-war career in industry, naval training and the charity sector. His school contemporary, **Peter 'Sam' Marriott (29–32)** DSO & DSC, having commanded three boats and spent all the conflict in submarines, rose to be a Captain RN and had much to do with the development of Britain's nuclear submarines. He retired from the service in 1964 and began a noteworthy second career in conservation in Norfolk. Described by the *Eastern Daily Press* as "a distinguished war hero," Marriott achieved a unique distinction during the war – captaining the only U-boat captured by the Allies that was used in operations against Germany.

Commissioned as *U570* in the Kriegsmarine in mid-1941, this submarine had been bombed by the RAF, damaged, and seized on the surface by RN ships on its first patrol. Made seaworthy again (see Chapter 2), re-named *Graph* and put into service with the Navy in September, the boat was found to have some advantages over Allied submarines. It could, for example dive as deep as 750 feet – far deeper than RN depth charges could reach at that

Peter Marriot.

time. Its rubber machinery mountings made it stealthier than British submarines and its underwater acoustic equipment was a significant improvement on the RN equivalent. Marriott was given the command, and made his first of three war patrols in *Graph* in October 1942. One afternoon about 60 miles north-east of Cape Ortegal in northern Spain, *Graph* was chased by a U-boat and fired four torpedoes back at it. Explosions were heard and Marriott believed that he had achieved a hit. "The irony of a U-boat sinking a U-boat caused great jubilation in the navies of the Allies" according to a report at the time. Marriott was awarded a DSO for "great courage, determination and a successful submarine patrol." After the war it became clear that the U-boat had been damaged but not sunk. Two further war patrols in *Graph* followed but mechanical defects, a shortage of spare parts and the RN's inability to replace the U-boat's batteries meant that in 1943 the vessel was placed in reserve.

Shortly after, Marriott commissioned a new-build submarine *Stoic,* took it out to the Indian Ocean and for the next 18 months in 1943–44 was involved in many engagements with Japanese vessels during seven war patrols off Burma (Myanmar), Malaya (Malaysia) and Java/Sumatra (Indonesia), sinking at least eight coastal vessels, a couple of tankers and one troop transport for which he was awarded a DSC. After the war, as the only RN officer who knew how to handle a U-boat, he took over a surrendered U-boat, *U776*, in May 1945, brought it into the Thames estuary – every dockyard crane dipped its jib as it passed up river – and berthed at Shadwell Dock. Large crowds appeared and he played host to 3,000 visitors a day before going to Northern Ireland where he took command of all surrendered U-boats.

Also awarded the DSO and DSC for his success as a submarine commander was **Russell Brookes (27–29)**. He served in eight submarines 1939–45, commanding six and taking part in 14 war patrols. It was in *Clyde*, alongside two other OPs in First Lieutenant **Peter Miles (34–38)** and Engineer Officer **George Gay (27–30)** – "a wonderful team" according to Brookes – that he was awarded his DSO "for bravery and skill in successful patrols in HM submarines." This imprecise citation actually

Russell Brookes.

referred to five highly dangerous "storage" trips taking aviation fuel and other supplies, including powdered milk, aircraft wheels and munitions, from Gibraltar and Beirut to Malta when the island was under aerial bombardment in 1942. "I consider her passages are comparable in risk to those undertaken by a submarine minelayer," wrote his commanding officer when recommending the DSO.

On one of these trips *Clyde* was in the Grand Harbour when a German air raid began. Only quick action by Brookes saved the submarine. Having dived instantly, it suffered damage to its after hydrophones and had to limp back into the harbour with batteries and air almost exhausted. On another occasion *Clyde* was attacked by an RAF Spitfire while outside the Grand Harbour. On his fifth storage trip, while returning to Beirut, he attacked and may have sunk a U-boat with *Clyde's* last torpedo – the stern of the German boat was seen "sticking up vertically" but Brookes did not hang around to discover more as another U-boat was nearby. His DSC had been awarded as First Lieutenant on *Triton* in April 1940 when the submarine sank two German troop carriers and a patrol vessel in the Skagerrak strait between Norway and Denmark.

Brookes was one of a number of Old Pangbournians, mostly anonymous, who contributed vivid articles about their experiences to the school magazine during the conflict. In his case his piece, "An Unusual Job," was signed "R.S.B." and appeared in the 1943/44 *Log*. It began: "Some while ago a besieged island was in dire need of certain essential armaments and stores. The outside of the island's harbours had been mined and most of the minesweepers had been damaged by enemy action. The Staff had, therefore, decided to use several of the larger types of submarines to penetrate the minefields and get stores to this island. My submarine happened to be one of the boats selected to carry out this job. Needless to say, we were not altogether thrilled with the idea as we should have preferred to be out on patrol hunting enemy supply ships – in fact, to do the real job a submarine is designed to do. However, this was a really essential job and it had to be done."

The article went on to describe how the crew, most of who were 'old stagers' who had served on *Clyde* (not named directly) for some time, adapted to work as stevedores. "It all seemed strange having to handle such things as Bills of Lading, Mate's Receipts and all the rest of the paperwork connected with cargo." Once the stores were on board "we sailed and as soon as possible dived…Many weary days passed" before Malta was reached. "Discharging nearly always was done at night and even with heavy air raids in progress. The crew worked like slaves, bombs or no bombs…Our cargo once discharged, we rapidly embarked a certain amount of ballast in the form of lead and copper ingots. These return trips were, in some ways, rather more exciting" as *Clyde* carried passengers – often up to 50 – usually a mixture of officers and men who had been stranded on Malta for one reason or another, including air crew and seamen sunk on merchant vessels. All told, Brookes was to navigate five months safely on these patrols before *Clyde* was sufficiently unseaworthy to merit a trip to the USA. Here it spent most of 1943 being repaired in Philadelphia Navy Yard.

Mostly, such exploits by submariners – far from land, silent, subject to censorship and often individual actions not part of a wider battle – went unrecorded in the national press. But early in the war, at a time when Winston Churchill, as First Lord of the Admiralty, was becoming exasperated by the seeming inability of the RN to hit back at the enemy, one submariner did achieve prominence. **Jack Slaughter** (19–20), in command of *Sunfish*, and part of the 2nd Submarine Flotilla, in April 1940 sank two German merchant ships and two German 'Q' ships (heavily armed, disguised merchant ships) – for which he was awarded a DSO the next month "for daring, endurance and resource." Hungry for heroes and anxious to boost naval morale, Churchill authorised national publicity for Slaughter and the *Sunfish* crew. A tall rugged man, he had a lurid reputation for highly descriptive Anglo-Saxon vocabulary. Eventually, Slaughter carried out 15 war patrols in *Sunfish* in the North Sea and Baltic Sea in the 12 months to September 1940. Subsequently, he commanded two submarine depot ships and ended the war as a Captain and senior officer of the 2nd Submarine Flotilla.

Numerous very young OPs served as officers in RN submarines too. Typical was **Oliver Lascelles** (34–38) who began as fourth hand on *Unruffled* in 1942 and ended as First Lieutenant with a DSC in 1945. In those three years *Unruffled*, with her famous ship's cat Timoshenko, sank 35,000 tons of enemy shipping in the Mediterranean as part of the 10th Flotilla known as "The Fighting Tenth." After the war Lascelles took command of a salvaged and peroxide-powered German submarine *U1407* – "not for anyone of nervous disposition" according to *The Daily Telegraph*. Explosions and fires were a daily occurrence but the boat's underwater speed was exceptional – 26 knots.

Another was **Kenneth Renshaw** (33–35) who had left the NCP to join P&O while continuing as an RNR officer. On the outbreak of war, he joined the submarine service and was Mentioned in Despatches in 1941 while serving in *Truant* in the Mediterranean and being awarded a DSC in *Truant* in March 1942 "for bravery and enterprise" after another Mediterranean war patrol. A second MiD came after he was in *Tuna* in July 1943 following a claimed sinking of a U-boat. Renshaw went on to command four submarines himself – *Sea Dog, H32, Vitality* and *Scorcher* before re-joining P&O after the war while remaining in the RNR.

Two articles by Renshaw appeared in *The Log* during the war under the by-line 'K.S.R.' The first, in the Summer 1943 issue, was titled Submarine Patrol and specifically highlights a hazardous patrol by *Truant* off Libya "along the enemy coast." A small enemy convoy guarded by a destroyer is spotted. *Truant* dives to 50 feet and rushes to intercept, fires at the destroyer, misses but hits a tanker in the convoy. The destroyer turns sharply towards the submarine which had got too close to the coast in pressing home its attack, "bumped the sand bottom and bounced to the surface." The Captain orders one of the compartments flooded and the damaged submarine comes to rest at 40 feet on the bottom – a sitting duck "in the calm, clear water" for any aircraft summoned by the destroyer. The captain tells "everyone what to do should the submarine be suddenly split in half by depth charges or ramming. Just at that moment there came an ominous sound…the rhythmic beat of a destroyer's propellers passing directly overhead. No one in the boat made a sound. Indeed, it was doubtful if they could have done so, the tension was so great." The destroyer raced back and forth overhead. *Truant* is stuck fast in the sand and "the stokers began to discuss the prospects for a run ashore."

For more than two hours the submarine lay wedged in the sand, mute and immobile. No depth charges were dropped by the destroyer – "Perhaps he had none left but more likely he wished to avoid killing the survivors from the tanker who may still have been in the water." Gradually, after continuous pumping and racing the motors, *Truant* began to move, navigating stern first for two miles to escape. After four hours, it surfaced "and raced away from 'the scene of the crime.'" It had already sunk three ships during the last week. "Down below, where dinner was being served, the crew were all laughing heartily at their very lucky escape and already discussing the prospects of another bag tomorrow."

The second article, in Spring 1944, titled 'Arctic Patrol,' tells the story of *Tuna's* sinking of *U644* in the Norwegian Sea in April 1943. It was so cold in the icy north that "it became hard for an individual to squeeze through the conning tower hatch due to the layers of clothing being worn." On the third day of the patrol *Tuna* ran into a blizzard, the wind was freezing, the seas "tremendous," life-lines had to be worn on the bridge and the ship lurched so violently that everything below deck "was in a complete shambles…. Every half hour hot water had to be poured down the voice-pipe to keep it clear." By this point *Tuna* was in waters where U-boats might be encountered. "It was all a matter of who saw (who) first now." Several U-boats were sighted in the next few days but never close enough to get a torpedo shot away. "At last, a chance came – a German submarine (was) 1,500 yards away coming towards us." Less than three minutes after sighting the enemy, torpedoes were on their way. "They could never know what hit them. There was a thunderous explosion, quickly followed by another, and the U-boat was no more than a swirling mass of oil and wreckage on the surface of the water. The only survivor gave up before we could reach him. Among the debris floated the cap of the German Officer of the Watch. The greatest thrill came a few days after when *Tuna* reached her base. As she slowly approached the depot ship the whole ship's company, who were lined along the decks, broke into a roar of cheering. It was a tremendous welcome home."

One OP submariner who was on the receiving end of enemy action yet survived to tell the tale was **David Abdy (25–28)**. He had entered the RN in 1929. By August 1941, aged 31, he was commanding the U-class submarine *P32*, 15 miles off Tripoli in the Mediterranean and racing to intercept an enemy convoy. Spotting five Italian merchant ships heading into Tripoli harbour under escort, he decided to run at full speed under a minefield probably laid by the Allies at a depth of around 70 feet. According to a vivid retelling of the episode in *Beneath the Waves* by A.S. Evans, the ploy failed and *P32* hit a mine eight miles out from Tripoli and sank. Eight of the crew forwards were killed instantly. All efforts to raise the submarine from the bottom failed. Abdy ordered the 23 survivors into the engine room. Escape through the conning tower hatch seemed possible but only by using the Davis Safety Escape Apparatus (DSEA). Abdy called for volunteers. Two stepped forward. Abdy's DSEA would not work but he went up anyway, holding his breath. He survived – at the time the deepest-ever underwater ascent without aid.

Emerging about five miles from the coast, Abdy headed for land with Coxswain Kirk. The third crew member had not been so fortunate. Nor had any of those who remained in the submarine as carbon dioxide poisoning took hold. It was about 5:00pm on a fine, warm sunny afternoon. Before long the convoy's escort plane spotted the swimmers and radioed for a rescue boat. One arrived after some hours and the RN pair became prisoners-of-war. After eighteen months in captivity, Abdy was repatriated by the Italians in a PoW exchange and resumed his naval career, captaining *Safari*, a training submarine, in 1944. For the rest of his life the loss of *P32* and 29 of its crew "greatly depressed him."

A rather different submarine operating in the Mediterranean was *Rorqual,* the leading RN minelaying submarine of World War 2. **Ian Stoop (34–38)** served in *Rorqual* for a year and a half from July 1942 to December 1943, latterly as First Lieutenant to its distinguished commander Lennox Napier, and left a rich account of its activities in a family memoir. During this period *Rorqual* laid about 500 mines in a dozen minefields and completed half a dozen vital storage runs to deliver ammunition, stores and petrol to the embattled island fortress that was Malta. "The cargoes they gave us to carry can hardly be called pleasant. Inside the submarine we had sacks of dehydrated cabbage, carbide and ammunition – the cabbage and carbine both evil smelling and the cabbage full of bugs. Outside the boat in our mine casing, we had eleven 1,000-gallon drums of petrol (100% octane) which was always a constant worry." On one occasion *Rorqual* encountered an Italian submarine "which had the nerve to fire three torpedoes at us, one of which exploded in our wake" and claimed it had sunk *Rorqual.* "It was a great day for us when at last a convoy managed to get through to Malta unscathed and we were relieved of our merchant shipping run."

To the crew of *Rorqual,* its mines were "eggs" and its torpedoes "babies." Both were very carefully cosseted. Having laid mines off Corfu on one operation, *Rorqual,* despite "strict instructions" to the contrary, attacked an Italian convoy including an armed merchant cruiser. Stoop described the firing of two torpedoes as "the most thrilling experience." One merchant vessel of some 5,000 tons was hit and sunk. Sixteen depth charges descended on *Rorqual* but it survived undamaged. For some months after, *Rorqual* was based in Beirut. The "dreaded part of these (mine-laying) operations West of Malta was passing through the heavily-mined Sicilian Channel. At times the enemy would discover the route we were using and put some more mines down. The result was that some wretched submarine had to blaze a new trail through the network. The job fell twice to us and we did not like it one little bit."

Off Cagliari, Sardinia, four torpedoes once passed right underneath *Rorqual* and missed. Soon after, it sank an Italian merchant ship and began its "most dangerous" minelaying patrol. Two days out of Malta, the submarine's mine doors jammed. The First Lieutenant and Engineer Officer, having persuaded the captain to surface that night in the Bay of Tunis, managed to get the doors open wide enough to allow mines to pass through. Had *Rorqual* been spotted, the submarine would have dived and "the two officers would not have had a chance." Both received DSCs. Diverting to the heel of Italy, *Rorqual* attacked convoys and merchant ships on three successive days without scoring a hit. Bombarding the railway line to Messina, it was fired on from the shore and a 3-inch shell went through the side of the bridge destroying the upper steering position – "a narrow shave." After repairs, *Rorqual* spent three months on a huge minelaying campaign off North Africa intended to harry Axis supply lines, forcing the enemy to change its convoy routes five times and preventing any Axis merchant ship reaching North Africa during the final three weeks of the

Ian Stoop.

land campaign. Meantime three "ace" T-class vessels had been lost which "shook the flotilla considerably. But it says something for the submarine morale that boats still went out on patrol with a smile."

Rorqual continued in this eventful mode to the end of the Mediterranean campaign, laying more minefields, sinking more enemy merchant vessels, being depth charged repeatedly, having to dive to 250 feet on one occasion, surviving assaults by shore batteries, bombarding targets in the Northern Aegean such as an iron works and a resin factory, and in pitch darkness delivering vital supplies, including a Jeep placed on the fore-casing, to embattled Allied forces "in a pretty bad way" on the island of Leros. After 25 war patrols in the Mediterranean and six storage patrols, *Rorqual* returned to the UK for a refit. Stoop and Napier came down with jaundice on the way back, reaching Portsmouth as passengers in late-December. "So ended 18 of the happiest months of my life," wrote Stoop. *Rorqual* had compiled an extraordinary record and was the only RN submarine to return from two full commissions in the Mediterranean. It also, as of the end of 1943, had laid more mines and sunk more shipping than any other RN submarine. Shortly after arriving home Lt. Ian Stoop was able to accompany Lt. Commander Lennox Napier to Buckingham Palace where Stoop received a DSC and Napier was awarded the DSO. *Rorqual* returned to service in 1944, moving to the Far East and completing a total of 33 war patrols.

Before *Rorqual*, Stoop had served in *Utmost*, a U-class submarine familiar to many OPs. **Patrick Joyce (32–37)** was one of them, taking part in countless hazardous operations in *Utmost* in 1941 including the sinking of about 70,000 tons of mostly Italian shipping in the Mediterranean and clandestine activities including landing Allied agents behind enemy lines. On one such occasion he was commended for his "brilliant" navigation when *Utmost* succeeded in locating and rescuing a downed RAF crew in a rubber dinghy off Malta. Later in the war he became the third OP to command the World War One training submarine *H44*.

To survive, submarines – craft designed to sink – demand, and must achieve, a degree of professional competence and teamwork from all on board that is rarely reached by surface ships. Fighting a war in such vessels thrusts a huge responsibility on the submarine's captain. His character becomes of crucial importance. Resilience, precision and resourcefulness are key, as is cunning and courage in battle when the odds can easily be against a submarine. The psychological side of such cat-and-mouse combat can be crucial; service on a World War 2 submarine represented "stress to the ultimate degree" according to Edward Beach, a US Navy veteran. Yet panics and breakdowns were unusual. In his book *Sea Wolves – The Extraordinary Story of Britain's World War 2 Submarines*, Tim Clayton reckoned that the "impact of (British) submarines in the war overall was "attritional and never easily measurable." In the Mediterranean, their role was "crucial – decisive in influencing the outcome of a land campaign that turned on logistics." The cost was very high – 42 per cent of Allied submarines in the Mediterranean were lost and roughly a third of all those (9,316) who served in British submarines during the war were killed. This level of loss was comparable to that in RAF Bomber Command, but had greater impact in a relatively small branch of the RN where many were acquainted. "Those who did survive," Clayton concluded "were often mentally or physically scarred by the experience.

Lt Cdr Clement Bridgman DSO portrayed by the artist William Dring in Londonderry in May 1943 five months before Bridgman was killed in action. (National Maritime Museum)

Surgeon Lt. Philip Evans G.M. sketched in hospital in 1943 recovering from his wounds by the artist William Dring. (National Maritime Museum)

A meeting of the VC and GC Association at Buckingham Palace in 2006.
John Gregson stands in the back row, fourth from the right. (VC & GC Association)

A digital image created by Dennis Andrews showing the forced landing of a
Swordfish aircraft carrying Pilot Ben Rice and Observer Ben Bolt ahead of the
battleship HMS Warspite, *off Cape Matapan 1941. (Iain Ballantyne)*

*Admiral Sir Frank Hopkins as depicted in a portrait
held by the Fleet Air Arm Museum, Yeovilton.
(© Heirs of Roderick Macdonald)*

*The Mayor of Villeneuve-les-Beziers honours the memory of
Rodney Rodgers at a ceremony in 2012. (Villeneuve-les-Beziers)*

*A 1920s WD & HO Wills cigarette card depicting Colin Laird,
the youngest-ever England rugby union fly-half.*

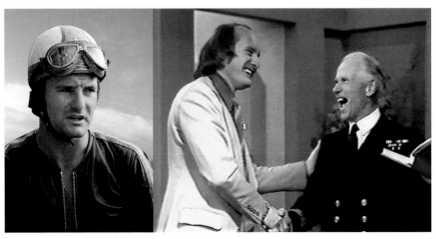

*Mike Hailwood in his
motorcycling gear in the 1960s.*

*Mike Hailwood meets his Pangbourne boxing instructor,
CPO Tiger Knights, on the set of* This Is Your Life *in 1975.*

Oarsman Peter Lowe in 1997 undertaking his transatlantic row. (OP Society)

Prop forward Daryl Marfo in action for Scotland versus New Zealand at Murrayfield, Edinburgh in 2017. (SNS)

The pairs rower Tony Garbett in his Team GB uniform ahead of the 2004 Athens Olympic Games. (Toby Garbett)

Andrew Simpson and Iain Percy sailing in the Beijing Olympic Games 2008. (World Sailing/sailing.org)

Colin Howard, Dhofar War 1971. (Colin Howard)

5

G.T.S. 'PETER' GRAY:
A NAVAL ENIGMA

— ◉ —

G.T.S. Gray (25–28) is an enigma. He so disliked his given names – Gordon Thomas Seccombe – that he was always known as 'Peter'. He made little mark during his three years at the Nautical College Pangbourne, yet was the only cadet in his leaving year to be nominated for entry to the Royal Navy. Much of his life he pretended that he was an only child, but he had two sisters.

As a husband and a father himself, and under the strains of war, he was somewhat remote from his family. Yet on all the ships he commanded in wartime, crew morale was high thanks to his sensitive leadership. Never a conventional blood-and-guts sort of 'hero,' Gray was nevertheless awarded the DSC and was Mentioned in Despatches no less than five times. But he never sought danger or courted awards. Reaching the rank of Rear Admiral after a 36-year career in the Royal Navy and marked out for still-higher rank, he resigned abruptly, fearing a deskbound future. The rest of his life was spent pottering about European canals and coastal waters in a motor fishing vessel with his wife. In a phrase, he was 'his own man' – someone who loved the sea and ships and was always a bit of a loner.

Gray's son, Nicholas, describes him as "a complicated character." Both 'Peter's' father and grandfather were clerics. The family are part of the Stewarts of Appin, a Scottish clan with the curious motto 'Anchor Fast Anchor' and an unusual crest to

'Peter' Gray in 1939.

go with it in the shape of a fouled anchor. The Gray family never had much money but previous generations, keen on fishing and shooting, lived as if they did. On his mother's side, 'Peter' Gray came from a wealthy Kettering line that owned much of the town and the local brewery; after the war, rather typically, he rejected the chance to take over the running of the business. Born in Hungerford in Berkshire where his father was Rector of the parish church of St. Lawrence, Gray felt bullied by his father, could not wait to get away from home and always wanted to join the Royal Navy. The Nautical College Pangbourne, 19 miles away from Hungerford, was a natural escape route.

If the NCP was a formative influence, it was not apparent in his adult life. He is not known ever to have returned to the school and does not seem to have kept any friends from his time there. His College record shows him winning prizes in 1926 and 1928 in Seamanship and Signals. A family story has him riding illicitly into nearby Reading on a teacher's motor cycle and being detected. His father was summoned and bicycled from Hungerford with a cane attached to the crossbar to give his son "a real thrashing." Despite this transgression, Gray became a Cadet Captain (prefect) in 1928 and is recorded in the school magazine as having taken part in several debates including one on the merits of a Channel tunnel and another on the impact of machinery on employment. At the time, education at Pangbourne, which had opened in 1917, can only be described as rudimentary and limited in scope. Throughout his life Gray – who became an accomplished artist and an excellent pencil line sketcher – lamented his narrow schooling and often felt excluded from the rest of his arts-loving family.

Transferring from Pangbourne to the RN gunnery training vessel HMS *Erebus* in 1928, by the early 1930s 'Peter' Gray had already experienced a variety of postings in the Mediterranean Fleet as a run-of-the-mill Midshipman, Sub Lieutenant and Lieutenant. Initially, at least, he may have found his mundane, regulation-bound naval existence hard to reconcile with the exciting life of one of his teenage heroes, Horatio Hornblower. Another family story, that cannot be verified, actually has him leaving his post as a Midshipman on one occasion in Algeria or Tunisia, walking across the desert and impetuously enlisting in the French Foreign Legion. A landing party from his ship retrieved him and returned him to his captain. Only a far-sighted decision by someone in authority would have averted dismissal from the service.

By August 1936 there is nothing in the record to suggest anything out of the ordinary in this young officer. Then Gray's ship at the time, the cruiser HMS *Durban*, was sent from the Mediterranean Fleet to support British land forces in Palestine which were attempting to quell an Arab strike and revolt against Jewish immigration and continued control from London. Gray was put in charge of a detachment of midshipmen, 15 ratings, a searchlight, two howitzer guns and a truck nicknamed 'Pip' and ordered to assist the 1st Seaforth Highlanders regiment at Nablus which was struggling to protect Jewish kibbutzim. Gray's unit soon came under attack from a band of twenty or so Arab snipers hidden on two sides of the Nablus-Jenin road. In an action that continued all day, four Arabs were killed, two taken prisoner and 250 decidedly hostile rounds fired into the landing party. Two days afterwards, Gray was involved in another action near Nablus when a roadside bomb exploded close to his "pom-pom" lorry and a firefight ensued. He remained with the Seaforths for a couple of weeks, sporting full Arab headgear, before returning regretfully to his ship just in time to board it before it sailed back to the UK to be de-commissioned. For his bravery and leadership, the 25-year-old was Mentioned in Despatches – the first of five such recognitions made in the next decade.

Admiring Lawrence of Arabia (T.E. Lawrence) as he did, Gray by now may have begun to toy with alternative careers. If so, the RN sensed it and gave him little room for manoeuvre. Back in England, he was posted far away to an RN gunboat on the Yangtse river in China. Here he was fortunate to be in hospital in December 1937 when the vessel was attacked and hit by a Japanese artillery unit. On his return home, he did his best to branch out and in 1938 qualified as a pilot and was granted a temporary commission as a Flying Officer on attachment to the RAF. The next year, as another European armed conflict neared, he was posted back to the RN but was actually stationed at RAF Gosport as part of a Fleet Air Arm training squadron. Flying, it seems, was to be his way ahead.

The outbreak of the Second World War in September 1939 changed everything. In October Gray married Sonia Moore-Gywn. He chose the day of his marriage, October 18, to inscribe in the front of his copy of Blackwood's *Tales of the Sea* some rather curious lines: "The two most beautiful things in the world are a ship under sail and a woman in love, but you must master them or they will drive you to hell. And if to hell I must go, give me a ship." Maybe the quotation came from him, maybe not. Maybe it was just the musings of a young man preparing uncertainly for war and marriage. Whichever is true, "it really says everything there is to say about my father," observed his son many years after the event. The very next month he reported for duty as First Lieutenant of the sloop *Stork* based at Rosyth in Scotland, initially escorting convoys on the east coast, and his war began.

HMS *Stork*, 266 feet in length with a displacement of 1,190 tons, had been launched three years earlier. Carrying a crew of 125, boasting a top speed of 19 knots and protected by a variety of weapons including depth charges and six anti-aircraft guns, in the right hands it was a potent small warship suited especially to a convoy escort role. To begin with, those were exactly its duties moving up and down the east coast of the UK. In May 1940, however, it was abruptly ordered north to assist in the hurried withdrawal of Allied forces from Norway. The immediate task was to escort to home waters a vulnerable troopship, MS *Chrobry*, which was lying in Vestfjord, not far from Narvik, in northern Norway. On board was a battalion of Irish Guards and some much-needed military equipment. Just before midnight on May 14 German Junkers 88 dive-bombers attacked the *Chrobry* three times, setting the ship on fire, exploding ammunition, and killing many on board. "Although the fire was spreading rapidly, stacked ammunition was exploding and all their senior officers had been killed, the battalion assembled on deck, company by company, platoon by platoon, with their arms and personal equipment" and showed amazing composure according to a newspaper report. Together with another RN ship, the destroyer HMS *Wolverine*, the *Stork*, with Lt. Gray on the bridge, now set about the hazardous task of rescuing the soldiers. Nearly 600 made it safely on to *Wolverine* as *Stork* sent up a withering barrage of covering anti-aircraft fire. Succeeding in driving the Junkers 88s away, Gray coolly nudged the sloop alongside the fast-sinking *Chrobry* and managed to rescue several hundred more men. *Stork* ended up being the last RN ship to leave Norway in June 1940. Gray, still only 28, was awarded the Distinguished Service Cross.

Some months after this episode, *Stork* was badly damaged by a torpedo dropped from a Heinkel He 11 bomber while at anchor in the Firth of Forth waiting to escort a convoy from Methil to London. Only in April 1941 did the ship return to escort duties, this time in the Atlantic where U-boats were running amok. After two months in this intense and incessant role, Gray took over temporary command when his captain, suffering from exhaustion and operational fatigue, had to be put ashore. A new captain did not appear until September – Commander F.J. 'Johnnie' Walker – tasked with leading the 36th Escort Group based in Liverpool and turning it around. In *Stork,* the near-legendary Walker was to prove himself one of the most able, imaginative and successful U-boat hunters of the war.

That December Walker was able to put his innovative ideas for convoy protection into practice for the first time when *Stork* took part in one of the most sustained convoy battles of the war. On this occasion an escort group of four destroyers was accompanying HG 76, a convoy of 32 ships, from Gibraltar to England. A ten-day running battle with a shadowing pack of nine aggressive U-boats and a number of ever-present German aircraft ensued after the convoy was spotted leaving Gibraltar by a German agent in Spain. The convoy got through to UK waters for the loss of two RN ships and two merchant vessels. German losses were greater – five U-boats and two aircraft thanks to the more aggressive, if controversial, tactics pioneered by Walker. Today the encounter is regarded as the first big convoy victory for the Allies in the Battle of the Atlantic.

Gray's part in the battle proved to be dramatic. Five days out of Gibraltar, one of the escorts, the destroyer *Stanley*, was torpedoed by *U-574*. *Stork* was nearby at the time, quickly gained an asdic contact (the early form of sonar) and made two depth charge attacks. Suddenly *U-574* surfaced two hundred yards ahead of *Stork* and an extraordinary eleven-minute chase began. Walker tried to ram the submarine but found that it could turn inside *Stork's* turning circle and was too low in the water to be fired on with any accuracy. "(Our) gun crews were reduced to fist-shakings and roaring curses," reported Walker. "The prettiest shooting was made by Lt. G.T.S. Gray with a stripped Lewis gun from over the top of the bridge screen. He quickly reduced the conning tower to a mortuary," Hard on the heels of this exploit, *Stork* managed to corner and ram another U-boat, scraping over the hull of the submarine and rolling it over. As the submarine emerged from under the stern of *Stork*, depth charges were dropped and blew it up. *Stork's* bows were crushed and bent sideways and the asdic dome under the hull smashed.

Meantime, with *U-574* fatally damaged, Walker ordered Gray to go on board, get into the damaged conning tower and seize any papers and documents he could find before the submarine went down. Armed only with a pistol, Gray scrambled down from *Stork* into the wrecked control room of the submarine. Here he grabbed whatever he could, including a wooden box containing a prized Karl Plath sextant that he kept for the rest of his life, before escaping back to *Stork*. Five survivors from the U-boat and 25 from *Stanley* were picked up by *Stork*. They did not include the U-boat commander, Dietrich Gengelbach, who was on his first war patrol. Following a heated argument after the initial depth charging with his Engineering Officer, who wanted to surface, Gengelbach is believed to have shot himself. For his role, Gray was Mentioned in Despatches.

Stork went on to sink several more U-boats during the war and 'Johnnie' Walker was to win the DSO and three Bars and achieve national fame before dying from ill health and overwork in mid-1944. More than a thousand people attended his funeral, and today a statue of him stands at the Pier Head in Liverpool. 'Peter' Gray, who turned 30 at the end of 1941, could not have had a more inspiring and skilful commander and mentor although he never spoke of Walker in these terms. His reward, aged 31, was his first solo command in March 1942 – a Hunt Class escort destroyer named HMS *Badsworth*, part of the 12th Escort Group.

Badsworth was a year old and had been ordered by the RN from Cammell Laird in Birkenhead three months after the outbreak of war. Adopted by the town of Batley, she was said to be named after a fox-hunt in Yorkshire. Slightly larger and rather faster than *Stork* but similarly armed, she had a crew of 164 men. Just a month after he joined the ship, Gray found himself uncomfortably part of one of the least successful combined operations staged by Allied forces during the war, code named Operation Myrmidon. *Badsworth's* role, as one of four RN destroyer escort ships, was to support a commando landing in the Bayonne River Adour area in southwest France by protecting two landing craft and shelling the harbour at St. Jean de Luz. From the outset, nothing went right. Intelligence about enemy positions was lacking, the weather was poor, there were no up-to-date maps, the attacking force knew nothing about tidal conditions on the river Adour, French liaison advice on the spot was ignored and even the time difference between the UK and France was overlooked. An officer from MI 19 (a section of British Army intelligence, related mostly to prisoners of war), who happened to be present at the briefing before the task force set off, pointed out many of these deficiencies but was criticised for doing so and side-lined.

Gray in *Badsworth* carried out his allotted tasks as planned but in shelling St. Jean de Luz inadvertently (due to the time difference) revealed the presence of enemy forces in the area "without achieving any positive result." Meantime, the commandos had faltered at the sand bar. After five hours, the operation was called off. Vice Admiral Lord Louis Mountbatten, just appointed Chief of Combined Operations, admitted after the operation that he knew Bayonne "quite well" and from the outset of the planning of the operation had realised that crossing a notorious sand bar on the river Adour was "the central difficulty... as it was in Wellington's attack on Bayonne in 1814." If so, he shared this knowledge with no one. Gray, emerged uncriticised and was commended by the force commander Capt. Maxwell-Hyslop (himself on *Badsworth*) who was struck by the "extremely efficient manner in which every operation called for was performed." Maxwell-Hyslop added: "I know of none that I would prefer to have under my orders in an operation."

'Peter' Gray had little time to reflect on this fiasco before he took part in one of the most eventful Arctic convoys the following month. PQ 15 was not the disaster that PQ 17 was to prove in

'Peter' Gray on Arctic Convoy.

June 1942. But all who took part in PQ 15 that May were tested in the extreme. *Badsworth* was one of eight to twelve RN ships (the number varied) providing "close" protection to 25 mostly American merchant vessels carrying vital war supplies to Murmansk and the Soviet Union. Generally unused to convoy work, the American merchantmen proved to be "steady and staunch" under torpedo attack and 22 of the convoy reached the Kola Inlet safely. But throughout the passage the convoy was harried and attacked by the Luftwaffe, a Kriegsmarine submarine *U-251* was always lurking in the neighbourhood, the weather was atrocious and gales and high winds never let up, visibility was often non-existent and speeds did not exceed a stately and vulnerable 7.5 knots.

The convoy formed up towards the end of April. *Badsworth* was positioned on the right rear side of the escorting screen with five columns of merchant ships to the left. Departing as a group from south of Iceland, the convoy was immediately detected and attacked by a German aircraft. Next day the escort destroyers collectively depth-charged a submarine that appeared to be shadowing the convoy – only to learn that it belonged to the allied Polish armed forces and had strayed badly off course. At midnight on May 2 in the grey Arctic half-light, a marauding wing of six Luftwaffe Heinkel aircraft suddenly appeared. Three merchant ships in the convoy were hit in what turned out to be the first torpedo bomber attack of World War 2. Gray in *Badsworth* rescued 61 people from the SS *Jutland* which had been torpedoed and was abandoned, and took on the distasteful job of sinking the badly-damaged SS *Botavon* by firing into her to prevent the crippled merchant vessel being seized by the Germans.

Next day, the gunners on *Badsworth* destroyed a Junkers 88 aircraft which flew directly at the ship from 9,000 yards at a height of 100 feet. A rare quiet day followed before *Badsworth* drove off a Focke Wulf Condor reconnaissance aircraft with more accurate fire from the ship's four anti-aircraft guns. Shortly after, *Badsworth* picked up Norwegian survivors from an earlier convoy attack. Sunk in their merchant ship five days before, these sailors had rowed 250 miles in an open boat in appalling weather and seas. As the relieved, but safe, convoy steamed into the Kola Inlet in heavy snow on May 9 *Badsworth* was almost out of fuel and ammunition. A report on PQ 15 subsequently commended Gray and *Badsworth* for "the efficient manner" the destroyer carried out her duties. "The ship was very quick to open fire on aircraft and moved out to force shadowing submarines to dive with considerable promptitude."

For nearly two weeks *Badsworth* remained in Murmansk. While ashore, a family story has 'Peter' Gray intervening at some risk to himself when a Soviet soldier threatened to shoot a British sailor who had given chocolate to a Russian sailor. Such common-or-garden fraternisation was strictly forbidden by the ever-suspicious Russians who offered no replenishments of fuel or ammunition to *Badsworth*. Gray, not surprisingly, formed a poor impression of his mistrustful allies. In the end, he scrounged 300 rounds of ammunition from the cruiser HMS *Trinidad* which was being patched up in the Kola Inlet having been bombed in convoy PQ 13. Husbanding its fuel as part of convoy QP 12 (a group of 30 empty merchant ships returning to the UK), *Badsworth* got as far west as 24 hours sailing time from Iceland before having to undergo an emergency refuel. Two of the merchant ships in this convoy were sunk by U-boats and the air temperature sank below 10 degrees Fahrenheit (-12 degrees Centigrade). But by the end of May, a month after leaving the UK, *Badsworth* and its rapidly-learning captain were back safely in British waters. Two significant developments were to follow from PQ 15, both of which made future convoys safer. Royal Navy ships equipped with anti-aircraft weapons were no longer placed in the centre of the convoys where they had often been unable to fire at attacking aircraft for fear of hitting vessels in the convoy; and more merchant ships were fitted with Bofors guns as British-made versions of the anti-aircraft weapon began to come into production in 1942.

Such was the pressure on RN resources in mid-1942 that, after only a week at home, *Badsworth* left for the Mediterranean at the start of June to protect convoy WS 19S on its journey to the besieged island of Malta. Described, post-war, as "one of the hardest-fought convoys to Malta," what came to be known as Operation Harpoon was one of two Allied convoys sent at the same time to re-supply Malta through the Axis-dominated central Mediterranean. Operation Vigorous set out from Alexandria in Egypt and Operation Harpoon began its journey from Gibraltar. Only two of the six ships in the Harpoon convoy completed the journey, at the cost of two Allied warships sunk by air attacks. *Badsworth*, in action against Italian warships on June 15, was badly damaged next day in her forward structure below the waterline. Nine of her crew, all stokers, were killed after the destroyer detonated a mine as she entered the Grand Harbour at Malta. A signals error to *Badsworth* about an allegedly swept and cleared mine-path was blamed. The Vigorous convoy never made it at all, being driven back to Alexandria by Italian air attacks. 'Peter' Gray was Mentioned in Despatches for a third time.

Towed to the Tyne to be repaired, *Badsworth* re-joined the North Atlantic convoy defence force based in Londonderry at the end of 1942. In December it accompanied an uneventful convoy to Freetown, Sierra Leone. Early in 1943, it began escorting convoys from Algiers and Tunisia carrying supplies across the

Mediterranean in support of the Allied landings in Sicily. On one of these trips in April the destroyer was mined again, this time near Bone in Algeria. Major structural damage to the aft section of the ship and to the starboard engine and steering mechanism resulted, and five ratings were injured. Gray managed to transfer most of the crew to a nearby ship before beaching *Badsworth* outside the inner harbour at Bone. Once the ship was re-floated and edged into the main harbour, Gray decided to act on his own initiative. Aware that cork was a major export out of Bone, he located a warehouse, bought the entire stock of unused cork planks on behalf of the RN and organised the crew into work details which spent a week packing as much cork as possible into *Badsworth's* flooded aft compartments. Buoyancy restored, the vessel was hauled off the beach, handed over to a salvage crew and towed back to Liverpool to be repaired. An enquiry by the Admiralty in London followed. Gray, according to family recollections, was given a hard time by his superiors not only for having fouled a mine but also, supposedly, for wasting tax-payer's money on an unauthorised expenditure – according to his son, a harsh judgement which rankled in his father's mind "for years to come."

If this capricious assessment harmed 'Peter' Gray's career, it is not evident. In September, as the Allied invasion of the Italian mainland commenced, he took command of another Hunt-class destroyer HMS *Lamerton,* at the time anchored at Malta. Its role at the outset was to provide naval gunfire support to Allied forces landing at Salerno in Italy. That achieved, the destroyer concentrated on deflecting attacks by fast-moving E-boats in the landing areas. Gray was again Mentioned in Despatches. After the Salerno landings Allied forces slowly edged up the Italian peninsula. *Lamerton* had no obvious role and was transferred to Alexandria to support operations in the Aegean and Adriatic following the Italian surrender and gradual German retreat from Greece and the Balkans.

One of the last naval incidents of World War 2 in the Adriatic was to involve Gray in a key role and lead to another Mention in Despatches. At the time the senior officer of the 57th Destroyer Division, he led a combined operation with the RAF at the end of 1944 against German positions on the island of Lussin off the coast of fascist-controlled Croatia. Not for the first time during the war, a ship commanded by Gray proved to be outstanding when it came to gunnery and crew efficiency. On this occasion, *Lamerton* expended all her ammunition (1,060 rounds) in the bombardment. Every known target was destroyed with the loss of one rating killed by German fire from the island. The citation for this fifth Mention in Despatches stated: "G.T.S. Gray was Senior Officer of the division of four destroyers... *Lamerton* shot with commendable accuracy from a concealed cove in Cherso island." The recognition was recommended for "courage, leadership and enterprise in command of a division of destroyers."

Convoy escort duties in *Lamerton* in the eastern Mediterranean and the North Sea followed before 'Peter' Gray's action-packed war years ended. Settling down to a peacetime routine with a wife who had barely seen him for five years and two young children proved tricky, as it did for many returning servicemen. Yet he never contemplated leaving the RN and, reckoned his son, "was never satisfied except when he had a posting on a ship." Fortunately, Gray had quite a few of these. As a Commander in 1951 he was appointed Executive Officer of the cruiser *Glasgow*, at the time Mountbatten's flagship as C-in-C Mediterranean Fleet. Promoted Captain in 1953, he took part in the ill-fated British-French action at Suez in 1956 and sailed his ship in the dead of night safely through the middle of the entire huge US 6th Fleet. That year, too, he took over as commander of the 5th Frigate Squadron in the Mediterranean in *Torquay* and was involved in offshore actions during the Cyprus Eoka emergency. In 1961 he became captain of *Osprey*, the naval air anti-submarine school at Portland. Here, 20 years after learning to fly, he qualified to go solo in a helicopter to understand better the pilots' challenges. In the mid-1960s he helped to plan the long-running Beira Patrol by the RN during the Rhodesian rebellion. His final naval appointment was as a rear admiral and Senior Naval Instructor at the Imperial Defence College.

Hating the prospect of a succession of desk jobs, Gray retired from the Royal Navy aged 54 in 1965. Ever after, he lived on his RN pension and spent as much time as possible cruising European waterways with his wife. At first, the couple owned a 50ft Dutch sailing vessel before switching in 1966 to a 25-tons 45ft "Gentleman's Motor Yacht" called *Sheemaun*. Over the next 14 years 'Peter' and Sonia would often spend six months a year on *Sheemaun* travelling as far east and north as the Baltic Sea, exploring canals and inland waterways in Germany and France and moving up and down the Channel and the English South Coast – "some of the happiest days of my life" Gray felt. When not sailing, his time was spent at cottages in Sussex and Dorset where he painted oils of square-rigged sailing ships or watercolours of nature and drew fine-line pencil sketches of the sea. In his seventies his health deteriorated and *Sheemaun* was sold – as it happens, to the Executive Officer at his old school, the Nautical College Pangbourne. He died in 1997, aged 85.

To 'Peter' Gray, "the least reflective of men" in the words of his son, the Second World War was always "that dreadful time." He spoke little about it and never attended reunions. In his eyes, his actions were not heroic – he just did what he had been trained to do. Stoic, diligent, relentlessly committed to his assigned role, he was widely regarded in the Royal Navy as "a fine naval officer and a fine commander of men" – not someone who would ever knowingly rock the boat, go against orders or let others down. His courage was of a peculiarly British type – understated, calm, unflashy and apparently unhindered by fear. Bravery, to him, was an abstract notion, subjective in concept and related inextricably to doing one's duty. Yet time after time, as his military record emphasised, 'Peter' Gray rose to the occasion in difficult circumstances showing, imagination, determination and leadership beyond that of many others.

6

THEY ALSO SERVED...

— ◉ —

Hundreds of Old Pangbournians served at sea in both the Royal Navy and the Merchant Navy during World War 2, apart from the destroyer and submarine commanders. Many of these men, too, performed bravely and courageously, from the youngest aged no more than 19 to the oldest who would have been 40 at most when the conflict broke out in September 1939.

Amongst the youngest was **Richard Pool** (37–39) who had joined the Royal Navy two years before war broke out. For more than three years during the fighting he was posted as "missing" and there were conflicting stories in the UK as to whether he was alive or not. When he reappeared in England, he wrote a long letter to Pangbourne in 1946 revealing that he had spent over three years as a prisoner of war in Japanese camps. "I shall not try to describe conditions and treatment as you cannot possibly imagine them and would not believe me. You may remember pictures of Belsen (concentration camp) – our sick, of whom there were tens of thousands, looked exactly like it. Men of 14 stones weight were reduced to seven and eight. I went down to six."

Richard Pool,
Midshipman, 1938.

It had, indeed, been an astonishing roller-coaster journey since Pool reported to HMS *Erebus* in the autumn of 1937 to begin training as an RN officer – one he recounted in an understated memoir *Course for Disaster* published in 1987. Still not 21 when war began, he was just 26 when he finally returned to England. During that period, which included 29 months on active service, three months "lost" on a tropical island and 38 months in Japanese hands, he was Mentioned in Despatches and awarded the DSC "for resource and bravery and initiative." He rose from the rank of Midshipman to Lieutenant, commanded small craft at Dunkirk, was sunk in a battle cruiser in the Far East and survived, operated patrol craft with Commandos on raids behind enemy lines in Malaya, and was one of the last RN officers to escape from Singapore before it fell to Japanese forces in February 1942.

Pool's tale is one of ingenuity and an enduring, dominant will to survive. Frequently, in his fledging RN career, he found himself in desperate situations in command of rag-tag crews of untrained volunteers and mechanically-defective craft where the only currency that counted was leadership and determination. For much of his brutal captivity he suffered from amoebic dysentery and was often close to death but nevertheless was forced by his cruel captors to undertake hard physical labour. "Being on the receiving end during those early years (of the war), there was a sense of bitterness towards the politicians who, between the wars, had allowed such a state of unpreparedness to develop," he observed with some restraint at the end of his book. But, he added, "for most of us, especially those under 30 years of age, the war was an exciting, and stimulating, time."

Action for Pool had begun with the Dunkirk evacuation. At the time, he was serving in the battleship HMS *Revenge*. Snatched from a torpedo course, he was ordered to skipper a Thames river steamer and get to France to help evacuate the British Expeditionary Force from the beaches. Just out of the Medway estuary, the steamer broke down as it ran into salt water and its boilers could not cope. So Pool commandeered a motor cruiser. No sooner had it left Chatham dockyard than the rudder fell off. Finally reaching Dunkirk at the third time of asking in an old water lighter, he ran into a scene of utter chaos. With no orders to follow, he headed inshore and rescued hundreds of French soldiers over the next five hours, taking them back to Ramsgate. Immediately he was sent back to Dunkirk in a motor launch. This time he was attacked by seven Junker 87s dive bombers, hit several times, lived to tell the tale and returned to Ramsgate fully loaded with 70 British troops. At this point, after 48 hours without sleep, his civilian crew declined to make another cross-Channel trip. But the next afternoon, with a new crew, Pool returned to Dunkirk for a third time and helped to retrieve another 70 men. His fourth and final rescue trip was made on the last night of the evacuation. Again fully loaded, his launch hit an underwater obstacle as it left Dunkirk harbour and had to be taken in tow. Pool was in the towing vessel when the tow rope broke and had to watch his trusty craft flounder in its wake (the launch made it back to Ramsgate).

Joining the aging, 38,000 tons battle cruiser HMS *Repulse* in September 1940, Pool was on board during the pursuit of the German battleship *Bismarck*.

Next, *Repulse* was deployed to the Far East as the Japanese threat to the Malayan peninsula grew. The day after Pearl Harbour was bombed, Japanese aircraft bombed Singapore harbour on December 8, 1941, where *Repulse* was at anchor. The invasion of Malaya began. *Repulse* and *Prince of Wales,* one of the Navy's most modern battleships, immediately left Singapore to steam up the East coast of Malaya to harry Japanese forces on land and at sea. Quickly spotted from the air, wave after wave of Japanese aircraft moved in for the kill next day deploying bombs and torpedoes.

Pool was Fire Distribution Officer on one of the gun platforms high up the port side of *Repulse.* He reckoned his 8-barrelled 2-pounder Pom Pom shot down two aircraft which had screamed in at point blank range. Hit by four or five torpedoes simultaneously, *Repulse* went down with the loss of more than 500 crew. Pool survived by walking down the side of the sinking ship and swimming away as fast as possible. When he looked back, "about 60 feet of *Repulse's* bow was sticking out of the water, the sun glittering on her light grey topside and on her red anti-fouling bottom. The ship seemed to hang poised for a few seconds and then, to the accompaniment of subterranean rumblings, *Repulse* slid under the surface." Picked up by a nearby destroyer, Pool helped to assist the many crew still in the water.

Another hair-raising interlude followed as the Japanese swept south through Malaya. Now without a ship, Pool skippered a small force of half a dozen patrol craft carrying commandos on raids behind enemy lines, going as far north as Taiping. Attacked several times from the air and always operating at night, this flimsy counter force had no protection. Pool was often ashore helping out. Ultimately, all involved had to escape south from Port Swettenham in a tug. By the time Pool reached Singapore, the island was on the point of surrender. Somehow finding a motor launch, he engaged in direct combat with Japanese vessels. By February 13, 1942, Allied military order on the island had collapsed. He was ordered to seize another motor launch, *ML 310,* embark the senior Admiral Malaya (Rear Admiral Ernest Spooner) and the senior RAF officer Malaya (Air Vice Marshal Conway Pulford) and navigate an escape to Batavia (now Jakarta) nearly 600 miles south on the Dutch-controlled island of Java.

So began the most challenging episode in Richard Pool's life. Before long *ML 310* was detected by Japanese naval forces, attacked by marauding bombers, further damaged after hitting a reef, captured, unexpectedly released, and marooned without means of escape on a small tropical island called Tjebia midway between Singapore and Java. On board *ML310* were 44 men. With its lagoons, palm-fringed beaches and luxuriant vegetation, the island seemed ideal for survival. But it lacked water, and the escapees had no fishing nets. Swarms of mosquitoes and sand flies plagued the group, day and night. Within weeks depression overcame the disparate party, malaria took hold and many began to lose the will to live. All attempts at escape failed. None of the men had medical knowledge, and gradually the weaker began to collapse and die. By the time Pool and a few others did manage to sail away in a painstakingly-rebuilt native boat, 18 had succumbed including Admiral Spooner and Air Vice Marshal Pulford. Pool wrote in 1987: "The three months spent there (Tjebia) were worse than the whole time as a prisoner of war."

Having managed to escape Tjebia, Pool ended up being handed over to the Japanese by locals on Singkep, a nearby island. From there he was transferred to Changi camp on Singapore, where prisoners were already eating anything that moved, and on to Selerang Barracks. In late-October 1942 he and thousands of other starving Allied prisoners were herded out of the barracks onto trucks for a four-day journey north to Kanchanburi in Siam (Thailand), a riverside town at the confluence of the rivers Kwai Yai and Kwai Noi. Over the next three years he moved up and down the infamous 258-mile-long Siam-Burma railway line forced to hack camps out of the jungle, build roads and lay rail track in searing 50°C heat. "The ferocity and intolerance of the (Japanese) engineers was beyond belief." Food, such as it was, grew worse and worse, work pressures were unrelenting and 18-hour workdays the norm. There was never time to recover from the inevitable debilitating illnesses. If a man could stand, he could work, was the Japanese mantra. "Get through today" was the prisoners'. By mid-1943 three-quarters of the men originally shipped north with Pool were dying.

Twenty-four at the time, Richard Pool was not immune to the privations and spent much of 1944 in PoW "clinics" suffering from amoebic dysentery. There were no drugs. Right to the day the Japanese surrendered in mid-August 1945, weak from repeated bouts of dysentery and forced to carry heavy loads through wild, hilly country on 60 grams of rice a day, he was shifted from one camp to another at the point of a bayonet. The key to survival was mental fortitude. "Those of us who survived all had one thing in common, 'a will to survive'" he reflected at the end of *Course for Disaster*. "If that 'will' was lost for more than a few days, you died." Returning to England in late-October 1945, the First Sea Lord, Admiral of the Fleet Sir Andrew Cunningham, asked to see him. Having heard his story, Cunningham suggested that Pool visit Admiral Spooner's widow to describe the events on Tjebia, which he did. Pool remained in the Royal Navy to 1958 before retiring and becoming a fruit farmer in East Anglia.

Other Pangbournians recounted varying encounters with the Japanese in South East Asia. **Richard Danger** (32–36), a Lt RNR, was captured when the Japanese seized Singapore. He, too, survived nearly four years in captivity in Siam (Thailand) on the infamous railway. **Hugh Darbyshire** (27–30), was among those hitting back and had what *The Daily Telegraph* characterised as a "hectic naval career in coastal forces in the Royal Indian Navy Volunteer Reserve." This included being Mentioned in Despatches after bombarding Japanese forces on the west coast of Burma 150 miles beyond the front line. A report in *The Times of India* recorded Darbyshire as saying: "The enemy for some time appeared to think that it was being attacked by bombers. By the time it realised the action came from the sea, we had vanished into a moonless night."

War, though, is not one-dimensional. In 1950 **J.B. Herklots** (50–53), at the time a 14-year-old who was to join the Royal Navy after Pangbourne, recounted his experiences in *The Log* as a young boy aged six to nine who was held prisoner from 1941–45 by the Japanese in Camp John Haye and Camp Holmes in the Philippines. Pre-war, his family had lived in Hong Kong. When the fighting began, his father stayed in Hong Kong whilst his mother and her offspring moved to the Philippines. Here they were captured by the Japanese. Only days earlier Herklots' mother had had a blood transfusion and throughout her imprisonment was very weak. In Camp Holmes, Herklots and his brother and sister learned how to sow seed and grow food to supplement a minimal diet of rice. Living conditions were basic and cramped. One night some Filipino guerrillas tried to rescue the family. "There was a lot of shooting but it came to nothing." After this, security in the camp tightened. As American forces advanced in the Philippines in early 1945, the camp inmates were suddenly moved to Bilibid prison in Manila, "stuffed like pigs into lorries. It was Hell itself." Young Herklots got dysentery and his life was saved only by a doctor begging the Japanese for serum. The Japanese plan, apparently, was to kill the captives as U.S. troops advanced. "At that time, we had a terrible Commandant. We were rescued a day before we were all to be machine-gunned. I spoke to General MacArthur myself. He saved our lives. Soon after we were rescued, a bomb was dropped on the prison by the Japs (sic). It hit a wall and, bursting outwards, killed five people. A month later we were taken to America and on to England by boat, ending my experience in a Japanese camp." The Nautical College in 1950 must have seemed like a holiday camp.

The tricky and often tense surrender of Japanese forces all over southeast Asia involved **David Smiley** (30–34) (see Chapter 8) and **Peter Hoare** (29–32). Hoare was commanding officer of the British frigate *Loch Eck* and led a four-man Allied

Mission to take the surrender of the Japanese garrison on the island of Bali. "The Japanese presented an impassive face and strictly formal manner throughout the proceedings, with much bowing and hissing," he wrote in an article in 1946. "Nevertheless, when it came to the actual signing, or rather, delicate dabs with a paint brush, the two officers showed marked signs of emotion." After two weeks Hoare returned in *Loch Eck* for a second surrender ceremony when a Dutch Occupation Force arrived in Denpasar, the capital of Bali. This time he received a Samurai sword for his pains. Having endured an hour-long event in blazing sun, afterwards he indulged himself with a spot of sight-seeing, remarking that "the natural beauty of the island has to be seen to be believed. In every direction (there is) a kaleidoscopic pattern of colour...Once visited, Bali is never forgotten."

Pangbourne had been set up in 1917 to improve officer training for Britain's Merchant Navy, and untold numbers of OPs served in largely-defenceless merchant vessels on the high seas throughout the war. Some 12 per cent of OPs killed during the conflict, or 21 MN officers, died from enemy action. Many others told amazing stories of survival. **Denis Foss (29–32)** wrote about his war experiences in a book titled *Shooting a Line*. Torpedoed in 1940, he was rescued by a passing Australian grain ship which, within six hours, was itself sunk "in mid-Atlantic with no S.O.S. and nothing in sight." Hauled on to one of the two lifeboats that had got away, Foss was lucky to be rescued by a passing RN destroyer. **W.N. Davies (37–40)** joined Union Castle in 1940 and was in *Roxborough Castle* the next year when a 500lb bomb passed through every deck while the ship was anchored in Liverpool, before exploding in the mud. "The force of the explosion lifted the ship upwards and forwards so that when she came crashing down her raked stern lodged on the quay and she broke her back...After eight nights of ceaseless bombings and eight days of hard work, we succeeded in re-floating her and getting her into dry dock." In his next ship, *Sandown Castle,* Davies survived when a couple of fire bombs exploding in one of the hatches.

John Lester (36–40) and **Poga Jones (36–40)** were two others to enjoy great good fortune. Cadets in the Union Castle's *Richmond Castle,* they were homeward bound with a cargo of frozen meat from La Plata, Argentina in 1942 when the ship was sunk by two torpedoes fired by *U-176*. The pair were pulled into one of the three lifeboats that got away, together with 16 others, some badly wounded. After ten days at sea, desperately short of water, they were spotted by an RN corvette called HMS *Snowflake*. By that point they had travelled around 500 miles in the South Atlantic, having square-rigged a sail using blankets stitched together and attached to broken bits of spar. The following year Lester was sunk again in

Desmond D.A.G. Dickens.

ss *Windsor Castle* 60 miles off Algiers – and again survived. **Desmond Dickens (38–41)** was another who had an amazing escape. A young cadet aged 19, his cargo liner, *Dorset* of the New Zealand Shipping Company, was part of the Operation Pedestal convoy to Malta. Repeatedly subject to German and Italian air and submarine assaults, *Dorset* became detached from the convoy. Pressing on unescorted, the vessel managed to evade an attack by a German torpedo boat near the island of Pantellaria. Re-joining the convoy, *Dorset* caught fire and was abandoned temporarily. Dickens helped to keep her afloat by pumping the holds and restarting the engines. After more hits, the ship had to be abandoned for good. Dickens transferred to the stricken tanker *Ohio*, one of only five merchant ships in the convoy that made it to Malta.

Another involved in Operation Pedestal (see Chapter 3) was **Frederick Treves (38–42)**. Post-war, he became a well-known character actor on stage and screen. Aged 17, he was a cadet in the Shaw Savill & Albion 13,000-ton freighter *Waimarama* which was carrying explosives and aviation fuel. Attacked by a dozen Ju-88s, it sank in flames on August 13, 1942. Treves managed to dive off the ship wearing a life-saving kapok suit and a helmet. "I bobbed to the surface like a cork," he recalled in *Lost Voices of the Royal Navy*. "I was quite a good swimmer. I saw the wireless officer, Jackson. He couldn't swim and I pulled him out (towed him away to a floating spar) because the ship was sucking him back into the flames. Then I saw my friend and mentor Bowdrey. He was standing on a raft, his arms were outstretched, he was screaming for help, he couldn't swim (and) he was drifting back into the flames. I started out towards him, but realised he was very near the flames and his raft would be too heavy to stop. I turned, and swam away. That

Frederick Treves.

has haunted me all my life. I was a coward. That affected me greatly." Others thought differently. Jackson described him as "a very brave lad." Treves was one of 27 out of 107 crew eventually rescued by the RN destroyer *Ledbury* and Roger Hill (see Chapter 3). For his actions, Treves was awarded the British Empire Medal. Similar bravery and resourcefulness were displayed by **Roy Wilson (24–26)**. Chief Officer on a P&O ship torpedoed and sunk in the South Atlantic, he was in charge of four lifeboats that got away with many on board. Sailing and rowing by day, keeping his boats lashed together at night, he made for the port of Freetown, Sierra Leone and got there after three weeks – as his obituary put it: "A great feat of leadership and skilled navigation." Within a month of reaching safety, Wilson was back at sea.

Thomas Fanshawe.

Miraculous sea escapes were not confined to those in the Merchant Navy. **Thomas Fanshawe** (32–35) three times survived when RN ships he was serving in were sunk by enemy action. On the first two occasions, in *Royal Oak* and *Iron Duke,* he happened to be in the ships' drifter coming back from shore when the battleships were torpedoed or bombed within three days of each other in 1939. At the end of that year, he was on his way to join the armed merchant cruiser *Forfar* when she was sunk by a U-boat. Late in 1942 he was awarded a DSC as First Lieutenant in *Rother* for his role in the Allied landings in North Africa. In his next ship he was twice Mentioned in Despatches while commanding the corvette *Clover.* Another unlikely survivor was **Os De La Casas** (36–40). Serving in the destroyer *Jupiter* in the Java Sea in February 1942, he was one of the few to escape alive after the ship hit a mine. Managing to evade capture by the Japanese, he got ashore on the north coast of Java, seized a small craft, took command of it and managed to reach Ceylon (Sri Lanka) with other members of the crew.

Jock Cunningham (34–38), according to a newspaper report in 2002, "spent most of the war in some of the thickest action in the Mediterranean." This began when, as a Midshipman, he was part of a fire-fighting crew sent from the battleship *Warspite* to put out a fire in a benzene-carrying barge in Alexandra harbour. Explosives needed to be removed from close to the fire as fast as possible. Cunningham, unhesitatingly and without protective clothing, took on the job. Three weeks on, in bad weather and in the dark, he dived ten feet into water to rescue two men drowning near a jetty. In February 1942 he displayed similar guts when *Cleopatra,* a light cruiser in which he was serving, came under attack from 50 Axis aircraft as the ship neared Malta. A bomb entered the forecastle deck without exploding followed by a potentially-fatal fire which broke out by a pile

Jock Cunningham.

Geoffrey Ward.

of ammunition near to the bomb. Cunningham took charge and, with others, hurriedly moved the ammunition, showing "resourcefulness and bravery." He was awarded a DSC. A similarly incident-packed war was experienced by **Geoffrey Ward** (27–30). An RNR officer, he made five trips to the Dunkirk beaches as commander of a small Dutch coaster. Appointed port control officer for Oban and the Isle of Skye, he was knocked down by a crane, hospitalised and declared unfit for further service. Discharging himself from hospital and taking his medical records with him, he went on to be awarded a DSC during the North African landings in 1942 when his ship was heavily damaged, take part in several Arctic convoys to Russia and command a corvette *Dahlia,* latterly based in Ceylon (Sri Lanka). At the end of the war, he was a member of a team that searched the Dutch East Indies for Allied personnel who had escaped from, or evaded, the Japanese.

For the renowned marine artist **David Cobb's** (35–37), Cunningham and Ward's experiences must have seemed part of a rather surreal OP pattern. He told his story to the Imperial War Museum on six hours of audio tapes made when he was in his eighties. Only 18 when fighting began, Cobb had grown up sailing in boats and barges from his home at Itchenor on the south coast of England. A rugby injury ruined his chances of passing into Dartmouth and, as war began, he was employed in an engineering workshop and belonged to the RNVR. Called up after Dunkirk, he was handed a motor yacht to skipper and ordered to join a Dad's Army group of a dozen similar boats anchored off the port of Ramsgate tasked each night with giving advance warning of any invasion to those on land. His defenceless craft relied on six large rockets to do the job.

David Cobb in HMS Hurworth, *Gulf War, 1990.*

Having proved his mettle, Cobb received an RNVR commission. At first, he was posted as No. 1 in an armed trawler undertaking escort duty in the stormy North Atlantic followed by similar tours with convoys sailing to and from West Africa. At this point a friend in the Naval Appointments Department remembered his knowledge of small boats and got him transferred into Coastal Forces Command and high-speed motor torpedo boats (MTBs). Skippering three of these vessels over two years from 1942, until he was shot and wounded in July 1944 and became an MTB Control Officer, Cobb was constantly in action, always at night, always in real danger. Sometimes he engaged the faster, better armed German E-boats directly, sometimes he laid mines in patterns off enemy-held ports such as Cherbourg and Le Havre, other times his MTB fired torpedoes at trawlers and smaller targets. "We lost count of the number of actions we took part in and the targets we hit. There was a great deal of luck in how well we did," he recalled on the IWM tapes.

The average age of his crew was very young – 18–20. Cobb himself was only 24 when the war ended. "You were at sea for 18 hours at a time, standing on an open bridge in the dark. One's vision adapted, but conditions were pretty rough. We became a kind of family, with a strong *esprit de corps*." Before the Allied invasion of the continent, German batteries along the French and Dutch coasts proved particularly adept at shelling MTBs and sank a fair number as well as killing the legendary commander of Cobb's flotilla, Lt Cdr Robert Hitchens, with a single shot at the end of a mine-laying operation off the Dutch coast in 1943. David Cobb was never decorated and ended the war controlling MTBs from a parent ship by radar. As the Royal Navy turned its back on small craft, he left the service in 1946 to begin an illustrious career as a marine and war artist as well as writing a number of books about the sea.

Another young Old Pangbournian, **R.A.G. 'Rags' Butler (35–39)**, was just 19 and serving in his first ship as a midshipman RNR when, in November 1940, he was awarded a DSC in the armed merchant cruiser *Jervis Bay* – the sole escort of a 37-ship convoy from Halifax, Nova Scotia. Attacked in the North Atlantic by the vastly superior German pocket battleship *Admiral Scheer*, and armed only with short-range guns made in the reign of Queen Victoria, *Jervis Bay* headed straight for *Scheer* in order to give the convoy time to scatter. "It was not a fight but a massacre" according to *The Daily Telegraph*. Rags Butler was on the after-bridge where he was directing the guns. He recalled: "There was a blinding flash and a ripping, rending sound like a thousand gongs. The man beside me literally burst into pieces. I felt my face warm and wet and looking down saw my hands and my coat red with blood, and stuck on it some utterly revolting pieces of flesh and gristle." Hit repeatedly by salvoes from *Scheer* and holed in several places, big fires soon got a grip below decks. After the *Jervis Bay* battle ensign was shot away, Butler helped a sailor climb

R.A.G. Butler.

the flagstaff to nail another ensign in place. The badly wounded captain of *Jervis Bay*, Fogarty Fegen, ordered 'Abandon Ship.' *Jervis Bay* sank three hours after the attack, so allowing the convoy precious time to get away (five ships were sunk by *Scheer*). One lifeboat and two rafts survived from the badly-damaged cruiser; Butler managed to reach one of the rafts; Captain Fegan was nowhere to be seen. That night a Swedish steamer from the convoy returned to the scene and picked up 68 men; 191 crew on *Jervis Bay* had been lost. Fegan was awarded a posthumous VC and Butler received a DSC.

A Royal Navy Board of Enquiry was held soon after in Halifax. Butler gave evidence in a notably neutral, matter-of-fact tone. Having carried out the Captain's orders to throw overboard loose cordite and smoke floats, "I returned to the after control. It had been hit and everyone was killed. The ship was now burning fiercely and I went further aft. I then heard that the order to abandon ship had been given and I asked the Navigator (Lt. G.L. Roe) if I should carry on. He said 'Yes' and I jumped overboard. I got hold of a piece of wood and in due course I got to a raft on which were a lot of men. I was the only executive officer and I took charge of it." A witness on the raft added: "He behaved exactly as one would expect a Midshipman to behave" including taking the difficult decision not to paddle back towards the sinking ship to look for a serviceable boat. But it was another witness who captured the full extent of Butler's leadership and courage. In the words of Leading Seaman H.L. Bonney: "I think the way Midshipman Butler behaved on the raft was magnificent. He swam a long way to get to the raft and was one of the last people to join it. He was very cold and having shaken himself to restore a bit of circulation, he took complete charge. One would have thought he was a seasoned naval officer instead of just a young boy."

Later in the war Rags Butler served in destroyers that took part in the Arctic convoys, in the Operation Pedestal convoy to relieve Malta and in the Sicily and Salerno landings in Italy. Near the end of 1943, as gunnery officer in the destroyer *Intrepid,* he survived after the ship was sunk in Leros harbour by German aircraft. Taken prisoner, he escaped three times by stealing boats and was recaptured twice. Reaching Beirut after the third escape, he caught a plane to Cairo which crashed on landing. In lieu of a Bar to his DSC, he accepted a year's accelerated seniority and promotion to Lieutenant, aged 22. In 1944 as gunnery officer in the minelayer *Apollo,* he took part in the Normandy landings. Two years after the war ended Butler accepted a regular commission in the Royal Navy, serving until 1967. He moved on to adventurous spells on oil rigs off Australia and in the Pacific for the Burmah Oil Company.

At least four Old Pangbournians took part in the famous St. Nazaire Raid – Operation Chariot – in May 1942. An amphibious operation launched by the Allies to destroy a dry dock on the Loire river used by German capital ships, it was a success – the dock was put out of action for the rest of the war – but a very costly one; only 228 of the 611 men who took part returned to England. One who had a miraculous escape was **Stuart Irwin (29–32),**

Stuart Irwin.

commanding officer of *ML7,* a motor launch with a top speed of 19 knots, a crew of eight and one 3-pound gun. A history of *Combined Operations 1940–1942,* published by the government in 1943, described vividly the dangers Irwin faced: "*ML7* had a roving but extremely hazardous commission. She (and another motor launch *ML8*) was to move up and down the river twice in each direction at high speed for the purpose of drawing the enemy's fire." Between 35–40 enemy guns, some mobile and mounted on trucks, and about the same number of powerful, penetrating searchlights, were concentrated on the small, poorly-protected vessels.

"The German machine gun barrage was very heavy. They *(ML7)* described directing their 3-pounder on a searchlight on the port bow which was flooding the *Campbelltown* (the obsolete destroyer chosen to ram the dock gates) and successfully dowsing it... Soon afterwards *ML7* was hit and her steering damaged, but it was repaired again after ten minutes of intense effort. Just as *ML7* was turning to go 'home,' she opened fire on a German trawler which was camouflaged, and quietened her down. *ML7* was under intense fire throughout the withdrawal and, with its engine damaged, (could make) a speed of less than ten knots. Motor Launches, with no armour, were hardly meant to resist the tornado of metal awaiting them at St. Nazaire. The heroism and skill of their crews cannot be over-praised. It was an experience approaching the limits of human endurance and they did not fail." Irwin was awarded a DSC. He went on to win a DSO in 1944 "for outstanding service in special and secret operations or bravery in raiding operations" as a member of the African Coastal ML Flotilla operating in the Mediterranean and Adriatic. This clandestine Beirut-based unit, made up of four vessels belonging to the 45th MGB Flotilla, carried out three covert missions into Greece on 14 August 1944 landing undercover units on Spilea and recovering one hundred Allied personnel. Irwin's DSO was dated the next day. After the war, he commanded eight Royal Fleet Auxiliary ships until he retired in 1973.

The war career of **John Russell (30–34)** merited obituaries in three national newspapers when he died aged 88 in 2005. On paper, he was a relatively junior Lt

Cdr in the Royal Navy who had won two DSCs. More to the point, he was a Fleet Air Arm officer before the war, scored several hits on a U-boat at extreme range as First Lieutenant and Gunnery Officer in the destroyer *Exmoor* in 1941 (for which he was awarded his first DSC) and commanded the elite RN Commando unit known as 'Nan' which planned and controlled troop landings from ships. During long months stuck on the Anzio beachhead in Italy, he volunteered to fly a Seafire plane at low level to reconnoitre other beaches. After a few sorties, he was caught on the ground by the long-range German gun known as 'Anzio Annie,' blown off his feet and had to have a leg amputated by an American medic. Russell received a second DSC "for courage, leadership and determination." Repatriated to England, "the years following his disablement were bleak" in the words of the obituary in *The Independent*. Latterly, he became manager of a grain merchants in Barnstaple, sailing regularly with the North Devon Yacht Club.

Not all Old Pangbournians who served at sea during the war, particularly those in the Royal Naval Reserve and Royal Naval Volunteer Reserve, felt fully acknowledged or respected by their RN colleagues, regardless of their exploits. One who falls into this category is **Colin Warwick** (27–29), an officer who joined the RNR in 1939 and commanded a 600-ton anti-submarine trawler *St Loman* for nearly four years. In that period, he was awarded two DSCs, sank five German submarines, evacuated and landed British troops in Norway, and took part in protracted U-boat hunts as far afield as the east coast of North America, across the South Atlantic and through the Indian Ocean. The work of these patrols was rarely exciting and life could be gruelling and monotonous. While the crew formed a strong bond under Warwick's tolerant leadership, his pleasure at taking command of a brand-new frigate *Rushen Castle* as part of the Gibraltar convoys in late-1943 spoke for itself – the only reserve officer commanding an escort group in the Western Approaches Command. Nevertheless, as an RNR officer and despite his considerable wartime achievements, he felt constantly under-valued by the pen-pushers in the Admiralty, ironically titling his post-war memoir *Really Not Required,* by which time he was working in advertising in the United States.

Colin Warwick.

A contrary view of life in the RNR is provided by the career of **Humphry Boys-Smith** (18–21). He ended the war as a Commander on the staff of the Second Sea Lord in the Admiralty along with a DSO & Bar, a DSC and a US Citation for "meritorious service" in the Allied landings in north Africa in October 1942 presented to him by General Dwight Eisenhower. One of his confidential reports described him as "the best type of RNR officer. He is exceptionally able, very keen, possesses a great deal of imagination (and) is a leader of the highest order." In his unpublished *Memoir,* held in the Liddell Hart Archive at King's College London, he expresses no interest in a peacetime career in the

Humphrey Boys-Smith.

Royal Navy and never seems to have resented his RNR status in wartime – rather the opposite if anything. A report in *The Daily Telegraph* after his death in 1999 put the matter succinctly: "In his audacious and energetic war service, Humphrey Boys-Smith epitomised the priceless contribution that was made by naval reservists between 1939–45."

The son of a New Forest country parson and the younger brother of a man who became Vice-Chancellor of Cambridge University, Boys-Smith got the sailing bug from a fisherman in Lymington harbour. At Pangbourne, he was awarded one of the first RNR openings, doing six months in *Orion* before joining the Commonwealth & Dominion Line (the precursor of the Port Line and part of the Cunard group) in 1922. He remained in the Merchant Navy for 12 up-and-down years, being made redundant while becoming an Extra Master and retaining his RNR status. He then spent "five happy years" as a pilot in Haifa, Palestine until war broke out.

Recalled immediately to the Royal Navy, he was given command of a converted trawler fitted with depth charges and Asdic to detect submarines and sent on convoy escort duty in the North Sea. After only three months, he was given command of a new corvette, *Anemone.* Before he could take over the ship, the Allied evacuation from Dunkirk intervened. Ordered to rush south from his base in Scotland, he made six trips to the French coast over the following week, rescuing more than 1,000 soldiers in four different craft. On one occasion his motor launch was riddled with machine gun fire by a German aircraft. On another, he was alongside the paddle steamer *Gracie Fields* when it was bombed and sank; Boys-Smith aided the rescue of 750 troops. His fourth, fifth and sixth cross-Channel trips were all made in the dark with different crews and without charts – and were "a nightmare." This bravery won him his first DSO.

In *Anemone,* Boys-Smith was in the thick of the action during the worst phase of the decisive Battle of the Atlantic. Bombed while still in a dock in Liverpool, it was "18 months of hard slog against the odds." He ended up admiring the courage and persistence of his opponent, the U-boat crews. But he never forgot the appalling conditions he and his crew endured on his small craft which was less than 1,000 tons in weight and 200 feet long. In January 1941, thanks to some skilled navigation, he encountered a lone U-boat shadowing a convoy and sank it with depth charges, winning his second DSO. Soon after, with another corvette, he was sent on what amounted to a suicide mission to detect the German battleship *Tirpitz* in the sea north of Iceland. Fortunately for Boys-Smith, *Tirpitz* never appeared and after six weeks he was recalled to port. Promoted to Commander to captain a new frigate *Spey* – "an accolade to his professionalism" according to *The Times* – he was Mentioned in Despatches in July 1942 after a combined three-ship Allied effort led to the sinking of *U-136* off Madeira. That November, *Spey* was part of the enormous assault convoy assembled to support the Allied invasion of North Africa. "Bullied about" by Axis torpedo strike aircraft, he managed to get an entire American infantry battalion ashore after all its landing craft had to be sunk by *Spey* during the 500-mile tow from Gibraltar to a beach near Algiers. The US Citation and a DSC resulted.

From early 1944 Boys-Smith was based in the Admiralty in London. One day he came as near as he ever did during the war to being killed when a flying bomb destroyed the Guards Chapel in St. James's just yards from his office; he had left the room moments before to take a phone call. Reflecting on the Second World War in the early 1980s, he spoke for many in saying that it had been "a sobering experience…a form of madness." Aged 35 when the conflict began, he felt that he had grown up during the fighting because it had taught him "to take executive responsibility without minding." Commanding a frigate in wartime is "very much a one-man band" Boys-Smith wrote, where the captain often had split seconds to make life-and-death decisions. This suited his temperament. Once, in the Mediterranean under aggressive German air attacks that lasted for hours, his crew sent a message up to the bridge. It stated that the ship's company had "complete confidence in my ability to dodge bombs. I doubt if they realised how much guesswork, as well as judgement, was involved." Yet there was no doubt how much Humphrey Boys-Smith had earned their trust.

7

IN THE ARMY:
LEADING BY EXAMPLE

— ▣ —

Fewer Pangbournians joined the Army than the Navy or RAF – a reflection, perhaps, both of the strong nautical ethos of the College before the Second World War and that generation's thirst for action, adventure and early command. By the end of the war, a handful had reached senior military rank – in itself, perhaps, an indication of the way the conflict evolved after Dunkirk and the slower pace of advancement in the Army, even in wartime. Yet the Army cohort of Old Pangbournians ended the war with seven DSOs, 22 Military Crosses, one Croix de Guerre and many dozens of outstanding and memorable feats of leadership, courage and endurance on land and in the air during the conflict.

This record stretched back to the first days of actual land combat. Early in 1940, **John Mackenzie (29–33)**, a Captain in the Gloucestershire regiment, was ordered by the commander of 3 Division, the redoubtable Major General Bernard Montgomery, to raise long distance patrols. "You will get the first German. Is that understood?" Montgomery, in his inimical style, ordered the young officer. That night Mackenzie set off on a patrol with two men along the front of the Maginot forts in the Saar region. Surprising an enemy group of about 20 men, "with great presence of mind he (Mackenzie) allowed the leading German to approach within ten yards when he fired his Thompson MG (sub-machine gun). The two leading Germans fell and the rest scattered." The Glosters returned to their outpost to reinforce, got back to the scene of the

*John Mackenzie,
a Brigadier aged 29.*

action and made it back to Allied lines unscathed, carrying with them one dead German. "Captain Mackenzie showed unusual qualities of judgment and leadership through both operations, not only in having secured the German soldier – of great value for identification purposes – but also in having carried out his dangerous task without his own party suffering any casualties." He was awarded his first MC for "skill, judgement and leadership with the result that there were no British casualties. This is believed to be the first German accounted for by the Infantry of the British Expeditionary Force." That year, he won a second MC during his battalion's epic 95-mile retreat in 83 hours, with little food or sleep, to the beaches of Dunkirk.

So began an illustrious military career. By the end of the war in 1945 Mackenzie had become the youngest Brigadier in the British Army aged 29, and fought more or less continuously from 1942–45 during "long and arduous" (his words) campaigns in North Africa, Sicily and throughout the advance up the heavily-defended Italian peninsula. Transferring in North Africa to the 2nd Battalion Lancashire Fusiliers – part of the famous 78th Battleaxe Division – initially as second-in-command, he took over after his CO was wounded in the Tunisian campaign. Landing in Sicily in July 1943, he was involved in bitter fighting all the way north through Italy. At the two-day battle of El Sangro, when Allied forces made their first attempt to break the Gustav Line (the main German defensive position south of Rome) and the Fusiliers attacked relentlessly, Mackenzie was wounded but carried on fighting and was awarded his first DSO. The Citation states: "For exceptional gallantry and leadership…The battalion captured all its objectives in spite of fierce opposition. The total prisoners taken during the two days was approximately 170 beside many killed."

Mackenzie seems to have been undeterred. Two subsequent engagements involving his battalion in Italy stand out. At Termoli, four days of intensive fighting in September 1943 against the formidable 16th Panzer Division was described in detail in an article he penned for *The Log* in 1946. "The battle was simply tremendous and very exciting. The Fusiliers had beaten the Germans to the high ground overlooking the town (of Termoli) and were having the shoot of their lives…a whole column of German vehicles came to an abrupt halt in front of us – a sight seldom seen…Three major counter-attacks were driven off, but that same night we (Fusiliers) were cut off but maintaining our position at all costs." Next morning, another German assault was beaten back after which a full-scale German retreat began. Mackenzie was sent for again by Montgomery who asked him to inform the Fusiliers that he "was very pleased with the great fighting stand at Termoli." He was awarded an immediate DSO "for outstanding leadership and conspicuous devotion to duty."

Following a three-week recuperation, the Fusiliers edged north and from January-May 1944 had a central role in what turned out to be one of the pivotal battles of the entire Italian campaign – the assault on German lines at the abbey, or fortress, of Monte Cassino. The encounter at the top of Monastery Hill abutting the abbey and very close to dominant German positions, and John Mackenzie's part in it, is brilliantly recounted in *The Monastery,* a short book published in 1945 by his second-in-command, the writer Fred Majdalany. Initially, the Fusiliers were deployed on one of the most exposed positions near the top of the hill for a month, taking 48 hours to reach it in stages. Here the battalion endured dire weather, constant shelling, minimal sleep, few medical facilities, basic hygiene, a lack of water, and being forced to live on iron rations perilously brought up to the outpost on mules by a Sikh support regiment.

Ostensibly occupying a forward defensive position, "there was never the slightest possibility of a sector which contained John ever becoming a quiet sector," wrote Majdalany. "John was allergic to quiet sectors. He held that defence was simply an irritating interval between attacks which must be used to promote the maximum amount of alarm and despondence on the opposing side. So, far from avoiding stirring up trouble, he would go without sleep, racking his brains for some new kind of trouble to stir up." At these times, noted Majdalany, he would sit at a little ops table, 18 inches square made out of odd pieces of wood, "peering at his maps and his air photographs through a magnifying glass, finding more places for the commander of his battery to fire at. 'Do you think you could hit that Harry?' Mac would say. 'Do you think you could give it a dossing now?' John would ask gently."

One evening, shortly after dusk, Mackenzie suggested to Majdalany "'Let's walk up to Snake's Head (a notorious hot spot and one of the Germans favourite mortar targets) and have a look.' He said it in the tone of voice in which you say 'Let's walk round to The Royal for a quick one before dinner.' An "ugly scene" confronted the pair – the littered human and physical remains of an earlier battle involving US soldiers. Ignoring snipers, "John casually picked up a nice map case not far from a dead American." After four or five days, Mackenzie felt confident he knew all the places where Germans might have sited gun positions. A couple of days on, he began to get restless and wandered about chatting with the soldiers. "Then he'd come back to his table and write a letter. Then he'd have an idea." One of his best was the 'Ghost Gun' which involved pointing and firing a remotely-controlled, moveable machine gun directly at windows in the monastery – to the evident fury of its German defenders. Not long after, the Fusiliers were reinforced by a battery of American-made 8" howitzers firing 350 lb shells on to the roof of the monastery. "John was beside himself with joy. Here was a plaything after his own heart! Someone christened the gun Horace and the name stuck."

After 30 days and nights on this brutally exposed hillside, the battalion was relieved by a Polish regiment whose commanding officer was twice Mackenzie's age – "They might have been father and son." The Poles, it turned out, "found it difficult to get used to the idea of a Colonel aged twenty-eight." Within ten days, the Fusiliers were ordered up to the front again for the decisive Allied attack in the Cassino sector which was intended to break out into the Liri valley, bisect Highway Six and open the road to Rome. "Get everything teed up. Then get some sleep," Mackenzie had ordered earlier. "I've got to be at Brigade at nine for the final conference. Don't suppose I'll be back much before eleven." At 4:00am next day, the battalion advanced quietly to the front. At 9:00am it began its attack. Over the next two days a fierce back-and-forth battle took place, often with both sides no more than 20–30 yards apart. Casualties were high. Mackenzie's iron nerve, and coolness under fire, held and after a week's fighting British and Polish forces linked up on May 18, 1944. Following the final stage of this battle Mackenzie successfully recommended that one of his soldiers, Fusilier Frank Jefferson, for the Victoria Cross after he single-handedly neutralised a German tank.

In the autumn Mackenzie was promoted Brigadier to command the 11th Infantry Brigade as it battled north through Italy. He advanced from there to help suppress the communist uprising in Greece in 1945–46 before attending the Staff College, Camberley. His subsequent post-war military career included spells in Korea, and Jordan where he succeeded Glubb Pasha as Commander of the Jordan Army Infantry Training Team. In 1962–3 he commanded the Nigerian Army during its deployment with the United Nations in the Congo (See Chapter 13). He retired from the Army in 1970 after three years as Commandant and Inspector of Intelligence at the Ministry of Defence. Known to everyone in the Army as 'Mac,' his obituary in *The Daily Telegraph* described John Mackenzie as "a thinking soldier, observant and open-minded who acknowledged that he often felt fear in spite of his outstanding record of courage. He created a battalion of superb quality and loyalty. His modesty and cheerfulness made him popular everywhere."

In retirement John Mackenzie wrote a war memoir *CO 2LF 78 Division* which was never published. But in 1997, two years after his death, an abridged version was issued by a friend. Mackenzie's innate modesty and shrewd focus on the things that matter in a land campaign shines through, along with his ruthless determination. His Lancastrian Fusiliers initially greeted him warily after he took over command in an emergency, not having even met some of the officers. By the time he left for Greece two years later, he could do no wrong. "Mac's back, have you heard! Yes, Mac's back" went the excited word when he returned to the battalion before the battle for Monte Cassino having been wounded seriously in his right leg on the advance to Sangro river, to his intense frustration. Awaiting evacuation, he had lain upright on a stretcher in his command post still giving orders. At Montgomery's personal request, he was not evacuated from Italy. The warm feelings in his battalion were reciprocated. Presented with a unique regimental pennant at his farewell parade, Mackenzie was driven away to ringing cheers, feeling "utterly depressed" at leaving Italy and his men before the campaign was over, and not in the least uplifted by becoming the youngest Brigadier in the British Army at the time. "Tears splashed down my face," he recalled.

Whilst at Termoli Mackenzie had run into **Peter Hellings (30–34)**, at the time second-in-command of the Royal Marines 40 Commando – "It was a Doctor-Livingstone-I-Presume situation," noted Mackenzie drolly. The previous night Hellings had landed with his men and raided the town where they surprised, and captured, 90 or so German officers and men dressed mainly in pyjamas and suffering the after-effects of what Mackenzie described as "a Bacchanalian orgy the previous evening." Next day, German infantry counter-attacked in strength supported by tanks but the commandos, backed by reinforcements sent in hurriedly by Mackenzie, held off the assaults for two days until support arrived from the British Eighth

Peter Hellings.

Army. For his action in clearing the harbour at Termoli, Hellings was awarded an MC to go with a DSC he had won in France in 1940 during the retreat to Dunkirk – possibly the only man ever to have received both awards.

The prolonged four-month stalemate around Anzio following the Allied landings in mid-January 1944 resulted in two OPs receiving immediate decorations in the field. **Jim Acland (33–37)**, a Major in the 1st Reconnaissance Regiment, King's Shropshire Light Infantry, was awarded a DSO "for gallant and distinguished services." The recommendation, written by his CO, reads: "Major Acland has been in action without a break between 24 Jan and 10 Feb. He has commanded his squadron with great distinction and has provided valuable information from patrols into enemy outpost positions. His squadron of 86 men subsequently took over a defensive position in the line from 400 US troops and held it for 8 days and nights. The position was under continual mortar and shell fire and was only 300 yards from the enemy. On the night of 4/5 Feb the enemy attacked in strength supported by mortar and MG (machine gun) fire but they were forced to withdraw by the determined defence. Maj Acland himself directed the artillery fire, giving corrections by observation on the line of the enemy's approach. By active patrolling into the enemy's positions, this squadron was able to establish a superiority over the enemy on his immediate front and so made a show of force which did not exist on the ground. During all this time Maj Acland was an inspiration to his squadron and completely disregarded his own personal safety. By his initiative and ability, he never allowed the enemy any respite or freedom of movement and it was largely due to him that the regiment was able to hold the defensive positions entrusted to it." Three days after this engagement, Acland's squadron was ordered to regain a lost river crossing. It did so, and held a bridge against strong opposition unsupported for five hours until the arrival of 3 Infantry Brigade.

Richard Hewitt (27–31), a Major attached to the Green Howards regiment, also was awarded an immediate DSO at Anzio. His battalion had landed in late-January but got stuck in reclaimed malarial marshland on a coastal plain surrounded by mountains. On May 23, a breakout was ordered. The Citation for Hewitt's DSO reads: "Major Hewitt was commanding 'D' Coy (Company). This Coy was the leading assault Coy and had been given the difficult task of making the initial crossing over the river Moletta followed by the subsequent assault over unknown anti-personnel minefields to the first key objective. The assault was a success and 27 prisoners were taken, but the Coy arrived at its objective with only 30% of its original strength. Throughout the day the position held by 'D' Coy was constantly shelled and machine-gunned from the right flank and, despite the provision of reinforcements, casualties continued to be heavy. At 2000 hrs the enemy launched a heavy counter-attack which drove in the forward company and by sheer weight of number surrounded 'D' Company.

"Knowing that his orders were to hold on at all costs, Major Hewitt rallied the remnants of his Company which now included elements of the forward company, a section of 2 Northamptons and a platoon of 7 Cheshires and succeeded in beating the enemy who withdrew to a position about 100 yards in front of 'D' Company, keeping up MG fire and throwing grenades during the remainder of the night. When orders were eventually received to withdraw his company across the Moletta, Major Hewitt organised his force into parties and successfully achieved a daylight withdrawal of some 70 men across the river within 25 yards of an enemy machine gun post…with the loss of only five men wounded and subsequently evacuated. Throughout the entire action Major Hewitt showed outstanding

Nick Knollys (left) and Charlie Daniel (2nd left) on patrol with two colleagues during the Dhofar Insurgency, Oman 1973. (Nick Knollys)

Rory Copinger-Symes photographed in Iraqi Kurdistan 1991. (Lori Traikos)

Angus Fair in Afghanistan before the start of Operation Panther's Claw in 2009 (Angus Fair).

The Falklands war: ss Canberra *in San Carlos Water. (Wikimedia Commons)*

The Falklands war: HMS Ardent *on fire as seen from HMS* Yarmouth *by John Plummer.*

The Falklands war: the nuclear submarine HMS Splendid. *(MoD)*

*West Falkland – a view from the farm on which
Miles Griffith was working in 1982. (Miles Griffith)*

A painting by Robert Lloyd of the sinking of mv Dara *off Dubai in April 1961. (Ian Tew)*

Rick Powell celebrates as a member of the winning GB wheelchair basketball team at the 2014 Invictus Games. (Getty Images)

Ian Shuttleworth at Goodwood one year, determined to enjoy life to the full (OP Society)

*Petty Officer Naval Nurse Alice Mullen who volunteered to work in a
Plymouth hospital during the first Covid lockdown in 2020. (MoD)*

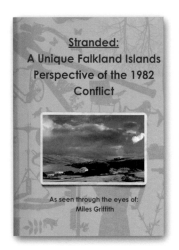

Stranded:
A Unique Falkland Islands
Perspective of the 1982
Conflict

As seen through the eyes of:
Miles Griffith

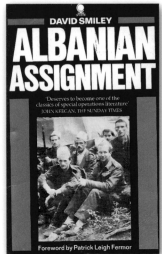

DAVID SMILEY

ALBANIAN ASSIGNMENT

'Deserves to become one of the
classics of special operations literature'
JOHN KEEGAN, THE SUNDAY TIMES

Foreword by Patrick Leigh Fermor

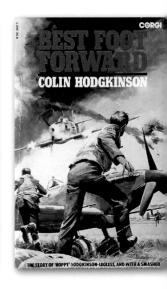

CORGI

BEST FOOT FORWARD

COLIN HODGKINSON

THE STORY OF 'HOPPY' HODGKINSON-LEGLESS, AND WITH A SMASHED

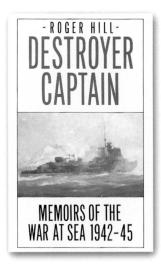

- ROGER HILL -

DESTROYER CAPTAIN

MEMOIRS OF THE
WAR AT SEA 1942-45

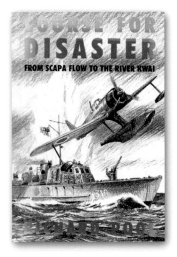

OURSE FOR DISASTER

FROM SCAPA FLOW TO THE RIVER KWAI

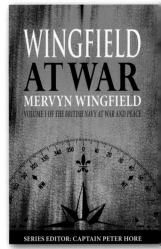

WINGFIELD AT WAR

MERVYN WINGFIELD

VOLUME 1 OF *THE BRITISH NAVY AT WAR AND PEACE*

SERIES EDITOR: CAPTAIN PETER HORE

leadership and resource and it was due to his constant encouragement at times when the situation was gravest that his very depleted force managed to drive off and hold its own against a very superior force of German para troopers." Another officer to fight in Italy and be recognised was **D.L. Roberts (30–35)**. A member of 43 Commando Royal Marines, he was Mentioned in Despatches following Operation Roast, a battle at Commachio in Emilia Romagna in the Spring of 1945 when he was badly wounded.

The Military Cross – the third-level military decoration awarded only to officers during the Second World War but to all ranks today – is granted in recognition of "an act or acts of exemplary gallantry during active operations against the enemy on land." Mostly, in 1939–45, it was received by those serving in the Army. Several Old Pangbournians, including **John Mackenzie (29–33)**, **David Smiley (30–34)**, **A.W. Innes (30–34)** and **J.A. McKee (31–33)**, won two MCs. Innes received his awards in 1943 and 1944 when fighting the Japanese with his regiment, the Royal Lincolnshire, in Burma. **Rodney Watson (18–20)** of the Royal Scots was awarded both the DSO and MC before being killed in action in May 1940 during the British retreat to Dunkirk. At the time he was commanding his battalion (see Chapter 10) and had already been wounded on three occasions.

Details of the actions involving most of these honours are scant but they include service in a whole gamut of Army units of the time including The Queen's Royal Regiment, the Rifle Brigade, the Royal Artillery, the Lancashire Fusiliers, The Glider Pilot Regiment, the Gurkha Rifles, the Royal Lincolnshire Regiment, the East Surrey Regiment and the East Yorkshire Regiment. **L. Allsworth Jones (28–33)** served in the Indian Army's 1st Dogra Regiment and was awarded his MC in 1944 during the Allied recovery of Burma. Subsequently, he led his regiment when it landed in Surabaya, Java in October 1945 to quell a nationalist uprising by militias seeking Indonesian independence. **Edward Palmer (24–27)** farmed in Kenya pre-war. On the outbreak of the conflict, he enlisted with the King's African Rifles and fought in the Somalia and Abyssinia campaigns and was Mentioned in Despatches. Towards the end of the war, he undertook jungle warfare training and campaigned in Burma until VJ Day in 1945, being awarded his MC there.

Ninian Hawken (24–28) of The Queen's Royal Regiment won an MC in France in 1940 "for gallantry in a very hazardous operation." In 1942 he was transferred to North Africa where his regiment took part in the battle of El Alamein as "Lorried Infantry." He was wounded during the capture of Tunis. Recovering, he fought in the Allied offensive to break the Germans so-called Gothic Line in Italy in 1943 "but enemy mortar fire seemed to have a fascination for me and I was wounded again – this time rather seriously in the chest." His Army record describes him as "Temporary Major, dangerously ill." That was the end of Hawken's wartime service. Some officers, of course, were never recognised. **Tommy Powell (29–32)**, for example, served throughout the war as an officer in the Wiltshire Regiment, fought at Normandy and was involved in the Arnhem operation before suffering the harrowing experience of being part of the British liberation of Bergen-Belsen concentration camp.

Several dozen OPs, mostly serving in the Army or RAF, became prisoners-of-war. Courage and stoicism, defiance and an abiding will to live proved to be crucial. **Ian Colquhoun (29–30)**, a Major in the 7th Gurkha Rifles, was captured by the Japanese after the fall of Singapore and spent three and a half years in a PoW camp in Sumatra. With him were three other OPs – **Jack Goold (18–20)**, **Gordon Spaull (19–20)** and **Patrick Langdon (25–28)**, all civilians living in the Far East when war broke out. Spaull died in captivity. So did **William Hutton (19–21)**, an officer in the Australian Army captured in Malaya who died in 1942. **Alan Walker (19–21)** survived more than three years in a camp in Siam but was never the same again after the war. In Germany in Camp Oflag 1XA four OPs kept each other company. One of them, **D.M. Barrett (28–32)**, an RAF officer, sent a post-card to the College in 1941: "Often, in the unfilled moments of our sojourn here, I think of the old times and wonder how you are all progressing up on top of that hill. There are four of us here who send good wishes to you all – **John Iliffe (26–29)**, **R.J. Lubbock (30–33)**, **Philip Boulnois (32–35)** and myself…If it is possible, please send out *The Log*. Our hosts are reasonably courteous and we organize ourselves and educate one another – and are, of course, full of spirit. Trusting we will meet again before long." At least four OP PoWs – **John Burfield (31–34)**, **R.A.G. Butler (35–39)**, **Ian McGeoch (28–31)** and **Robert Ramsay (29–31)** – escaped successfully and a few were repatriated due to illnesses or wounds.

Conventional warfare by regular infantry officers was supported throughout the Second World War by "irregular" or unconventional Army-authorized and supported operations. One Pangbournian who seems to have had no other role – and is probably the only Australian-born cadet ever to attend the Nautical College – was **Victor Fretwell (19–21)**. He received no decorations and his wartime contribution was unknown until well after his death – yet he never forgot his time at Pangbourne, and the values he had absorbed in far-away Berkshire. After the NCP, Fretwell had remained in England and the RNR for five years, being noted as "a good seaman for his age" during training one year in the destroyer *Venomous*. From there, he joined the Asiatic Petroleum Company (which became part of

Royal Dutch Shell) as a clerk. At the end of 1926 he was posted to Shanghai in China. Here he played rugby for a few years for the expatriate Shanghai Rugby Club, marrying an Australian in 1940 nine years after meeting her. The following year his wife gave birth to a daughter in Melbourne and never returned to China. At the end of 1941 the Japanese invaded the international settlement in Shanghai but Fretwell had left for India. That September he was commissioned as a 2nd Lieutenant in the British Army.

Precisely what happened over the next four years can only be discerned in outline. As a fluent Mandarin speaker, Fretwell was soon in demand for behind-the-lines roles as Japanese forces swept through China and Burma. *Old Pangbournian Notes* in the Spring 1943 issue of *The Log* records that he had been deployed "in Burma in a 'hush hush' unit until the Japanese occupied the country. He complained that the unit had been removed to China "too early." In August (1942) his small force (probably the Special Operations Executive-backed 204 British Military Mission to China known as Tulip Force) "was buried in the heart of China and had almost lost touch with the outside world." A letter from Fretwell to *The Log* after the war revealed that the unit had operated against Japanese lines of communication. For ten months the local population, fearful of reprisals, did their best to starve and obstruct the force. Malaria and typhus took a toll. "We had some pretty tricky problems in navigation, too, in persuading our stores to ascend mountain streams, 80 miles in 18 days, in which officers and men waist-deep had literally to tow the boats up and over rapids. Being Adjutant, and with advanced headquarters (having) gone ahead and overland, I escaped the towing gang and saved my modesty. On another river, rafts had to be used. Any dish of rice figures will never again be popular with the survivors of this small force."

By 1944 Fretwell was listed as a "Staff Army Officer" based in India. That July he was given a code name, BB227, and transferred to Force 136 (another element of the SOE) "to be specially employed." Force 136 had been established to run and supply resistance movements in enemy-occupied territory and to undertake some clandestine sabotage operations. Led by British officers, it relied on indigenous manpower, and much of Fretwell's time seems to have been spent sorting out the loyal from the two-faced among its recruits. From November 1944 to early February 1946, he was stationed in Chungking and Kunming in southwest China. Here he was designated "second in command" with the rank of Captain according to a file in The National Archives, although his commanding officer was rarely present. His base was 13 miles outside Kunming by a lake at Shi Shan under the Western Hills; about 15 British and Chinese signalmen worked there, relaying messages from agents in Japanese-occupied parts of Burma and China. Fretwell oversaw 204 missions in this period, and was described as "very efficient – a hard-working and reliable officer…suitable for office or operational work" in a confidential report written on the last day of 1944.

When Fretwell relinquished his commission on 28 April, 1946, he was given the rank of Honorary Major by way of thanks. At the end of that year, he was back at work in China as manager of the Tsingtao branch of the Royal Dutch Shell company, lasting in this role until the communist takeover in mid-June 1949. Shell then seconded him to the ill-fated groundnut scheme in colonial Tanganyika (Tanzania) for two years. He recalled his war service disparagingly in 1946, remarking that he had "added no lustre to the impressive record of honours gained by OPs and so many of my term-mates in First Medway." That was, perhaps deliberately, to downplay his clandestine role. As the Editor of *The Log* added: "Fretwell must have had a very uncomfortable war, joining a Commando Force formed in Burma in 1941 to operate against Japanese lines of communication in China…and later having 'fun and games' behind Jap (sic) lines when the war ended." After his stint in Africa he returned to Australia, settling near Sydney where he died in 1975.

Unconventional warfare was the speciality, too, of another outstanding warrior and very determined Pangbournian, **George Chatterton (25–29)**, a former Chief of the College. Described by contemporaries as charismatic, driven, progressive, self-confident and a tough disciplinarian, by 1946 he was a Brigadier aged 33 – at which point he retired from the Army after just eight years in the Service. On leaving the NCP he had gone into the RAF, become a Flying Officer and taken part in flying displays. But after a nasty accident in 1935, he switched Services and became Lt. Chatterton of The Queen's Royal Regiment (West Surrey) – the senior English line infantry regiment. Deployed to France in 1939 in the British Expeditionary Force, he returned to England before the evacuation from Dunkirk in June 1940. Bored with a lack of action at home in the year following, in late-1941 he volunteered to join the new 5,000 strong Glider Pilot Regiment (GPR) that Churchill had ordered be formed following the success of the German airborne invasion of Crete in June 1941. Immediately chosen to command the nascent 2nd Battalion, Chatterton took over the 1st Battalion after its commanding officer was killed in a crash

George Chatterton.

in 1942. A firm believer in the axiom that "a good regiment is a smart regiment," Chatterton reckoned he had been heading for a clash with his predecessor who, while a brave man and an expert parachutist, had no experience of night flying and favoured a looser, more relaxed approach to training and discipline than did the self-avowed "spit-and-polish" Chatterton.

After the war Chatterton wrote a disarmingly frank memoir titled *The Wings of Pegasus* which was published in 1962 and tells the story of the GPR. In an Introduction to the book General 'Boy' Browning, the overall commander of British Army's airborne forces during the Second World War, praised "the imagination, the foresight and the inter-Service knowledge" of Chatterton. He might have gone a lot further. As an obituary in *The Daily Telegraph* puts it: "The regiment owes more to Chatterton than to any other single figure – his leadership and stubborn refusal to be beaten by difficulties enabled it to play a vital operational part in the war."

From the outset Chatterton set down the exacting standards required for service in the GPR. In his words: "If the pilot of the glider had to get out and fight at the other end of the flight, he must have what amounted to a dual personality. First, the flexibility of the pilot for his long tow to the target. Secondly, the *esprit* and discipline and all that went with it in order that he should stand up to the rigours of battle at the end of his journey." Therefore, he decided that his pilots – most of whom were Non-Commissioned Officers who had passed the RAF Aircrew Selection Board – would be subjected to a punishing training regime overseen by two Army Brigade of Guards Sergeant Majors. At his first briefing for the new recruits, he was blunt about what was expected of them. "I make no apology for talking to you like this. May I add that I shall be quite ruthless. Only the best will be tolerated in loyalty and discipline, apart from anything else." Called a 'Fascist' by a poorly-informed Member of Parliament, the Army bureaucracy investigated. Chatterton refused to back down, was supported by the War Office and was proved resoundingly right by future events. As a *Times* obituary put it: "He was hard as nails and a tough commander."

With a more-or-less blank sheet of paper to work on once he took over the 1st Battalion, and supported by his own flying skills and unusual military background, Chatterton devised many of the battle tactics used by the GPR. Among his innovations was the concept of landing gliders on top of enemy positions instead of miles from the target. He made his pilots wear dark glasses in training so they could land with limited vision. After much study, he rejected mass glider landings in favour of smaller tactical ones where the casualties and associated damage were greatly reduced. In pilot training he put the emphasis not on flight hours but landings – the moment of greatest danger for the pilots – and pioneered the use of overlay aerial photos of airfields to help Army commanders unfamiliar with the organisation of landing zones for gliders. He was the first glider commander, too, to recognise the importance of "target" gliders painted in bright colours to lead landings by the rest of a glider force. Always hampered by a lack of gliders and tow aircraft on which to train, his ingenuity constantly overcame obstacles. But he was never a reckless do-or-die type, on occasion challenging orders and resisting suicidal missions proposed by Army commanders who knew nothing of glider capabilities or needs, and cared less.

Four main operations defined the combat record of the Glider Pilot Regiment during the Second World War – the invasion of Sicily (Operation Ladbroke) in July 1943; the invasion of Europe in June 1944 (Operation Overlord); the attempt to seize a road bridge at Arnhem in Holland (Operation Market Garden) in September 1944; and the mass Allied crossing of the river Rhine (Operation Varsity) in March 1945. Sicily proved to be Chatterton's nadir, even though he was awarded a DSO, while D-Day was a "95 per cent success" in his estimation. Arnhem, he reckoned, resulted in "horrendous" casualties as a result of his tactical plan being ignored, dissension among Allied commanders and lack of cover from the RAF. The airborne-led crossing of the Rhine was, he felt, the culmination of all the GPR had learned and was deemed a resounding success, helping to hasten the end of the war in Europe.

Right from the start of the GPR's involvement in the planning to invade Sicily, Chatterton was uneasy and found himself at odds with Army commanders who displayed a woeful lack of understanding of the potential of gliders – and of their limitations. At that point the GPR pilots had an average of two hours' flying experience, had never flown at night, had never seen or flown the 500 American-made Waco gliders the GPR was loaned to use in the invasion, and had never cooperated with ground troops in a live action against the enemy. The stony, walled small-field terrain chosen to land the gliders and their cargo – a brigade of troops with all its arms and equipment – on the Sicilian coast was spectacularly unsuitable. And, by the time the gliders did reach Sicily, many of the pilots were exhausted by trying to keep their gliders on track in a 45mph gale during a 300-mile tow from North Africa. Some of the gliders had actually been sabotaged earlier by a disaffected Italian-American mechanic in the US Army; fortunately, this was detected before take-off.

Threatened with being cashiered by the officer commanding Airborne Forces, who had sold the airborne element of the invasion to the equally uncomprehending

General Montgomery, Chatterton faced a "ridiculous dilemma." He concluded that he had no choice but to proceed. "I was deeply apprehensive" he wrote 18 years after the event. On the night of the invasion, Chatterton's glider was hit by enemy fire about a mile short of land and had to be ditched in the sea. Swimming ashore, he was fired at but had no way of fighting back – all his weapons had sunk with his glider. Reaching a beach and finding a colleague, "I lay there paralysed with fear and shock…We felt helpless and I, for my part, was utterly dejected and despondent. All the planning and training exercises in the world could not have foreseen this situation."

Somehow, Chatterton linked up with an SAS (Special Air Services) landing party led by the formidable Paddy Mayne and was involved in the capture of 100 Italian soldiers that night. Fewer than one-fifth of the 1st Airborne Division had been dropped in the right place at the right time, but despite this some GPR objectives were achieved including the capture of a key bridge. Nearing the city of Syracuse, the surreal took over when Chatterton and a friend and fellow officer were invited to a sumptuous lunch with plentiful Chianti wine by a welcoming Italian-American family glad to see the back of the Fascists. The pair had arrived at the hosts' villa in a requisitioned fire-engine of 1900 vintage complete with brass fittings and a six-pounder anti-tank gun attached to the rear. Explosions, set off by the advancing Allied 8th Army, resonated in the background as lunch was taken. For a time after the invasion recriminations reached such a pitch that the future of the GPR itself was threatened. Calmer heads prevailed; Chatterton was promoted to full Colonel and decorated. The Citation for his DSO states: "By his personal disregard for his own safety at all times, Lt. Colonel Chatterton set an example of courage and determination which, together with his outstanding leadership enabled the 1st Battalion Glider Pilot Regiment to carry out its first operation with such distinction and gallantry."

After such a dramatic and costly battlefield debut, D-Day proved to be almost the antithesis of Sicily for Chatterton and the GPR – a well-planned, exhaustively practised operation that went off like clockwork. The regiment was better-equipped by now and was using British-made Horsa gliders and the heavy Hamilcar glider. Its role was to convey battalions, weapons and an entire armoured squadron with tanks to landing areas six miles behind the enemy frontline, in the dark, mostly in the hours before the amphibious invasion on the morning of June 6. Much to his frustration, Chatterton was made to remain in England coordinating airfields and GPR operations. More than 1,000 gliders were involved, including 250 on D-Day itself – "a formidable force." Seven thousand men of the 6th Air Landing Brigade reached France. Much of the parachute deployment before the gliders landed went awry due to high winds, yet most of the gliders landed where they were supposed to, at the designated hour, and the whole operation was deemed a success.

The battle of Arnhem in September 1944, by contrast, proved to be another disaster. About 9,000 men and 1,126 glider pilots belonging to two American and one British airborne division were dropped at three points in front of the advancing 2nd British Army. The role of the British 1st Airborne Division, supported by the GPR, was to capture the heavily-guarded bridge at Arnhem. The strong German presence around Arnhem – in particular two panzer divisions refitting in the area – was overlooked or discounted. Such was the German anti-aircraft power around Arnhem, however, that the dropping and landing zones for the gliders ended up eight miles from the target bridge. Ninety per cent of the GPR took part and nearly 600 gliders had to be landed with their precious loads. The glider landings were successful, but subsequently just about everything that could go wrong, in what had been billed as a two to three-day operation, did go wrong. After nine days the 1st Airborne Division had been wiped out and the surviving Allied forces ended up withdrawing under extreme pressure. The Glider Pilot Regiment emerged from this ordeal "tremendously proud but desperately reduced." A total of 1,262 members of the GPR flew in, 219 were killed and 511 wounded or taken prisoner-of-war – some 60 per cent of those involved. "For the regiment this was all-but a death blow" in Chatterton's words. Afterwards, and for years to follow, reproaches and accusations of betrayal surrounded the battle.

Chatterton played a front-line role at Arnhem, flying in the commander of the British airborne units, General 'Boy' Browning, his batman, doctor, cook, jeep and tent close to what became Browning's headquarters in the Reichswald Forest. He was present at several crucial meetings of senior commanders during the battle and at one point in *The Wings of Pegasus* gives an illuminating picture of Browning, someone he rather admired. "He came to the glider immaculately dressed in a barathea battle-dress with a highly-polished Sam Browne belt, knife-edge creased trousers, leather revolver holster, all gleaming like glass, a swagger cane in one hand and wearing kid gloves. He was in tremendous form because he realised that he had reached one of the climaxes of his career. There was immense gaiety everywhere." Inside the glider, Browning perched on a beer crate by the pilots' door. The landing ruined a Dutch family's precious vegetable allotment containing row upon row of cabbages. The Germans, taken by surprise, barely reacted until Messerschmitt aircraft arrived on the scene and killed an RAF photographer standing alongside Chatterton. Soon after, at a meeting with US commanders, Browning and three Guards' Colonels with him, "wore a most amazing air of nonchalance and gave the impression that this was not a battle but an exercise near Caterham Barracks." Another OP was at Arnhem, **R.M.F. Giles (32–35)**, a Pilot Officer in the RAF. He described Chatterton as "a great leader when the day came."

Badly mauled, what was left of the GPR got back to England in October 1944. Chatterton was "at a loss to know how to reorganise." The following month he was summoned to a conference in London by the newly-appointed American head of the 70,000-strong Allied Airborne Army, General Lewis Brereton, and instructed to prepare a huge glider force to take part in the crossing of the Rhine the following March. Lacking manpower and gliders, he turned to the RAF which reluctantly provided 1,500 under-employed officer and NCO pilots. In the following four months he recreated, through intense training, the GPR *esprit de corps* and managed to integrate the newcomers with his Army pilots. In the end a huge assembly of aircraft was involved including almost 1,800 troop-carriers conveying parachutists and 1,300 gliders with supplies.

Learning from Arnhem, Brereton backed Chatterton to the hilt and the result was one lift, with the bulk of the airborne force landing a short distance behind German lines, after initial amphibious landings. Those landed were reinforced as soon as possible by supply lifts. A number of targets, rather than a single one, were selected. GPR casualties were again heavy – more than 100 pilots killed, missing or wounded. But within 24 hours all the objectives had been achieved and within three days there were 14 Allied divisions on the east bank of the Rhine. "This time," wrote Chatterton, "nothing had been left to chance, everything had been tied up completely. It resulted in an astounding victory." The Supreme Allied Commander, General Eisenhower, was exultant and maintained that Operation Varsity was "the most successful airborne operation carried out to date."

Even so, the cost had been very high. In late-July 1945, survivors of the GPR marched behind a band through Stedham, near Midhurst in Sussex, on their way to an evocative, emotion-filled memorial service in a little church at the east end of the sprawling village. Four hundred voices thundered out 'Fight the Good Fight' and 'Abide With Me.' Chatterton gave a Tribute. A description of the occasion was printed in *The Evening News:* "Simple, too, was the Brigadier's farewell address. He spoke without histrionics of 'the things I have watched as Commander of this Regiment – the wonderful qualities of the patience, discipline and fortitude of all concerned. I have always wanted you to have the better qualities which are given to men. By that I mean simplicity, faith, and that good courage on which you would have to fall back when the real trial came – and you had them.' He recalled old memories and abiding comradeship. There was nobody in that church who was not intensely moved."

Just a year on George Chatterton retired from the Army with his Glider Pilot Regiment garlanded in honours and recognition. A total of 3,302 men served in the regiment during the Second World War of whom 1,301 (40%) were listed as killed (551), wounded (200) or taken prisoner-of-war (550). More than 170 awards for courage and bravery were received. By 1957 the regiment had been disbanded and its expertise integrated into the Army Air Corps as helicopters replaced gliders. Chatterton was a stockjobber by then, working in the City of London selling securities wholesale to brokers. In 1980 he received an OBE for his herculean efforts in raising more than £1 million for the Lady Hoare Trust for child victims of thalidomide. He died in 1987. George Chatterton never forgot the values of leadership, man management and self-discipline that he learned first at Pangbourne, returning to the College several times in war and peace to address awestruck cadets. "Nothing is Impossible" was the motto he devised for the Glider Pilot Regiment. It applies equally to his life and career.

8

"COURAGE IS THE THING. ALL GOES IF COURAGE GOES!"[2]

— ◉ —

David de Crespigny Smiley (30–34), LVO, OBE, MC and Bar, was a remarkably courageous, adventurous and fortunate man. In a long, action-packed life, he survived countless near-death experiences, broke most bones in his body, lived for months in dreadful conditions behind enemy lines, scouted German-held towns during the Second World War, took the surrender of a Japanese army division, rescued French hostages, liberated a prisoner of war camp, commanded a force that seized a mountain redoubt unconquered for centuries, and counselled monarchs and prime ministers without fear or favour. Ever his own man, yet a staunch loyalist to king and country with many connections in the right places, he was often let down by those in authority, rarely rewarded publicly for his services and frequently blind-sided by political machinations. But he soldiered on when many others would have given up, taking huge personal risks for three decades. Given a mission, Smiley was someone who would always see it through to the end.

By his own reckoning he was the only British officer ever to have commanded both Soviet and Japanese troops. As a regular soldier he took part in an Allied invasion of Iraq in World War 2 which captured the country in two weeks. Next, he fought the Vichy French in Syria. Not long after, in the North African desert, he opposed

2 Sir J.M. Barrie in 1922.

the Germans with cardboard dummy tanks. Some of his exploits seem scarcely believable today. On one occasion during the war, he spent ten days in the Iraqi desert shooting sand-grouse and drinking a stock of 1928 Heidsieck champagne he had chanced upon near Kirkuk. On another, having given a Thai gun-running boatman in his employ a Japanese sword as a prize for services rendered, the man promptly used it to decapitate a robber.

The subject of an exhaustive academic biography published in 2019, and the author of three volumes of memoirs, Smiley was nevertheless not given to introspection. Yet certain defining characteristics stand out. Modest and self-deprecating about his achievements, he knew his own worth. Whilst a serious risk-taker, invariably he calculated the odds with great care. Scrupulously fair in his treatment of all the men he led, be they irregular partisans or regular soldiers, at the same time he was a tough and sometimes ruthless fighter who condoned looting and the destruction of rebel-held villages. Hating the decline of British influence in the world, he loathed many of the policies which, in his view, dominated U.K. foreign policy after 1945 while generally leaving politics to others.

"Smiley lived for action alone and was happiest on a dangerous reconnaissance, or on those expeditions which gratified his passion for blowing things up," wrote Julian Amery, his friend and colleague in Albania, in his book *Sons of the Eagle*. Smiley echoed this rather black-and-white assessment in his book *Irregular Regular*, observing that "there was something very satisfying to me about being in contact with the enemy, whether visually or more violently." Over the years his reputation as an exceptionally brave individual has only grown as his exploits have become better known. At the time the recognition and rewards seemed meagre. Recommended for a DSO on three occasions, he was denied the award each time, on the last occasion leading Queen Elizabeth II to complain – in vain. A Croix de Guerre awarded him by the French for his undercover role in Laos was blocked by the British government on the grounds that World War 2 had already ended. Mentioned in Despatches in 1941 for actions in the Middle East, he was awarded the LVO for services to the monarch having commanded the sovereign's escort at the Coronation in 1953. More typically, for his success in commanding a brigade-size force of local and British troops and defeating a persistent rebellion in Oman, he was given a coffee pot by the niggardly Sultan.

David Smiley went to Pangbourne, like many of his contemporaries, because he had not got directly into Dartmouth and the Royal Navy from his prep school, failing the entry exam due to a badly-timed bout of chickenpox. The youngest of four children, he came from a loose-knit but relatively well-to-do family that lived across the river Thames from Pangbourne near Whitchurch. His father, who died when he was 13, knew Commander Tracy, the Captain Superintendent of the Nautical College at the time, and his uncle Commander Philip de Crespigny had begun to steer him towards the Navy. So he entered the NCP in 1930, staying for four years and doing well in sports such as fencing, fives and swimming but not standing out. A heart complaint led him to miss a term at a crucial moment and he failed the Dartmouth exam again in 1934. Instead, he decided to enter the Army and passed into RMA Sandhurst. Here, horses and point-to-point riding dominated life and he gravitated to the cavalry, joining the Royal Horse Guards (known as The Blues) in mid-1936. Something of a gilded life of ceremonial duties, polo, skiing, point-to-point riding, flying and partying ensued for the next three years. "Officers were encouraged to seek adventure on leave," he recalled matter-of-factly; three to four months' a year away from regimental duties was not unusual. Smiley took full advantage. Ice-tobogganing at St. Moritz was a favourite diversion regardless of the risks involved; in the 1950s he held the record for the most consecutive crashes (five) on the Cresta run.

When war broke out in September 1939, The Blues remained in the UK for five months before heading to the Middle East with their horses in February 1940. "I was a pretty bolshie officer at this stage, certainly enjoying my leave more than my duty," Smiley remembered. After eight months doing very little in Palestine and becoming increasingly frustrated at the lack of action, he used his connections to engineer a move to the Middle East Commandos. A 600-strong collection of misfits, the unit Smiley joined included criminals and deserters and trouble-makers other regiments wanted removed. Within a month, Smiley led the poorly-trained, unruly group on a successful night raid into Italian-held Abyssinia – his first of many excursions behind enemy lines. No medals were awarded – "Gallantry was supposed to be normal duty," he noted drily. It was in Abyssinia that he killed a man for the first time when an armed local popped up from behind a rock and he had to shoot first. As significant in the light of future events, he ordered a badly-wounded local ally to be shot to end his suffering. As he put it: "I feel I did the right thing."

Re-joining The Blues a few months on, Smiley saw action in Syria, Iran and Iraq, helping to relieve a besieged British garrison and being Mentioned in Despatches for reconnaissance work in ruins near Palmyra in Syria. Around this time, another OP, **A.R.W. Burbury (18–22)**, was serving in The Blues and wrote a letter to Pangbourne in which he described Smiley as "a gallant youth, a good officer and destined for the VC if he doesn't get killed." True to type, back in Palestine Smiley went on a "cloak-and-dagger" course designed to train behind-the-lines teams in case the Germans occupied the territory. Service with his regiment as part of the 8th Army in the Western Desert followed including a minor role in the battle of El Alamein which was cut short when The Blues were told to pull back. When it was learned that the next deployment would be garrison duty in Syria, it proved to be a decisive turning-point in Smiley's life. Aged 26, and encouraged by his lifelong comrade-in-arms, Billy McLean, he volunteered to operate behind enemy lines for MO4, the Middle East branch of the Special Operations Executive (SOE).

Smiley's destination was the isolated and mountainous Balkans backwater of Albania. The intention was to find, and link up with, any guerrilla movement that might be fighting the Italians, who had invaded the country in 1939 and, if contact was made, to train and supply the partisan fighters. Little or nothing was known by MO4 about the real political or military situation on the ground. Smiley, accompanied by McLean and two others, and suitably trained in parachute jumps, the use of explosives and captured Italian and German weapons, bridge-blowing and skills such as mine-laying, lock-picking, safe blowing and writing in secret inks, dropped into the country on his 27th birthday, April 11, 1943. Very soon he found himself in a morass of competing and fickle tribal and ideological factions, a pervasive Nazi presence after the Germans invaded the country, an incipient civil war and vague and sometimes contradictory instructions from Cairo, Bari (MO4's headquarters after the Italian surrender in September) and London.

On this first mission Smiley was to remain in Albania for seven months as one of a number of British Liaison Officers (BLOs), supported by a radio specialist, an explosives expert and an interpreter – about a month longer than was deemed sensible since the psychological strain of living rough behind enemy lines caught up with the strongest-willed in time. It was an existence full of danger, constant movement, frustrating negotiation, frequent changes of plans and objectives, and some physical hardship as food supplies dwindled in the icy winter months. Smiley, against all orders, kept a diary and took photographs wherever he went. As a rule, his "uniform" was a British battle-dress top, often crowned by a white Albanian fez., and baggy corduroy trousers that hid a variety of weaponry. Soon after his arrival meetings took place with Enver Hoxha and Mehmut Shehu, the future communist dictators of Albania. Hoxha, he found, had a bad temper and a sense of humour whereas the more dour, ruthless Shehu disliked and mistrusted the British and made no effort to conceal it. Despite training some 800 partisans in guerrilla tactics such as mine-laying and ambushes and supervising many parachute drops of much-needed machine-guns and ammunition to establish British good faith, it became apparent that the communists were reluctant to attack Italian or German military units, instead preferring to hoard their arms and ammunition for the civil war they assumed would follow any Allied victory in the war.

Before long Smiley was working mostly with the so-called Zogists – a smaller group of supporters of the exiled King Zog. No keener to fight the Italian-German invaders than the communists, and equally difficult to pin down, the Zogists at least proved to be friendlier. Within weeks a frustrated Smiley was taking matters into his own hands, launching a series of hair-raising attacks on bridges across central and southern Albania and taking part in destructive ambushes, usually with a small escort. On one occasion he found himself stranded on the wrong side of a river having blown up a wooden bridge prematurely. Swimming across the river, he was machine-gunned by German troops before, wet through, he scrambled along a goat track and trekked for two hours up a high ridge, chased all the way by the Germans. Finally throwing off his pursuers, his reward was to be met by a furious Hoxha who demanded to know why he had blown the bridge without asking his permission. Never a diplomat, Smiley's blunt reply was that he "was fighting the Germans, which was more than I had noticed his partisans doing. He (Hoxha) left me, incensed."

Exactly how many bridges Smiley destroyed or ambushes he took part in during this chaotic April-November 1943 period is hard to pin down. It must have been dozens. At one point he linked up with a third guerrilla group, the Bali Kombetar movement (republicans, but not communists, known as Ballists), to undertake an ambush on the Korca-Leshkovik road in southeast Albania, his main centre of operations on this first foray into the country. Eighteen Germans were killed, one 88mm gun and its trailer seized and three trucks destroyed with no losses to the guerrillas. Shortly after, the Ballists and communists were at each other's throats and many of the BLOs began to despair.

On another occasion, following the Italian surrender to the Allies in early September, he marched alone in British uniform up to an Italian barracks and brazenly negotiated the disarming of the soldiers there with the commanding officer. Ordered to evacuate for a break in November, he and Billy McLean slogged for days to the Adriatic coast through enemy-held territory, passed hundreds of Italian soldiers dying of starvation and saw scores of villages burned by the rampaging Germans. Near to the town of Ducati, he and McLean commandeered a damaged, sinking dinghy and paddled it to the open sea where they were collected by a waiting Royal Navy motor torpedo boat. On leave for a month in Cairo – "my happiest time of the war" – Smiley was awarded an immediate Military Cross.

Returning to London (and rather typically staying in the Ritz hotel), Smiley's immediate future in early 1944 was unclear. During his leave, in his words, "disaster intervened." The entire headquarters staff of the SOE mission in Albania was betrayed to the Germans. In severe winter conditions most of its members were killed or captured or scattered. McLean was ordered back as senior BLO, together with Smiley, with a personal brief from the Foreign Secretary, Anthony Eden, to go to the north of the country to encourage local leaders there to fight the Germans. Disillusion with the partisans was widespread on the Allied side by this stage and civil war between the various factions had begun in the south of the country. Making matters worse, in SOE HQ in Bari there were ideological divisions with several officers avowed communists and antagonistic to further support for the Zogists. Nevertheless, it was felt in London that another effort involving Allied arms drops was required to stir up local opposition to the Germans. "Keep the pot boiling" said Eden. It was, essentially, a political mission.

Parachuting into Albania near Bixha, east of the capital Tirana, in April 1944 Smiley, McLean and Julian Amery again linked up with the Zogist leader Abas Kupi. No arms would be given, Kupi was informed, until he began fighting. A compromise was reached and Smiley, who was itching for action, was allocated a 12-strong Zogist team to help him blow up a key bridge at Gjoles. This was no ordinary bridge but the third largest in Albania. Made of reinforced concrete, it carried the main Tirana-Durazzo road to the coast. Nerves of steel and considerable skill with explosives were required and Smiley now displayed both. On reaching the bridge, he reconnoitred it in civilian clothes and found that he had insufficient explosives. A 48-hours delay ensued, which he used to conduct a survey of German transport moving along the Tirana-Scutari road. Once sufficient gelignite arrived, he and a colleague crept under the bridge to fix the charges, only to be disturbed by a German truck that stopped above them. A soldier got out of the vehicle to urinate over the side of the bridge, unaware of the two Britons crouching under him. "We were in very different ways relieved when he got back on board and the lorry drove off," recalled Smiley. Setting the charges took two long hours. Having withdrawn to a safe distance, the explosions went off late. But in the end a "tremendous blast" rocked the area. When the smoke cleared, an entire span of the bridge lay in the river. The party returned happily to base. "Sat up late drinking cherry brandy," Smiley wrote in his diary. "Do not feel very tired in spite of an 18-hour march, no sleep for 36 hours and much mental and physical strain." McLean recommended Smiley for an immediate DSO. Instead, months after, he received a Bar to his MC.

The Gjoles attack had little impact on swaying SOE opinion in favour of the Zogists. Shortly after, communist and Zogist fighting broke out in the central area of the country and Smiley's base was overrun by the communist partisans and its supplies captured. He escaped, but by July he was sure the mission was over. Wearing a captured Albanian gendarme uniform, he moved to the coastal area and began searching for suitable pick-up points, walking along main roads and even hitching a lift in a German truck (in which he was attacked by RAF aircraft and ended up in a ditch alongside a fist-waving German soldier). At this point the Zogists changed tack and decided to assault the port of Durazzo; Smiley was sent to the town to carry out a reconnaissance mission clothed in "a shabby civilian suit with my white Gheg fez." Following several nerve-shredding encounters, including passing through four road blocks undetected in a German truck, he concluded that Durazzo was far too heavily defended by the Germans to be captured by the rag-tag Zogist guerrillas.

Not long after, in another surprise turn of events, he supervised the surrender of more than 70 "German" soldiers. In fact, they were tough Tajiks, Uzbeks and Kazakhs who had murdered their Russian officers early in the war, deserted to the German side and been sent to the Balkans as garrison troops. Starved of money and food, they had murdered their sergeant major. McLean and Smiley decided to use some of them to attack a German artillery camp. Smiley provided covering machine-gun fire as the base was assaulted and destroyed – the first of a number of successful actions by the Zogists and the so-called "Turkestanis" in the next weeks. "I had my first action in command of the Turkestanis when we went down to the main road, blew a bridge and shot up a German convoy," he remembered in *Albanian Assignment*.

During another such attack, the unit found itself assaulted from the rear by Hoxha's partisans. The communists, it transpired, had orders to kill McLean and Smiley on sight. At the same time the Germans began to pull back. It was time to leave Albania to its fate. After more than a month on the move, trying to dodge both the Germans and the partisans, blowing up more bridges, providing target co-ordinates to raiding RAF bombers and venturing as far north as the border with Montenegro (where he crossed the river Drin in a hollowed-out tree-trunk), Smiley, together with McLean, Amery and most of the remaining BLOs in northern Albania, left for Italy at the end of October in an RN motor launch from an isolated beach north of Cape Rodonet. Within a month, Enver Hoxha entered Tirana – the start of a 50-year paranoid communist nightmare that isolated Albania from the world.

Throughout this seven-month period in 1944, betrayal had been Smiley's constant close companion. He spoke little Albanian and had to rely on translators. He had no transport except for a faithful mule. The Bari headquarters of SOE Balkans was riven with ideological divisions; on his return he was astounded to learn that his mission was seen as "fascist" by some in the left-leaning Albanian section, because of its ties to the Zogists. Always, he knew that his British Army uniform was no protection if he was caught by the Germans who long before had decreed that Allied commandos were saboteurs and not covered by the Geneva Convention. Somewhat disillusioned – "I have completely wasted four months... life for me is bloody. Nobody here talks of fighting the Hun" he claimed in his diary one day – he returned to Cairo for leave in December thinking that he might re-join The Blues as his regiment advanced through Belgium and Holland in Montgomery's 21st Army Group. A chance meeting changed all that.

Before the war Smiley had lived for a time in Virginia Water in Surrey and got to know the abdicated Siamese (Thai) monarch and his family who were housed nearby. In Cairo he happened to meet one of them – Chin Savasti, a brother-in-law of the abdicated king. A regent in charge in Bangkok had declared war on Britain in 1942 under pressure from the Japanese who dominated the country. Chin had been recruited by SOE to organise a Free Thai resistance movement and was on the lookout for helpers. Would Smiley, Chin asked, drop into Thailand to work with Force 136, as the SOE Far Eastern section was known? He needed no second offer and accepted at once. Carrying only an American .30 carbine and a Colt .45 automatic pistol, he parachuted into Thailand at the end of May 1945, returning to London in January 1946.

Over the following seven months, even by his standards, Smiley experienced the full gamut of incidents that any behind-the-lines operative must expect in wartime. Unlike Albania, he had a brief of specific tasks. These included organising and training guerrilla groups, receiving arms, sending intelligence reports on Japanese troop dispositions and locating Allied prisoner-of-war camps. Most importantly, with the Allies planning an all-Asia drive against Japanese forces, he was ordered: "At all times remain clandestine and on no account take any action against the Japanese." As a result, he never fired a shot in anger in Thailand before two atomic bombs were dropped on the Japanese mainland by the US in August. "When the war ended," he recalled in 1994, "quite a different situation existed and I saw my first action."

In the steamy jungles of northern Thailand where he landed, the Free Thai movement was numerous and ubiquitous but always under Japanese pressure.

Cheerfulness was a critical requirement as well as resolution since relentless monsoon rains poured down for months on end. Constantly on the move around his large area (one-third of Thailand, known by SOE as Candle), and often hunted by Japanese patrols, he liaised with 12 Free Thai camps and the 1,000 or so guerrillas in each of them. Everywhere, arms were in short supply. At the end of June his first foray into Thailand was cut short. Hurriedly evacuating his base camp one day as Japanese soldiers closed in, an armed briefcase carrying confidential documents blew up, badly wounding Smiley's face, arms, knees and hands. He got away, but in great pain had to be flown out to India, not returning to Thailand for six weeks.

While recovering in Calcutta, the A-bombs were dropped on Hiroshima and Nagasaki. No one knew if the Japanese in Thailand would fight on. Since he was able to pinpoint Japanese garrisons in Candle, Smiley – still not properly recovered from his first-degree burns – persuaded Force 136 to send him back to Thailand. An exceptional period followed during which, wearing a British Army uniform but lightly armed, he personally liberated a large PoW camp at Ubon holding more than 3,000 British, Dutch, Australian and American prisoners (immortalised in the 1957 film *The Bridge Over the River Kwai*). Smiley took an emotional parade at the camp during which the Japanese garrison surrendered formally. For the next month he ran the camp with the help of its ex-prisoners, negotiated the concentration and disarming of 9,200 regular Japanese troops in the Candle area, identified war criminals and even oversaw brothels outside the Ubon camp. To supervise all this, he equipped himself and his staff with looted Japanese goods, including, much to his delight, a huge Straight Eight Cadillac and a Chevrolet drophead coupé, and dealt with a string of potentially combustible incidents on a daily basis. These included truculent and suicidal Japanese officers, drunken Japanese soldiers, PoW violence towards the former guards, a lack of condoms for the PoWs, and prostitutes claiming they had not been paid in sufficient parachute silk (prized on the black market) for their services. None of this fazed Smiley who soon had Japanese officers re-imposing discipline on their troops and reporting daily to his house.

The Candle region was bordered on the east by the river Mekong. In Thakhek on the other side, three-quarters of a mile away, lay French Indo-China (today Laos). Here Vietnamese Annamite rebels were trying to drive out returning French colonialists and had seized a number of civilian hostages including women and children. Ostensibly, the Japanese remained in control but were not respecting the armistice. Disregarding all orders, Smiley decided to mount a rescue mission with two colleagues. After some spine-tingling moments, including being marched "ignominiously" down several streets by the Japanese to the house where the hostages were being held by the Annamites, a release was agreed. It took place the next day.

Hearing of more French civilians held in Boneng to the north of Thakhek, he drove there. Threatened all the way by the hostile Annamites, he succeeded in releasing the hostages, including a French army officer, taking seven civilians and two wounded Lao soldiers back to Thailand with him. Not long after, Smiley's tour in Thailand came to an end – but only after a macabre incident in November when he was living in Nong Khai, across the Mekong from Vientiane (future capital of Laos). One day he presented a Japanese sword to a boatman who had done a good job gun-running for Force 136. As dinner was finishing that evening, the man rushed into the room with blood dripping from the sword. Excitedly, he announced that he had caught a robber in the storehouse and had cut off his head. "We went to look. He had."

Once again Smiley was denied the recognition that was his due. Force 136 did not exist officially, so Whitehall red tape ensured that no decorations were given. "We thought this a bit mean" observed Smiley mildly in his diary. Only 29, he had now been recommended for a DSO twice, latterly for "activities in Thailand and Indo-China." Instead, he was given a military OBE, normally reserved for desk officers at staff headquarters. General Philippe Leclerc, the French commander in the Far East, wanted to award him a Croix de Guerre; the Foreign Office intervened to say that the war had ended and Smiley did not qualify. His biographer, Clive Jones, subsequently wrote: "The OBE gave no formal acknowledgement to the risks he (Smiley) had taken, the lives he had saved or the near-fatal injuries he had suffered during his service in Thailand."

For the next dozen years Smiley tried to adapt to the post-war world, passing the Staff College exams in 1946 that all regular Army officers had to if they wished to command their regiment, and marrying Moyra, an independent-minded war widow with two young children, in 1947. Twice he took on military attaché roles, first in communist Poland (where he was expelled), next in neutral Sweden. He was dragged, too, into two hush-hush SOE-type operations sponsored from London – *Embarrass* in the Mediterranean, where he was part of a four-man team that was assigned by the Attlee government in 1947 to thwart illegal Jewish emigration by sea to Palestine (see Chapter 13); and *Valuable* in 1949 in Malta, where he trained Albanian exiles in the use of explosives and Moy worked as his cipher clerk. He led his regiment, the Royal Horse Guards, riding escort at the funeral of King George VI in 1952 and Sovereign's Escort by the back-right wheel of Queen Elizabeth II's gold state coach at her Coronation procession the following year. In late 1954 he stepped down after three years as commanding officer of The Blues. With Moy, he decided to change direction and farm in Kenya after first completing a three-year attaché posting in Sweden.

Out of the blue, early in 1958 he received a call from his friend Julian Amery, Undersecretary of State for War in the Conservative administration led by Harold Macmillan. Would he consider a final job for the government – a three-year tour as commanding officer of the Muscat and Oman Field Force, at the time in desperate need of leadership, reorganisation and training as a Saudi-backed rebellion gained traction? He knew nothing about isolated, backward Oman – a friend and strategic partner of Britain since the days of the East India Company – or its cranky, autocratic ruler. Yet Moy was keen, the terms seemed attractive and, at the age of 42, David Smiley was ready to apply all he had learned about subversive warfare to counter an uprising. The poacher had turned gamekeeper.

Oman proved to be the pinnacle of Smiley's military and post-war career. "I found myself faced with a difficult war," he wrote disarmingly. Rebels, based in the inaccessible Jebel Akhdar range, up to 10,000 feet high with a base of over 800 miles, were running rampant in the largely undeveloped country, mining roads, attacking oil company vehicles and terrorising villagers in remote areas. Discontent and poverty were widespread. The Sultan, on the throne since 1932, refused to spend money or to build a locally-recruited Omani army or air force for fear of a coup. Smiley took over a demoralised force of 848 men and 23 contract (mercenary) officers, split in two regiments, with almost no modern weaponry. He spoke only bare bones Arabic and had never led Arab troops. Soon he was at odds with his nominal British superiors in Muscat and Bahrain, who favoured a do-nothing approach and, while personally sustaining cordial relations with the Sultan, he was never able to persuade the eccentric potentate to act decisively. Totally undeterred, he ploughed ahead, commanding decisively from the front.

Much more aggressive training and patrolling was introduced and he led patrols himself around the Jebel Akhdar rebel stronghold. An SAS squadron from Britain was recruited with Amery's help, and a unit of Life Guards with Ferret armoured cars brought in to boost mobility. Aerial bombing of the mountain hideouts by the RAF Special Duties Squadron began.

Astute and sensitive leadership by Smiley also encouraged some defections from the rebel ranks.

David Smiley.

At the end of January 1959, after a copybook deception manoeuvre (part-planned by Smiley), a decisive assault was launched by the Sultan's revitalised forces that rooted the rebels out of Jebel Akhdar and ended the rebellion there with minimal loss of life. In October 1960 he wrote to his old school: "The job here has been very interesting, especially the first year when there was quite a lot of violent activity. But now, except for an occasional mine or bomb going off, the main role of the forces is to combat the gun-running and the hit-and-run tactics of the locals who do not like my master (the Sultan). They receive a lot of help from outside – mainly Saudi Arabia and Egypt, and, more recently, Iraq. Several OPs have come my way. The Adjutant of the Muscat Regiment is **Neil McNeil (40–44)** of the S.A.S., and a Royal Marine, **Jeremy Coulter (48–53)**, were here in 1958 – he won a well-earned Mention in Dispatches."

Yet again, however, at what was "in many ways the apogee of Smiley's military career," in the words of his biographer, Smiley was let down in London. A recommendation (his third) for a DSO was never made by his unsympathetic superior in Bahrain and in any case would have been blocked by the Foreign Office which claimed he had been working for the Sultan, not the UK, whereas others involved including his deputy were awarded the medal. All publicity about the success – a rare one in the Middle East for Britain in the post-Suez era – was discouraged. For his part, the miserly Sultan gave Smiley his coffee pot and no more; a decade on, he was overthrown by his son in a coup master-minded by British Army officers as the Dhofar rebellion flared (see Chapter 13). Smiley remained bitter about his lack of recognition for the rest of his life. He left Oman in 1961 "utterly cheesed off." Offered the command of Britain's three SAS regiments in April, instead he resigned his commission when the War Office refused to promote him to brigadier. In Oman, as a full colonel, he had been commanding a force bigger than a brigade. It seemed to be, and was, the sad end of a highly unorthodox military career.

Like a cat with nine lives, Smiley bounced back within two years. His oldest friend, Billy McLean, an MP since 1954, was now advising the UK government about events in the Arabian Peninsula. Here Yemen was in the middle of a civil war. Egypt and its nationalist and anti-British president, Gamal Abdel Nasser, backed the rebels and had deployed 60,000 troops in the country. Neighbouring Saudi Arabia supported the incumbent, feudal Imamate and his loyal mountain tribes. In Britain a pessimistic view prevailed about the Imamate's prospects, offset by a desire in some quarters to blunt Egyptian ambitions in the peninsula and avenge the Suez humiliation. Julian Amery, now Minister of Aviation, led those in power in London urging support both for the Imamate and the Saudis. In October 1962 Amery despatched McLean to Yemen to assess the Imam's political strength. Seven months later, sent back to prepare a military assessment, McLean asked Smiley – at that point working part-time in England as an inspector for a food guide – to accompany him. Aged 47 and stuck in a rut, he needed no second invitation.

David Smiley in Yemen, 1963.
(Smiley family collection)

Over the next four years Smiley made 13 trips to Arabia, each lasting two to six months. Initially, his official cover, arranged by Amery, was that of a special correspondent for *The Daily Telegraph* among other media outlets. Articles appeared under his name from time to time, although he was never paid by the newspaper. Often disguised as a local, he travelled for weeks on a donkey through rough, hazardous territory, sometimes trekking for miles along narrow mountain passes, surviving as best he could without proper hygiene or decent food and always accompanied by fleas and diarrhoea. On two occasions he supervised covert arms supply drops to the Imam's troops by Israeli military aircraft, and several times witnessed at close range haphazard and inconclusive actions by the royalist forces. Then, with the blessing of the Saudis, he was given command of a small British mission inside Yemen – a lucrative contract that allowed him four months leave a year. A stream of candid reports flowed back to the Imam and the Saudi defence minister as well as to several parts of the UK government including MI6, Britain's Secret Intelligence Service. "He won the admiration of his colleagues, both Arab and British, for his toughness, bluntness and shrewdness as an adviser," noted Smiley's obituary in the *Telegraph*. "King Faisal, whom Smiley greatly admired, personally expressed his appreciation."

As in Albania, Thailand and Oman, Smiley's lasting impact in Yemen were undermined by factors beyond his control. In London, the new Labour government from 1964, and especially the Foreign Office, was openly hostile, favouring a hands-off approach to the Yemen civil war and to British withdrawal from Aden. In Saudi Arabia, many of the King's close advisers became wary of too deep involvement in a conflict the kingdom could never win on its own as Soviet influence in Yemen grew. In the end it was the outbreak of the Six Day War between Israel and Egypt in 1967 which resolved matters in Yemen when Nasser withdrew his forces and the Imam survived -- though not for long. Subsequently the Yemen conflict ended – at least for a while – in what Smiley called "a draw." To that extent, his efforts bore fruit. Long before that point, Smiley admitted in letters that he was "increasingly disillusioned...by this whole job out here." Reaching 50 in April 1966, his health was suffering from his lifestyle and he had begun to pine for a more settled existence. Needing the money, he remained on the Saudi payroll until 1969 making six trips to Yemen 1966–68. It was to be his swansong experience of a 'hot war.'

Never a man to do things by halves, Smiley used the money he earned from the Saudis to leave England with Moy and buy land to grow almonds, olives and avocados near the east coast of Spain. It was to be his base for the next two decades before old age caught up and drew him back to Somerset and, latterly, London. Three volumes of memoirs appeared and in 1991, together with Amery and Alan Hare (another SOE WW2 colleague; Billy McLean had died in 1986) he made a nostalgic visit to Albania at the invitation of the leader of the Democratic Party, Sali Berisha, who was governing in an uneasy coalition with the former communist rulers. Frequent holidays in Oman for winter sun were another trip down memory lane, as was a 2002 visit to Sana'a, the capital of Yemen, at the age of 86, to help with the compilation of an official history of the country. Meantime, his health slowly deteriorated. He died of pneumonia in London in 2009 aged 92. As Moy put it: "He was greatly irked by the infirmities of old age...and was really ready to go."

Exactly what motivated David Smiley throughout his remarkable life has long been a topic of discussion. Moy used to tell told her son Xan, half in jest, that "David had no imagination and that's why he was so brave." But this seems to be only part of the explanation. His friend Julian Amery reckoned that he was "more interested in things than in men" while Alan Hare described him as "not very reflective." He certainly held his feelings in check from a young age. The only time in the entire Second World War when he was reduced to tears, he once confided, was when he had to have his dog put down in England before he left with his regiment for Palestine. He was never reckless, much more a calculated risk-taker. Often, for him, the end justified the means, not least because he so often found himself alone in no-win situations burdened by vague orders. Others have tended to dismiss his evident virtues – integrity, honesty, modesty, patriotism, loyalty – as both anachronistic in the modern world yet commonplace in his era. In practice, living so much of his life on the edge meant that such values always served David Smiley well and gave him the motivation and bravery to persist long after others would have given up. His was a very particular form of courage and bravery sustained over many decades – one that armchair, revisionist critics may find easy to mock today, but real enough for all that.

9

THE FLYERS:
OVER LAND AND SEA

— ⊙ —

Flying, whether in the RAF, the Fleet Air Arm (FAA) or at private flying clubs, was one of the growth areas of British life in the 1930s – and a large number of Old Pangbournians flocked to take advantage. Many came ashore to do so, having first served in the Merchant Navy for a few years. Others moved across to the FAA from the main branches of the Royal Navy. Some joined the RAF straight from the Nautical College. And many took up flying as a weekend hobby as small aircraft became available to hire or buy through private clubs. "Flying was great fun. In a biplane you could look over the side and wave," recalled one who joined the RAF Volunteer Reserves in the 1930s. What attracted them all, as the technology improved, was the newness and exhilaration and adventure of soaring up in the clouds, free and alone, unrestricted by class or hierarchy or irritating rules. Risk was coupled with reward. It proved to be a heady mixture. When war broke out many of these weekend-flyers rushed to join the RAF, perceived to be an organisation truly based on ability and merit. "There never has been, I suppose, in all the world, in all the history of war, such an opportunity for youth," mused Winston Churchill early on during the Second World War. By 1939, scores of young OPs had seized this opportunity and were aloft in one or other branches of the flying Services.

The first OP to join the Royal Air Force and go to RAF Cranwell for officer training actually had done so sixteen years earlier. He was **Vickers Eyre (20–23)**. In an article for *The Log* Spring 1925 he wrote that life at Cranwell "consists of three main items – flying, play and work – and this is the order in which we would have them." He continued: "Cranwell offers a career in what, although it is termed

Vickers Eyre, killed in an air accident in 1929.

the junior service, is now generally considered the future first line of defence of the Empire." In 1928 he made the national press when, trying to pick up his map from the floor of his aircraft, he tipped the machine over and fell out at 2,000 feet, parachuting to the ground. "His face was covered in mud but he was very cool," a farmer who found him informed *The Morning Post*. "He lit a cigarette and said 'I wonder where my kite has gone?' We saw the aeroplane some distance away." Eyre, a Chief Cadet Captain who was remembered at the College for his "sound character and cheerful disposition (and) above average ability," never had the chance to test his views in action. Practising a manoeuvre for the RAF Pageant in 1929, he put his single-seater fighter into a deliberate nose dive, the plane got into a spin, appeared to recover but went into a second spin and crashed. This time he did not survive. The sadness of his death cast a gloom over Founders' Day at the College that year.

Over the next decade at least a hundred OPs followed Eyre into the RAF and more joined once war was declared. What attracted them, wrote an OP cross-over from the RN FAA, the redoubtable **Colin Hodgkinson (33–37)**, was the sense of excitement. "Life in the Navy had been very English, and by comparison very tame, more gentlemanly, less vital. (In the RAF) there was more cut and thrust, a cosmopolitan bustle. Here I would have to fend for myself; no one was going to wait on me in the RAF." By the end of the war, OPs in the RAF had been awarded two DSOs, 23 DFCs, nine AFCs, one DFM and one Croix du Guerre for a variety of actions in Europe and the Mideast that collectively can be described as either "conspicuous bravery" or "gallantry in the air." About 30 OPs received these awards, several more than one. Casualties, at 44, were second only to lives lost by OPs in the Royal Navy. The majority served in Bomber Command in which the average number of operations before being killed was fourteen, four in ten died, and the survival rate was less than in the trenches in the First World War. Yet a youthful sense of indestructability seemed to prevail.

Four OPs in the RAF who were all awarded the DFC became prisoners-of-war – **Anthony Dickinson (35–38)**, **William Grime (38–40)**, **Robert McGregor (31–33)** and **David Marwood-Elton (25–28)** – having survived after their aircraft were shot down. For some of the time in Stalag Luft 3, sited in a pine forest 100 miles southeast of Berlin, Dickinson was accompanied by McGregor – who had been awarded his DFC in 1942 for taking on four Me 109s near Bir Hacheim, North

Africa and downing one before crashing in flames. "Uninjured, he immediately proceeded to send in his report from the nearest telephone." With Dickinson and McGregor in Stalag Luft 3 was the unfortunate **John Iliffe (26–29)**. Iliffe was a Lt RNR and Flight Observer in the FAA who had been shot down over Norway on his second-ever sortie in early 1940 and spent the rest of the war in captivity. Another OP RAF officer who became a PoW was **D.M. Barrett (28–32)**.

Group Captain Marwood-Elton had the dubious distinction of becoming the most senior RAF officer taken prisoner by the Germans. A Halifax of 578 Squadron in which he was flying, despite a general order to senior officers not to take to the air, was shot down early in 1944. Despatched to Stalag Luft 1 camp in northern Germany on the Baltic coast at the end of March, he became the senior officer. A history of 578 Squadron takes up the story: "He remained a thorn in the Germans' side for the rest of the war. Arrested by his captors on August 17 1944 after issuing an order that PoWs should not acknowledge the Nazi salute but only proper military salutes. Considered an act of mutiny by the Nazis. Marwood-Elton was sent to a naval detention barracks to await trial and was tried on November 15 1944. Found guilty after a farcical trial, he was taken to a prison in Stettin (but) eventually sent back to Barthe (Stalag Luft 1) before being freed by the advancing Russians." His exploits are recorded in a book about the RAF, *Footprints on the Sands of Time.* Among other disruptive efforts, he had tried to cut himself out of the camp in May 1944 using wire-cutters fashioned from ice-skates only to be interrupted by an Allied bombing raid and having to give himself up. Earlier, in one of the 22 different Wellington bombers he flew during the war, Marwood-Elton crash-landed in Loch Ness in a snowstorm on New Year's Eve 1940, paddling ashore in a dinghy. The main section of 'R for Robert' weighing 74 tons was raised 230 feet from the bed of the loch for a television programme in 1985.

The official awards system during times of conflict has always been hit-and-miss, and in the RAF in the Second World War this proved to be the case more than ever. Some RAF officers, such as the gallant war photographer **Ian Matheson (30–34)** or **Patrick Lowe-Holmes (19–21)** or **Denis Wood (34–35)**, served in important roles throughout the fighting without any recognition, despite being involved in many dangerous missions. Yet one individual who was recognised repeatedly was Group Captain **Mike Foster-Pedley (29–33)** DSO, DFC, AFC. Known as "Pepperbox Pedley,"

Mike Foster-Pedley, IWM.

he saw action over the Channel, in France, in the Western Desert in North Africa, in Italy and in Greece and lived to tell the tale. Once, he was the proud recipient of a double-edged compliment from a superior: "Pedley, I don't think you're the cleverest man I have ever met, but I believe you are the best officer."

The Citations for Foster-Pedley's DFC in 1942 and his DSO in 1945 hint at his courage. In September 1942 he was a Wing Commander in 131 Squadron flying the Spitfire Vc. "Within the past three months, this officer has participated in 38 operational missions including shipping reconnaissance. During the combined operations (raid) at Dieppe on 19th August, 1942, he displayed great keenness and a fine fighting spirit. In the evening, when the enemy attempted an air attack in the vicinity of one of our aerodromes, they were intercepted by the squadron led by Wing Commander Pedley. At least two enemy bombers were destroyed. This officer is a squadron commander of outstanding ability." In March, 1945 his DSO Citation stated: "This officer has completed much operational flying. During the fighting in Tunisia, he participated in very many sorties and shot down two enemy aircraft. Throughout these operations he displayed the highest qualities of determination and devotion to duty. In later operations he has commanded larger formations of aircraft with conspicuous success. His leadership has been of a high order."

Foster-Pedley, though, was more than the sum of his citations. When war broke out, he was a senior flying instructor in the RAF and did not take part in the Battle of Britain. A year on, he received command of a Spitfire squadron based at Tangmere, and immediately led from the front, quickly gaining a reputation as an extremely aggressive pilot. His sobriquet followed a successful lunchtime "peppering" of the gasworks at Le Treport in Normandy. In the Dieppe action he made five sorties in seven hours of combat and notched up at least three of his eight wartime "kills." Aged 28, he was given command of 337 Wing in 1944 and assisted in the capture of Athens airport and the British reoccupation of Greece. After that, he flew in operations against communist fighters in Greece and, following the war, had a similar role in Malaya before retiring from the RAF in 1957. At the age of 70 he took up parachuting. Aged 80, he made his last flight in a hot air balloon in New Zealand. Desk jobs were not his style. He lived for the challenge and the risk.

David Yorke (27–30) was cut from a similar mould. After the war he became a Group Captain in the RAF by 1950, before spending 25 years involved in grand prix and sports car racing. At one time he worked closely with Stirling Moss and the Vanwall team. Before the war, he had joined the RAF in 1934 and by 1939 was a Flight Lieutenant and member of 16 Squadron. Flying a Lysander, he was deployed to France in April 1940 and won a DSO within weeks.

Initially, Yorke was recommended for a DFC by his commanding officer, followed by a bar to the DFC after a second mission. An intervention by Air Vice-Marshal Blount, the office commanding all RAF units in France, changed the recommendation to a DSO. The original commendation ran: "On 17th May 1940, this officer was detailed to ascertain troop dispositions on the Cambrai-Le Cateau road, which had been ordered to be bombed. He ascertained the positions of the French motor transport on the road, and proceeded to locate the enemy tank concentration, despite very heavy anti-aircraft fire, and descended to a very low altitude in order that the numbers might be accurately discovered. The information obtained very materially helped in the ensuing operations. Within a few days he again successfully carried out a supply dropping sortie to Calais in spite of encountering very heavy anti-aircraft fire. I cannot too strongly recommend this officer for the Distinguished Flying Cross."

Two weeks after, Yorke's commanding officer added: "On 1st June this officer was ordered to undertake an artillery reconnaissance sortie with the object of bringing to bear the artillery of the retiring British Expeditionary Force on the enemy batteries shelling the troops embarking from the beaches to the east of Dunkirk. This officer succeeded in locating two enemy batteries and, in spite of a continuous and accurate stream of anti-aircraft fire, calmly went through the necessary procedure for carrying out an air shoot as far as the second call for fire in each case. This officer was not perturbed when, in the middle of the shoots, a formation of nine Junkers arrived on the scene to carry out a bombing raid on the troops. His aircraft was narrowly missed by a salvo of bombs jettisoned by the enemy aircraft when attacked by our own fighters." The same day (June 3) Blount minuted this recommendation: "This officer has proved himself to be a commander and organizer of exceptional merit. Having regard to my previous recommendation that he be awarded the DFC, and (after) this additional recommendation that he be awarded a Bar to his DFC, I recommend that he be awarded the DSO in place of a Bar to his DFC."

Pigeon-holing all RAF pilots as dare-devil risk-takers is, nevertheless, a mistake. Many were cool, calculating, analytical and cautious, and the characteristic RAF bonhomie on the ground was often a "carapace over sorrow" as losses of youthful colleagues and friends mounted. Some asserted after the war that they did not have long enough working with other pilots to make real friends, and few seem to have kept personal records or forged lifelong relationships with other pilots. Even fewer thrived on administration. Yet one who did, participated bravely in a dozen bombing operations, and emerged unscathed was **Royd Fenwick-Wilson (28–32)** who ended the war as a Wing Commander with a DFC and AFC.

Royd Fenwick-Wilson.

Perhaps Fenwick-Wilson's background – he came from a family of poor homesteaders grinding out a living in an isolated hamlet called Rock Creek in British Columbia on the southern Canadian boundary with the United States – had something to do with it. Aged about ten, his mother deposited him with relatives in the UK. In 1928 he was enrolled at the NCP. By 1934 he had joined the RAF and was training in a bomber squadron. When war broke out in 1939, he was an RAF flying instructor. Within a year he had been promoted to command 12 Flying Training School outside Grantham. Here his "personality and splendid qualities of leadership" inspired others and led to the award of an AFC. In August 1941 he was given command of 405 RCAF Squadron, the first Canadian squadron to form in Bomber Command, flying Vickers Wellington Mk.IIs. Over the next five months he made half a dozen bombing raids over northern Germany and appeared on the front page of Canada's leading newspaper. A liaison spell in the USA followed before he returned to England and took command of 218 (Gold Coast) Squadron in February 1944 – a front-line "heavy" bomber unit that flew the powerful Short Stirling aircraft.

More hazardous operations followed and among them was Operation Glimmer, an important diversionary action before D-Day. This spoof mission was intended to convince the Germans that a large invasion convoy was heading to the French port of Boulogne, well away from the Normandy beaches. It involved hours of dangerous precision navigational flying by 218 Squadron in long circles above strong German fortifications. Fenwick-Wilson took personal charge. There were no casualties and the deception reinforced the Nazis' belief that the Allies would invade near Calais. After D-Day, the squadron mined the sea off Le Havre and attacked railway yards in northern France. Having switched to Lancaster aircraft, Fenwick-Wilson ended his war bombing German targets as far east as Stuttgart. Retiring from the RAF in 1946, he moved back to British Columbia and became an immigration officer before transitioning into a visa officer in the Canadian foreign service and working in Italy, Yugoslavia and Germany. In retirement, like so many of his peers, he rarely mentioned the war. When, unexpectedly, he died of a heart problem in 1982 he was hailed by the Mayor of Osoyoos, his home town, as a very fine example of the "greatest generation."

Somewhere between Foster-Pedley and Fenwick-Wilson, in attitude at least, was **Dennis Mitchell** (33–36) who ended his career with a knighthood as a much-decorated Air Commodore, Captain of the Queen's Flight, ADC to The Queen and managing director of two Belgian aviation companies. Mitchell had gone straight into the RAF via Cranwell from the NCP and honed his flying skills over the treacherous North West Frontier in the late-1930s. Once, providing cover for British trucks supplying forts guarding the Khyber Pass, he was brought down by a tribesman's chance shot which hit the radiator of

Dennis Mitchell.

his Hawker Audax aircraft. Luckily, he was soon rescued by an armoured car. This prevented the rebels presenting the infamous "goolie chit" which was carried by RAF pilots and offered the bearer a handsome reward in gold if they returned any pilots they caught with their manhood intact.

Mitchell's operational war began at the end of 1941. Posted to a fighting squadron on the Indian sub-continent, he was awarded an AFC in 1943 for the crucial part he played in testing new Curtiss Mohawk American-made medium-range bombers. Never seen before by Mitchell's squadron, these aircraft had been sent to India to bolster the unit. Returning to England at the end of that year, he was put in command of 226 Squadron which flew US-made Douglas Mitchell aircraft. The following year, he took part in dozens of perilous cross-Channel daylight attacks and bombing raids far into the German heartland.

In July 1944, with a Navigator, he was awarded the first of his DFCs for his role in covering the D-Day landings. The Citation for the pair stated: "These officers, the pilot and navigator respectively, of an aircraft (were) detailed to attack a target in Normandy recently. When approaching the target, their aircraft was heavily attacked by anti-aircraft fire but despite this a successful attack was made. The excellent results achieved were due mainly to the fine leadership of Wing Commander Mitchell and the navigational skills of Flying Officer Farquhar. Their courage and determination in the face of heavy enemy opposition was most praiseworthy." His second DFC Citation came in 1945 for "intensive bombing operations prior to the final offensive on the German army." This citation paid tribute to Mitchell's "inspiring leadership, untiring efforts, courage and (the) high standards of operational efficiency in squadrons under his command." It was reflected in a Croix du Guerre awarded by the French for his part in the liberation of France.

The war ended, and Mitchell began to ascend the RAF promotion ladder including a spell in Brussels advising on the needs of the future Belgian Air Force. Here he met his wife, a Belgian Comtesse, before being posted unaccompanied to the U.S. Tactical Air Command Headquarters in the United States. Unbeknown to his new wife, while there he volunteered to fly with the USAF in the Korean War and took part in four operational missions. Ever the efficient, loyal, understated officer who could get things done, in later life he managed to modernise The Queen's Flight without controversy – a considerable feat of diplomacy – during a seven-year involvement.

The roll-call of other courageous OP flyers is long, but the detail is often sparse. **George Bliss (24–27)**, to give one example, was awarded a DFC & Bar flying with 21 Squadron in Blenheim aircraft for Bomber Command. The Citation for his first DFC in 1944 simply states: "This officer has completed a very large number of sorties as air gunner and, more recently, as navigator. He has destroyed one enemy aircraft and has shared, with his pilot, in the destruction of a third aircraft. He has displayed great skill and tireless enthusiasm for operations." **Geoffrey Millington (27–32)** had originally joined the Army but ended up flying tactical reconnaissance missions as commander of 225 Squadron in North Africa, winning a DFC in 1943 having "displayed courage, keenness and devotion to duty worthy of high praise." In the Italian campaign, his 285 Wing and its five squadrons of mixed aircraft provided gruelling tactical support as Allied armies edged north. After the war Millington, too, rose to the rank of Air Commodore before retiring from the RAF and beginning a second career advising newly-independent governments in Zambia and Singapore about their air force requirements.

One OP in the RAF was involved in an improbable coincidence. **Richard Gates (29–31)**, a Wing Commander, was awarded a DFC in 1944 for sinking a U-boat (*U-608*) in the Bay of Biscay. "The vessel was submerged but could clearly be seen from a certain angle," stated his citation. "Wing Commander Gates promptly delivered a well-conceived attack, straddling the submarine with a number of depth charges. Afterwards, the surface of the water became covered with a large patch of oil." The full story did not emerge until *The Log* of Michaelmas term 1946. Two issues before, **A.D. Hunt (35–37)**, a Lt. RN who was to become Cunard's Marine Superintendent, wrote about his 18 months as Navigator in the sloop *HMS Wren* during which "we were in at the death of 22 U-boats." This prompted a letter from Gates. "I think one of many U-boat kills which he (Hunt) attended must have been one in which I shared. This was in the Bay (of Biscay) in August 1944. I had a go at the U-boat and flew over to 2EG (Second Escort Group) and called the *Wren* to assist. They came in and sat on the U-boat – which by this time was leaking badly. They gave it a good going-over and shortly after midnight (some 12 hours after the first attack) it surfaced and *Wren* took off most of its crew as prisoners.

I was commanding No. 53 Squadron Liberators and was Captain of Aircraft C53." Indeed, all 52 crew in the U-boat were picked up which, by that stage in the war, had become unusual.

S.J.McK. Newman.

Charles Newman (31–36), a former Chief of the College who only joined the RAF after his older brother, Stanley Newman was killed on active service in Iraq in the RAF in 1935, was awarded a DFC in 1944 having "completed very many sorties and invariably displayed great courage and resolution." A Squadron Leader in 613 Squadron (a tactical bomber unit flying Mosquito aircraft), "in April 1944 he participated in an attack on a target in Holland. This operation called for a high degree of skill and this officer played a worthy part in the success achieved. He has rendered most valuable service." The Citation was referring to a daylight raid on the Dutch Central Population Registry building in a large white structure in The Hague where the Germans held their Dutch Gestapo records.

Newman wrote vividly about his time in 613 Squadron for *The Log*. "The aircraft would take off from base and form up into echelons of six, deployed to port or starboard, depending on our tactics. Flying to the English coast at about 1,500 feet, we would get 'right down on the deck' 15 to 20 feet above the sea and make the crossing of the Channel to keep out of radar range as long as possible." On reaching the coast of France or Holland, tactics varied. On D-Day the squadron had the job of patrolling the Cherbourg Peninsula and "creating as much nuisance as possible to the Germans by bombing and strafing any movement seen, or railways and roads. The weather was vile." After D-Day to the end of 1944, when Newman left for another command, his "normal" job was to attack any movement on the roads or railways or canals of France and the Low Countries. If none was seen, as happened often, he would bomb cross-roads, railway junctions, bridges and 'dumping points' selected by the Army. Often, this work was "very disheartening" for long periods reflecting a lack of targets. Suddenly, "somebody would strike lucky, giving hope and encouragement to the rest (of us)." On Christmas Eve 1944 "the Wing that I was with attacked a total of over 50 trains in the course of the evening…This night work was carried on continuously from D-Day to VE-Day with the occasional interruption for really bad weather and sometimes a pause for a long-distance, low-level daylight raid, usually against the Gestapo." Newman ended his piece, characteristically, by paying tribute to the ground crews who had kept his squadron in the air.

One aviator, **Robert Connell** (36–38), joined the RAFVR from the MN in 1940 and spent his entire war in the Far East, becoming a Flying Officer, piloting a variety of Hurricane aircraft, winning a DFC and being involved in a succession of tough encounters with the Japanese as a member of 17 Squadron. Arriving in early 1942 as enemy troops neared Rangoon, he flew defensive patrols during the Allied retreat to India, took part in the siege of Imphal and supported Orde Wingate's Chindit expedition. Returned to the Arkan (Burma) front in November, 1944, he destroyed two Japanese aircraft in dog-fights and put two trains and other transports out of action as the Allies re-took Rangoon. The Citation for his DFC stated: "This officer has shown outstanding keenness and has set an exceptionally high standard of flying and navigation in the face of arduous conditions." Post-war, Connell was to die in 1951 test-flying a Hawker Sea Fury while based at the Empire Test Pilots' School at Boscombe Down.

Scores of Old Pangbournians also flew in the Royal Navy's Fleet Air Arm. Formed in 1924 as part of the RAF, which was operating aircraft embarked on RN ships, the FAA only came under direct control of the Admiralty a few months before fighting broke out in 1939. During the Second World War, it ran aircraft on ships and on land where its role was to protect the RN's shore-based facilities. On occasion, notably during the Battle of Britain in 1940, it supplemented the RAF. But for at least the first four years of the war it was poorly equipped. Not until the summer of 1943 did American-made fighters like the Corsairs and Hellcats, with 2,000hp engines, start to be available under the Lend Lease programme.

Despite these handicaps, four OPs in the FAA achieved widespread renown – **Frank Hopkins** (24–27), **Charles Owen** (22–25), **C.R. Bateman** (27–30) and **Ben Bolt** (21–22). Two of the quartet became influential Admirals, two established important links with the U.S. Navy and two became leading advocates in the post-war world of naval air power and the Fleet Air Arm. Much of what each did in the Second World War is somewhat obscure. As a post-war file in The National Archives puts it: "The wartime history of a Naval Air Squadron is a difficult thing to collate. Many records have been destroyed (and) the memory of squadron members can be hazy…But (these) squadrons gave good value for money despite W.S.C.'s (Churchill's) rather poor opinion of the worth of the FAA."

Frank Hopkins is probably the best-known. In time, he became Vice Admiral Sir Frank Hopkins KCB, DSO, DSC and Bar and was twice Mentioned in Despatches. His obituary in *The Times* described him as "an extraordinarily modest man of great charm and the personification of kindness…He always led from the front and his thoughts were constantly for those who followed him."

Maybe reflecting innate reticence, or his rather introspective character, he left little publicly-available material such as personal papers or a memoir. But two books published in the 1980s do fill in some of the gaps – *Night Strike from Malta* by Kenneth Poolman, and *Voices in the Air* edited by Laddie Lucas, himself a leading wartime RAF fighter pilot.

Frank Hopkins.

Hopkins joined the Royal Navy in 1927 and until the outbreak of war served in surface ships including aircraft carriers. In 1934 he qualified as an Observer and in the late-1930s was flying in the Fleet Air Arm's array of Swordfish and Albacore torpedo bomber biplanes. By 1939 he was on the staff of the Naval Observers School. As a member of 826 Squadron, he covered the Allied evacuation from Dunkirk in May 1940 and won his first DSC. After Dunkirk, the squadron concentrated on cross-Channel raids, mostly against shipping convoys and inland military facilities. A contribution he made to *Voices in the Air*, recounts what happened next.

"Nearly all the various operations we carried out between June-October 1940 were at night. The Albacore's speed of 90 knots made daylight raids too expensive (in men and machines). For example, on our trip to Texel (an island off the coast of Holland) on June 21 we were intercepted by Me-109s (Messerschmitt 109s, one of the workhorses of the Luftwaffe, with a top speed of 400 knots) – about a dozen of them. We had no fighter escort and there was no cloud cover. Result: three Albacores were shot down and most of the rest were damaged. We did shoot down two Me-109s with our single Vickers .303 machine gun mounted in the rear cockpit. We also set some storage tanks on fire." After the war Hopkins was told by a Dutchman that the commanding officer of the Me-109 squadron was sacked after this episode for allowing such "ancient, out-of-date biplanes to waffle in, in broad daylight, bomb the oil tanks and lose two (109s) to these ridiculous aeroplanes." The group was not sent out in daylight again for three months. This time it attacked German ships off Calais and was escorted by six RAF Blenheim aircraft. Again, there was no cloud cover and "long before we entered the target area, we could see swarms of 109s taking off inland." No targets were hit, four of the six Blenheims were shot down along with three of the six Albacores. Hopkins was awarded a second DSC, but FAA/RAF relations were not improved.

Late in 1940 Hopkins embarked in a new-build aircraft carrier, *Formidable,* and sailed at top speed to the Mediterranean via South Africa, arriving in time to take part in the Battle of Matapan at the end of March 1941. During the engagement, 826 Squadron made three torpedo attacks on the Italian battleship *Vittorio Veneto.* "The attacks were most unpleasant and not something I would wish on my worst enemy," he wrote. He was Mentioned in Despatches. *Formidable* was severely damaged two months after during the evacuation of Allied troops from Crete and had to be withdrawn for repairs. Hopkins and his FAA colleagues, with their remaining Albacores and Swordfish, disembarked to the Western Desert and operated with the 8th Army, mostly on night bombing attacks against Axis tanks.

In December 1941 Hopkins took command of 830 Squadron in Malta after it had lost five Swordfish and its commanding officer on one sortie. The Swordfish was considered obsolete in 1939 but lasted the war and proved to be enduringly destructive in the right hands. By the start of 1942, 830 Squadron had only two serviceable Swordfish left. Soon after, it was one. Hopkins insisted on using it to attack an Italian troop transport convoy, was ambushed by a vastly superior Ju-88 but managed to escape. By mid-January the squadron strength was up to eight aircraft. Running battles, night after night, were fought against German and Italian convoys moving by sea to Tripoli. On January 23 Hopkins located a large group of Axis ships but, short of fuel, had to return to Malta to refuel. The squadron crews, exhausted by six hours' fighting and flying and concerned about the deteriorating weather conditions, were reluctant to go aloft again. Hopkins, "a master of the Mark-11M ASV" (airborne sea-surface search radar), called for volunteers and set off with four Swordfish, finding his target 30 miles off Misrata before signalling to his three torpedo-droppers to attack. One merchant vessel, a famous pre-war 14,000-ton Italian liner, now a troopship called *Victoria,* was sunk. The four planes made it back to Malta after flying an hour beyond their usual limit. "Hopkins himself had flown for a total of nearly 12 hours in conditions (lashing rain, heavy cloud) which normally would have been considered impossible. He received an immediate DSO "for leadership and relentless determination," as described in *Night Strike from Malta.* He left 830 Squadron for a post in Washington DC in June 1942.

Hopkins went on to qualify as a pilot in the USAF in 1944 and was lent to the United States Pacific Fleet, flying from two aircraft carriers and being present at the defeat of the Japanese Navy at the decisive battle of Leyte Gulf – the largest naval battle of World War 2. During the clash, he witnessed sustained *kamikaze* attacks on Allied carriers, noting: "The two sources of damage are the petrol tanks in the plane and the bomb." Both, he observed, caused extensive harm to the flight deck, to parked aircraft and to personnel on the hangar and flight decks who were hit by splinters. During his post-war career Hopkins took part in the Korean War as Commander (Air) on the carrier *Theseus,* directing 12 war patrols and many dangerous actions inland against Chinese and North Korean ground forces. For this, he was Mentioned in Despatches a second time (see Chapter 13). His last RN job was as Commander -in-Chief Portsmouth before he retired to Devon and Hawaii in 1967.

Charles Owen, a near-contemporary of Hopkins at Pangbourne, won the DSC and the American Bronze Medal and had the remarkable and alarming experience of being sunk, and surviving, four times during the Second World War. Initially, he served in destroyers before qualifying as a Fleet Air Arm Observer in 1936 and flying the cruiser *Berwick's* Walrus seaplane in 1939. Until early 1941 he was attached to the RAF before re-joining the Royal Navy and spending the rest of the war in aircraft carriers. In *Ark Royal* at the end of 1941, he survived the sinking of the ship near Gibraltar for which he received a DSC "for courage, resolution and devotion to duty" even if he reckoned that all he did was to save the money that was on board.

Charles Owen.

By May 1942 Owen was in *Eagle* ferrying aircraft to Malta and took part in Operation Pedestal to relieve Malta. *Eagle* was sunk north of Algiers but he survived. By 1943 he was in *Victorious* in the Pacific as Air Staff Officer, helping to re-equip the carrier with American aircraft and planning the ship's air actions for the next two years. In February 1945 he was appointed British Pacific Fleet Liaison Officer with the US Navy Fast Carrier Task Force. Aboard *USS Bunker Hill* when it was sunk by kamikaze aircraft that May, he was rescued from the water by the *USS Enterprise* – only for the *Enterprise* to be sunk shortly after. Once again rescued, Owen was recommended for Presidential and Navy Unit citation ribbons only for the US Navy department in Washington to reject the awards on the grounds that these awards were restricted to American citizens. Instead, Owen received a Bronze Medal Star in 1946.

Amazingly fortunate, and brave too, was **Dick Bateman.** He had joined the Fleet Air Arm after Dartmouth and in the 1930s flew seaplanes and fixed wing aircraft from Malta and Leuchars in Scotland. Early in the Second World War he was in the battleship *Rodney* and was catapulted off the vessel in a snowstorm in a Walrus seaplane to search for the German battleship *Scharnhorst* – only for the snow to thicken and force him to land in neutral Norway. Here he was interned for three months until the country entered the war on the Allied side in April 1940. On return to London, he met Winston Churchill (First Lord of the Admiralty) and gave him information that the Norwegians wanted to be passed on. Posted to the *Prince of Wales* in 1941, he was in the battleship in August for the historic Newfoundland meeting between Churchill and Franklin Roosevelt. He was still serving in the ship when it was sunk by the Japanese off Malaya that December. But by a stroke of luck, he had been catapulted off *Prince of Wales* that morning to fly papers to Singapore. Two months afterwards, he escaped from Singapore before it fell and subsequently flew many types of aircraft in the FAA during the rest of the war, surviving unharmed. He went on to a post-war career flying commercial helicopters.

Far away in Canada in 1943 **R.S. Henley** (31–34), another FAA pilot who had been awarded a DSC in 1942 and completed a full tour of operations, was training future FAA pilots. His cohort that year included three OPs – **Michael Hayward** (33–37), who spent the war on carrier operations, ending in the Far East; **E.V. Speakman** (33–36) who was killed in action in 1944; and **R.M. Rodgers** (32–35),

Ben Bolt.

another who was killed in action (see Chapter 10). In contrast, **Ben Bolt** survived the conflict and went on to become Pangbourne's first Admiral in 1956. During a 37-year career in the Royal Navy he was awarded the CB, DSO, DSC and Bar. He had qualified as an aircrew Observer in 1931 and spent the next eight years developing his skills – dive-bombing, torpedo attacking, night attacking using flares – which became standard in the FAA as the war went on. One of these skills earned him a DSC in 1940 after flying in a Wellington bomber at 50ft over the sea to sweep magnetic mines laid by the Germans. One of the bombs on the Goodwin Sands exploded under the aircraft knocking Bolt off his seat and stunning him.

A key moment in Bolt's wartime career occurred in March 1941 in the action between the Allied Mediterranean fleet and the Italian fleet off Cape Matapan. Thanks to accurate reports Bolt sent back to *Warspite* from a Swordfish floatplane, British commanders had some idea of enemy dispositions. But his aircraft ran low on fuel, so had to be landed in the sea ahead of *Warspite* and taxied at 18 knots alongside the battleship as Bolt climbed onto the upper wing to hook on to *Warspite's* crane and be hoisted on board. After the Swordfish was recovered,

Bolt and his pilot, Ben Rice, "readily agreed to take off again" according to Rice's obituary in *The Daily Telegraph* in 1994. Just after 6:00pm Bolt sighted the battleship *Vittorio Veneto* and was able to report back to *Warspite* and broadcast "copybook enemy sighting reports." Guided by this information, the British fleet attacked after dark and overwhelmed the Italians. By then it was too late for Rice and Bolt to land on *Warspite*, so Rice diverted to Crete and used his own flares to create a landing patch. Bolt was awarded a Bar to his DSC.

From 1942 he worked in the Admiralty, ending up as director of the Naval Radio department. Five years older than Frank Hopkins, he achieved his first sea command as a Captain after the war ended in 1947. In 1950 he worked closely with Hopkins in the light fleet carrier *Theseus* during the Korean war. This ship set all kinds of records for operational sorties and Bolt was awarded a DSO (see Chapter 13). Subsequently, he became Director of the Naval Air Warfare Division and was involved in the planning to fit aircraft carriers with angled flight decks and to introduce turbojet aircraft into the FAA. In retirement in the 1960s and 1970s, he campaigned tirelessly for the Fleet Air Arm when its existence was threatened by defence cuts and new technology.

One notable flyer who spanned the different worlds of the FAA and the RAF was **Colin Hodgkinson** (33–37), one of two legless Allied pilots in World War 2. Hodgkinson's father had won an MC & Bar in the First World War as a pilot and "excited" his son's ambition to fly. A fine rugby player and natural disrupter who, by his own admission, found it "impossible to keep on the right side of authority" both at the NCP and in adult life, he joined the Royal Navy as a Midshipman FAA in 1938. There was one problem: in training he discovered that he had a claustrophobic distaste of flying. One day in 1939 he crashed into another plane at 500 feet and ended up having both his legs amputated. His instructor was killed. Before long, he had been invalided out of the RN, lost his girlfriend, was living on a pittance and had no idea what to do next. Then war broke out.

Whilst recovering from his accident, Hodgkinson ran into the world-famous plastic surgeon Archibald McIndoe who described him like this: "A red-headed, thick-set man, face badly scarred, his eyes reflected bitter desperation mixed with wariness...In 1939 he was 6 feet

Colin Hodgkinson (Daily Express).

1 inch tall and weighed 13 1/2 stone of solid and well-trained bone and muscle. In 1940, following a near-fatal air crash, he was 5 feet 10 inches tall, minus two legs, and weighed 12 stone." McIndoe got to work and patched Hodgkinson up so well that, in time, there was little physically that was beyond him. One day he saw a press story about the well-known pre-war legless pilot Douglas Bader returning to serve in the RAF. Determined to prove himself to himself, and to take part in the war, he began a long, persistent campaign to re-join the FAA, to re-start flying in the FAA and, finally, to transfer to the RAF and qualify as a Spitfire pilot.

Two things about the RAF appealed to Hodgkinson. He could fly from an airfield since operating from a ship at sea was impossible for him in his legless state; and the RAF's diversity and "loose, almost improvised discipline" suited his maverick temperament. In his revealingly honest memoir, *Best Foot Forward*, published in 1957, he pulls no punches about his fragile mental state during much of the war and spares no one, including himself. He never loved flying and by his own admission was no more than an average, somewhat cautious, pilot. Yet he was well qualified, very determined and courageous. Wangling his way into the RAF and Fighter Command in 1942, he joined 131 Squadron at the end of the year and became known as 'Hoppy' – one of the boys. In 1943 he flew almost one hundred sorties in various squadrons led by two illustrious Battle of Britain aces – 'Johnnie' Johnson and Laddie Lucas. He was credited with two 'kills' and a number of 'damages' as well as destroying two tank trains and two canal barges carrying tanks, undertaking secret missions, twice helping to rescue downed colleagues from the North Sea and Channel and once surviving on his wits when his Spitfire engine cut out at less than 1,000 feet 140 miles from land.

Colin Hodgkinson meeting King George VI (Daily Express).

Hodgkinson's luck finally ran out just as he realised that he was feeling the strain of so many operations and narrow escapes. Asked to undertake a last, lone reconnaissance sortie over German rocket sites in the Pas de Calais region before a spell of leave, he flew too high, blacked out at 31,000 feet from lack of oxygen, turned his Spitfire on its back and crash-landed in France. In a coma for four days, he awoke in a German military hospital in St. Omer to discover that his tin legs had been removed. One of the doctors looked at him in amazement and said: "You must hate the Germans very much." Transferred to Germany, he ended up for a few weeks in the Stalag Luft 3 camp with other OPs, before being repatriated at the end of August 1944. More painful medical operations followed on his face and legs and the war in Europe ended before he could get back to the front line.

Like many of his generation, Hodgkinson found it hard to settle into a peacetime existence or to come to terms with why he had been fighting. The world had changed too much. Flying did not return to his life for 11 years until a horrendous experience, by coincidence again at 31,000 feet, when the pressure inside a Caravelle jet aircraft failed on a trial flight as he was supervising an advertising shoot. Returning in one piece to *terra firma,* he collapsed. "Then, as if brushing something for ever from my mind, I sat down calmly…Flying had returned to my life, not to fill, but to enrich it. I feared the air no longer and, with that fear lost, no longer feared myself."

10

THE SUPREME SACRIFICE: NOT MERE WORDS

— ◉ —

In mid-December 1941 British forces in Malaya were driven into headlong retreat down the 700-mile peninsula by a large Japanese invasion force. Twelve miles from the Siam (Thai) border, the 2nd Battalion East Surrey Regiment was positioned in a rubber plantation. A 28-year-old officer, Alastair Hill (28–32), commanded Rifle Company B. Caught ill-equipped and unprepared for the rapid Japanese advance from the coast on December 8, the battalion headquarters were overrun within five days and the commanding officer put out of action. Hill, the senior company commander still alive, gathered the remnants of the battalion together and began a long, debilitating and humiliating trek south through the jungle towards Singapore. Reaching a village northeast of Taiping, an account lodged in the archives of the Queen's Royal Surrey Regimental Association states: "He (Captain Hill) was now in a state of complete exhaustion and would go no further. He insisted the party should move on without him and they left him in a woodcutter's hut near the village of Kampong Lasah. He was not seen again."

At around the same time, off the east coast of Malaya, the Royal Navy battlecruiser *Repulse* and the battleship *Prince of Wales* were hurrying north as part of Force Z to try to head off Japanese reinforcements, unaware of the strength of the enemy air force they faced. Among several OPs serving in the ships was **John Watson (36–39)**, a 19-year-old Midshipman in *Repulse*. He was killed in one of the relentless waves of Japanese air attacks on December 10 – just one of 1,233 men to die in the 27,000-ton vessel which sank in six minutes having been hit by several torpedo bombs.

Over the six years of the Second World War 178 Old Pangbournians are known to have been killed in action or died as a result of wounds or training accidents or in captivity – equivalent to an entire generation of cadets, or about 10 per cent of all boys who had passed through the school by 1945. So relentless was the tide of carnage that many of these OPs have no memorial. One reason, above all, explains the relatively huge loss. At the start of the war virtually every OP, except for the medically unfit, served automatically in one of the armed services or in the Merchant Navy. Even in Spring 1941, when an audit of OPs leaving the College since 1939 was published in The Log, the oldest OP in the conflict was under 40. By the time in early 1947 that a final Roll of Honour was published, the oldest OP to die was reckoned to be only 42.

The official fates of these men, especially the many who served in the Merchant Navy or in RAF Bomber Command, varies little – "Lost at Sea" or "Lost in a raid over …" – and the detailed records of the air operations and particular voyages are generally sparse. Those awarded decorations or Mentioned in Despatches – about 50 – are easier to trace. Many of the casualties were extremely young including 16 teenagers, the youngest of whom, John Benn (41–43), had just turned 17. An Apprentice in the Alfred Holt cargo ship ss *Empire Lancer*, he died after it was torpedoed at the northern end of the Mozambique Channel by the German submarine *U-862* while sailing unescorted from Durban to Aden in 1944. A number of OPs died serving in the same ship at sea, many were killed in the same theatre of war and in one tragic incident two OPs piloting a BOAC aircraft requisitioned by RAF Ferry Command were shot down near Plymouth by Polish pilots attached to the RAF who mistook the Liberator transport aircraft for an enemy plane.

Each death was an individual tragedy. Collectively, they stunned the College. At first, the caring chaplain, R.T. Sheills, read out names as they reached the school during daily prayers. As the number increased, this was done once a term. A Memorial Service for the fallen was held at St. Martin-in-the-Fields in London in March 1947. The huge church was packed to capacity as the Roll of Honour listing 175 names (the total at the time) was read out. During the war a fund had been set up to raise money to build a chapel in memory of the dead. Money flowed in, but insufficient to build a suitable place of worship, and it was decided instead to commission a memorial window. Designed by a Mr. Cole of William Morris & Co., it depicts the figure of the risen Christ and four uniformed figures gazing inwards – an Army commando and a Merchant Navy officer on the left, a Royal Navy officer and an RAF pilot on the right. It was dedicated in 1951. Today the window hangs at the rear of the Falklands Islands Memorial Chapel above a plaque listing the names of all OPs who lost their lives during the 1939–45 conflict.

To mark the dedication, *The Log* of Summer 1951 published a poem by Christopher Daniel (47–51), a Fifth Former shortly to enter the Merchant Navy. It reads:

"Revealed, at last, to light this sacred place,
In memory of those who fought and died.
It was for us that Death they went to face
And many times the enemy defied.
It is for them, for those who gave their lives,
This window in their honour stands – its rays
To pierce the gloom, in countless sapphire knives,
When 'ere the Sun the stained-glass displays.
For all to see, it flashes many shades
And lights the Altar-cloth with green and gold;
At Even, only then, the purple fades,
The red is dimmed, for them the day is old.
But yet, the window shall be lit again,
A symbol of our men, in battle slain!"

The first OP to die in the Second World War was **Michael Roupell** (28–32) in October 1939. A Lieutenant in the Royal Navy, he was serving in *HMS Royal Oak* when the battleship was torpedoed by a German submarine in Scapa Flow, Orkney. Two months later came the second death – that of **Humphrey Woods** (18–22), a Royal Marines Captain in *HMS Exeter* who was killed during the high-profile battle of the River Plate off Montevideo, Uruguay. Three OPs were killed in the April-June 1940 phase of the Norwegian Campaign. One of them, **Reginald Levinge** (33–36), a Sub Lt RN, was serving in the destroyer HMS *Glowworm* when its captain won the first Victoria Cross (posthumous) of the war following a desperate, no-hope clash with the much better armed German heavy cruiser *Admiral Hipper* during which *Glowworm* rammed *Hipper* and exploded, killing most of its crew. **Henry Maidlow** (31–34), a Lt RN, took part in an equally heroic action when another RN destroyer, HMS *Hunter*, raided Narvik harbour after the German invasion of northern Norway and fired all its eight torpedoes at the massed, anchored German invasion fleet which had arrived in the port the day before. On retreating, *Hunter* ran into five German destroyers at close range outside the harbour and was sunk. Most of the crew were killed. Even further to the north, **Reginald Law** (32–36) probably died of exposure after his ship, the destroyer HMS *Acasta*, sank with the loss of 160 men having encountered the German capital ships *Scharnhorst* and *Gneisenau* far above the Arctic Circle south of the Lofoten Islands. Law was a Sub Lt RN aged just 21.

The Norwegian campaign led to the first deaths in the Fleet Air Arm – something that was to become distressingly commonplace. **Ronald Benson-Dare** (32–34) was flying a Walrus aircraft off HMS *Devonshire* when he was attacked by a German Heinkel bomber. Diving to 100 feet, he evaded the Heinkel for a quarter of an hour before his fuel tank and engine caught fire and the plane crashed into the sea. **Grenville Hampden** (32–34) was in HMS *Furious* providing anti-submarine cover off Narvik when he was shot down. **Robert Dundas** (26–28) was flying a Sea Hurricane from the aircraft carrier HMS *Glorious* when he was killed. HMS *Ark Royal*, another major RN carrier, bore witness to the death of a number of OPs before being torpedoed itself in November 1941. One was **John Harris** (31–34) who took part in a disastrous attack by the ship's Skua aircraft on the *Scharnhorst* at midnight on June 13, 1940. After flying 40 miles over enemy-occupied Norway through intense flak (anti-aircraft fire) to the target, all surprise was lost and eight of the 15 attacking planes were shot down.

So emerged a grim pattern for the rest of the war. Old Pangbournians fought and died across the globe – from the icy wastes of the Arctic Circle to the plains and forests of northwest Europe, in the Mediterranean, in the North and South Atlantic and the Indian and Pacific oceans, across the deserts of North Africa, up the rugged Italian peninsula, in the Balkans and the Middle East, in East Africa, and in Burma, Malaya and Singapore. The circumstances varied hugely. A few of those who lost their lives were decorated posthumously – around 30 – although the number Mentioned in Despatches was rather greater. Most were aged under 30. In a couple of cases the men were killed along with a family member. At least three died in prisoner of war camps.

Information about those who died sailing in the British Merchant Navy – 21 by most counts – is not plentiful. Given the scale of MN losses in the war– 32,952 registered seamen lost their lives, or a 17.8 per cent loss of the total MN strength, compared to a 9.7 per cent loss of RN personnel – and the lack of record-keeping among the various shipping companies (now almost all defunct), this is not surprising. During 1941 alone, 3.6 million tons of shipping were lost, 60 per cent to attacks by German submarines. Once torpedoed, the odds of a merchant seaman surviving and being rescued, let alone leaving a record of the event, were poor. Those who were not killed outright in the explosion might be badly injured. Many drowned or were suffocated by oil or paralyzed by the cold seas. Others who did make it to a lifeboat or raft were often left behind by the convoy they had been part of since it was too dangerous for another vessel to stop and pick them up. Allied naval escorts did their best to help, but their priority was to prevent further losses from circling Axis submarines. Many survivors therefore faced a lingering death from starvation or exposure or both. At some periods of the conflict less than half of all merchant seamen survived a sinking.

A "typical" death at sea in the Merchant Navy was that of **Ralph Ansell (24–26)**. Chief Officer on the cargo steamer ss *Glen Head* belonging to the Ulster Steamship Co. Ltd., Ansell was in Convoy OG63 going from Liverpool to Gibraltar. The day before reaching Gibraltar the ship was bombed and sunk southwest of Cape Vincent. All 23 crew on board were killed. A similar fate befell **Douglas Clegg (18–20)**, a Master Mariner who worked for the New Zealand Shipping Company. Chief Officer in ss *Rotorua*, Clegg was making the long and perilous run carrying refrigerated goods from Lyttleton, on the South Island of New Zealand via Australia and the Panama Canal to Halifax, Nova Scotia and on to Avonmouth in England. Sailing between Australia and Panama, *Rotorua* was repeatedly attacked by a shadowing U-boat but not hit. About 110 miles west of St. Kilda (an outpost of the Hebrides Islands), *Rotorua* was torpedoed again. This time there was no escape and the vessel sank in 15 minutes. "The ship went down stern first and stood up like a tall skyscraper before sinking slowly into the deep sea," recalled a survivor. Clegg was not among the lucky ones who got away in lifeboats and were picked up by a passing trawler.

Two young OPs, **John Benn (41–43)** and **William Pink (40–43)**, aged 17 and 18, were killed within three days of each other by the same submarine *U-862* in different cargo ships sailing through or near the Mozambique Channel. Three OPs died serving in converted troopships. One was **Denis Gordon (36–39)**, a cadet in mv *Warwick Castle*, which was sailing back to the UK from North Africa with 300 soldiers on board when it was torpedoed by a U-boat 200 miles west of Portugal. The second was **Richard Dennis (19–22)**, Troop Officer in ss *Duchess of York* (a Canadian Pacific Steamship Co. liner). Sailing in a small convoy from Scotland to Freetown, Sierra Leone, *Duchess of York* was attacked by three German aircraft about 300 miles west of Vigo. More than 700 crew and troops were on board. Dennis was not among the 620 who were rescued by an escorting RN ship. The third was **Frank Cox (18–19)**, Chief Officer in ss *Strathallan*. This well-known P&O liner/troopship had just taken part in the Allied landings in North Africa in November 1942 and was returning to the UK with more than 5,000 men and women on board when it was torpedoed on the side of the engine room. An initial evacuation got 1,300 people off the ship. A tow to Oran in Algeria at five knots followed. Then the vessel exploded, caught fire and had to be abandoned. Thousands managed to scramble off the stricken ship. A skeleton crew remained on board for another 14 hours but 12 miles off Oran the 23,700-ton vessel finally capsized and sank, drowning the 16 people still on it. Cox is thought to have been killed in the initial torpedo explosion.

Peter Brendon (29–32) was particularly unfortunate. A Lt RNR, in March 1941 he was returning to his base in Ceylon, where he was an officer in the armed merchant cruiser HMS *Hector,* with his wife and children in the steamship ss *Staffordshire* after leave in the UK. One hundred and fifty miles northwest of the Butte of Lewis, the *Staffordshire* was bombed. Brendon and at least one of his children were killed. Another death, that of Peter Whitaker (30–33) 3rd Officer in the cargo steamer ss *Automedon*, may have had major ramifications. Attacked by the German surface raider *Atlantis* 250 miles northwest of Sumatra in November 1940, *Automedon* was hit but not sunk by four salvos at the bridge which killed all the officers. Before scuttling *Automedon*, the captain of *Atlantis* ordered a thorough search. This unearthed secret documents, intended for the British Far East Command. Passed to the Japanese, these papers may have aided the invasion of Singapore and Malaya the next month.

In May-June 1940 numerous OPs were involved in the Allied retreat through Belgium and France and the evacuation at Dunkirk. Seven are known to have been killed – three serving in the RAF, two in the Royal Navy and two in the Army. Among the RAF deaths, that of Bruce Skidmore (33–37) stands out since the loss was detailed. Aged 20, a member of 88 Squadron and a Pilot Officer, Skidmore was flying a Fairey Battle monoplane bomber – a relatively slow aircraft with a limited range and two machine-guns. Considered "highly vulnerable" to enemy fighters and anti-aircraft fire, both the Battle and 88 Squadron suffered "very heavy losses" during the fight for France. On the day Skidmore was killed, seven of eight Battles sent aloft by his squadron were destroyed – shot down near Liege in Belgium while attacking German troop columns. Within four days, 88 Squadron had written off most of its aircraft, the Battle's career as a day bomber had ended and what was left of the unit was withdrawn to England. Just five days after Skidmore's death a similar debacle involved Leslie Thornley (27–30), a Flight Lt. in 615 Squadron. A member of a unit flying the outdated Gloster Gladiator biplane, the aircraft proved to be easy meat for the enemy. At the time of death, Thornley was based at Moorsele in Belgium. The squadron record for May 1940 states simply: "A very intense ten days of combat began on May 10 with some of the squadron pilots flying six or seven sorties per day." Thornley was one of three 615 Squadron pilots killed on May 16.

When he died in France, Army officer **Thomas Onslow (30–34)** was attached to the 1st Bn Herefordshire Regiment. A regimental history entry for May 20, 1940 records: "During the morning Lt. T.P.R. Onslow, the Battalion Liaison Officer, had been sent to Brigade to report progress, but was never seen again. He was later reported to have been killed in action. The inaccuracy of the map (provided) probably caused him to lose his way and run into the enemy." As it happened, Onslow had been wounded, taken prisoner-of-war and was to die of his injuries in captivity in July. **Frederick Colville (27–30)** was another caught up in the chaos of retreat. An officer in the 1st Bn Gordon Highlanders, Colville was fighting with 51st Division which, despite its lack of ammunition or weapons, had been left behind near Dunkirk to delay the German advance. The battalion ended up being trapped and most of its soldiers had no choice but to surrender. Exactly what happened to Colville is unknown. Today he is buried in the cemetery at St. Valery-en-Caux, Seine Maritime – one of many Commonwealth War Graves Commission cemeteries in northern France.

At sea, some notable examples of courage and bravery were displayed during the Dunkirk evacuation. Those who paid with their lives included **Clifford Carter (25–26)**, a Lt RN serving in the minelaying destroyer HMS *Esk,* who made six cross-Channel trips and helped to rescue 4,500 troops. His commanding officer wrote the recommendation for the award: "(He) has outstanding ability as an executive officer. In addition, his personal courage on several occasions was a fine example." Carter was awarded a DSC. Three months on, still in *Esk,* he lost his life when his ship hit a mine northwest of Texel, an island off the Dutch coast, while rescuing survivors from a second RN destroyer which, too, had hit a mine. **John Percival-Jones (31–35)**, a Sub Lt in HMS *Wakeful,* was another who was involved in the Dunkirk evacuation. By May 29 *Wakeful* had already embarked some 1,200 Allied troops and made one successful cross-Channel crossing when it was torpedoed outside Zeebrugge harbour by a German E-boat. More than 700 men were on board at the time. Only 27 survived.

Post-Dunkirk, the Royal Navy played a critical defensive role in Allied strategy by bottling up German capital ships in French and German ports, gradually countering the U-boat menace in the Atlantic and helping to keep the sea lanes to the UK open, so ensuring the country did not starve or the British war effort grind to a halt for lack of resources. Battles, clashes and chance encounters took place initially in the North Sea and Arctic seas, later in the North Atlantic and, finally, in the Mediterranean, Pacific and Indian Oceans. Casualties at sea rose correspondingly.

In 1942, four OPs were killed in the Arctic region on Russian convoy duty. **Vyvyan Manfield (32–36)** was a Lt (E) aged 23 who had joined the RN in 1937 and was one of two officers in the cruiser HMS *Edinburgh* killed in April in a torpedo attack. *Edinburgh*, part of convoy QP11, was carrying gold bars worth £70 million in today's money back from the USSR in part-payment for previous American and British arms deliveries. Not until the 1980s was most of this gold retrieved. Another OP, **Patrick Massy (30–33)**, lost his life when flying a Sea Hurricane from the carrier HMS *Avenger* as part of the flotilla escorting convoy PQ18. As many as 70 German aircraft attacked PQ18 on September 14, 1942. *Avenger's* ten aircraft did well, but the numbers told and Massy was among those killed. Having been awarded a DSC and Mentioned in Despatches in the previous two years, this time he was awarded a posthumous DSO "for gallantry and skill in HM ships escorting an important convoy to North Russia in the face of relentless attack by enemy aircraft and submarines" as the Citation in the *London Gazette* put it.

Clement Bridgman (20–22), an RNR Lt Cdr captaining the frigate HMS *Itchen,* was killed along with 227 others in his ship in September 1943 south of Iceland. *Itchen* was escorting an Atlantic convoy westward when the frigate was torpedoed by *U-666*. *Itchen* had picked up survivors from the Canadian destroyer *St. Croix* two days earlier and was overloaded with the wounded and disoriented. Few had much chance of getting away. The German submarine involved was itself sunk by a FAA Swordfish early in 1944. Bridgman had won a DSO in 1942 "for skill and devotion to duty in action against enemy submarines" while commanding the destroyer *Dianthus* in the North Atlantic and sinking *U-379* which was "attempting to slink away" from convoy SC94 after torpedoing two merchant ships. In a brutal no-holds barred war of this sort, in which saving life was a secondary factor, it was notable that *Dianthus* picked up 175 survivors from four ships sunk in this convoy. Bridgman had begun the war in Gibraltar in the Contraband Control Service, progressing in 1940 to command of "quite a nice large steam yacht" before moving to *Dianthus.*

Two OPs died in the destroyer HMS *Somali* – part of convoy QP14 – when it was torpedoed by *U-703* in the Arctic and hit in the engine room on September 24, 1942 foundering after five days with considerable loss of life. Of the 102 men on board, 80, including **Martin Hunt (20–21)**, Cdr (E), initially remained on board as a skeleton crew while the ship was being towed by *HMS Ashanti*. Forbidden to go below on the badly damaged vessel, Hunt was Mentioned in Despatches "for brave or skilful conduct while escorting or protecting a convoy" but drowned when the ship sank suddenly. Only 35 of the crew survived. Pre-war, Hunt had lectured in engineering at BRNC Dartmouth. **John Longhurst (35–38)**, a 21-year-old Sub. Lt in *Somali*, perished on the same day in the icy Arctic waters. Near the end of the war, in February 1945, **Douglas Hill (37–41)** was killed when his ship, the corvette HMS *Bluebell*, was torpedoed and sank in 30 seconds in the Kola Inlet off Murmansk while convoy RA64 was assembling to return to Scotland. Only one of the crew of 86 survived. A second ship to be torpedoed and claim two OP lives was the cruiser HMS *Charybdis* in October 1943. **Oswald Moseley (30–34)** and **John Phillips (33–37)**, both Lieutenants, were serving together when *Charybdis*, attempting to intercept a German merchant vessel carrying rare commodities for the Third Reich, was hit by two torpedoes during a night sweep of the Bay of Biscay. The ship sank in half an hour with the loss of 426 men – and the suspicion has lingered that, in the words of a survivor at the time, "someone had talked – they were ready for us."

Anthony Stott.

Three sets of OP brothers died. **Anthony Stott (30–33)**, a Lt RNR, took part in one of the epic one-on-one naval clashes of the war when the armed merchant cruiser *Jervis Bay*, captained by Edward Fogarty Fegan, although massively outgunned, took on the German battleship *Admiral Scheer* to protect convoy HX84 steaming from Nova Scotia to northern England in November 1940. The action lasted an hour before *Jervis Bay* sank with the loss of 186 of its crew. Fogarty Fegan was awarded a posthumous Victoria Cross. The length of the hopeless fight allowed 32 of the 37 ships in the convoy to slip away and reach Liverpool. A handful of survivors from *Jervis Bay* were picked up from rafts within three days by a neutral Swedish ship. Anthony's twin, **John Stott (30–33)**, died at sea in 1944. Second Officer in the Shaw Savill vessel ss *Mataroa*, used mainly in the war as a troopship, he was lost overboard and is listed as "Missing at Sea."

Two brothers who died serving in the Army, both in the Royal Tank Regiment, were killed in the desert war in North Africa. One, **Ronald Rawlins (22–25)**, was a 33-year-old Acting Lt. Colonel in 42 Royal Tank Regiment when he died in late-1941. He is buried in the Commonwealth cemetery at Halfaya Sollum on the coast road from Mersa Matruh to Libya. The other, **Geoffrey Rawlins (27–31)**, was killed in action at the First Battle of El Alamein in July 1942. He was a Lieutenant in the 5 Royal Tank Regiment and is buried in the El Alamein cemetery. In the RAF, Flying Officer **John Lascelles (34–37)**, aged 20, was lost while piloting a Lockheed Hudson long range patrol aircraft over the Atlantic in October 1940. Within three months, his older brother **David Lascelles (24–26)**, a Wing Commander, was sailing across the North Atlantic in a merchant ship to a new position in the USA with his wife Diana, when the vessel was torpedoed and sunk. It is hardly possible to imagine the grief of all the parents concerned.

In the Mediterranean-North Africa theatre 20 OP deaths were recorded in a short period before the centre of Allied operations moved north in mid-1943 with the invasion of Sicily and the Italian peninsula. **Frederick Renny (18–19)**, a Lt Cdr RNR, was the recipient of a DSC and Bar as well as being Mentioned in Despatches before he was killed. His first DSC had been won at Dunkirk where he commanded *Skoot Hondrug*, a 227-ton Dutch coaster, and made four trips to the beaches, landing 1,442 troops back in England. The next year, now commander of the corvette *Samphire*, he sank *U-567* northeast of the Azores and shot down an attacking German aircraft near Algiers; he was Mentioned in Despatches. Early in 1943 while off Bougie, Algeria, *Samphire* was torpedoed and sunk while escorting a troop convoy reinforcing the Allies in North Africa. Renny and 44 of his crew were killed. He was awarded a (posthumous) Bar to his DSC "for bravery and skill in the hazardous operations in which Allied Forces were landed in North Africa." Other older OPs to die in the Mediterranean included **Wilfred Cooke (21–24)**, commanding officer of the minesweeper *Algerine*, **Gyles Andrews (24–26)**, a Lt Cdr in the battleship *Barham*, and **Kenneth Bloomer (21–24)**, captain of the destroyer *Panther* – the first two following submarine torpedo attacks and the third after an attack by a Ju87 aircraft, the first-known Stuka bomber victory over a Royal Navy ship.

Four OPs died in submarines in the Mediterranean including one, **Michael Willmott (22–25)**, a Lt Cdr RN and captain of HMS *Talisman*, who had an exceptional record and had been highlighted in national newspapers as "one of the most daring men in the service." Willmott, "an alert and resourceful officer," assumed command of *Talisman*, a T-class submarine, in July 1941 and carried out five war patrols in the Med. He won a DSO in December 1941 following "a remarkable and highly successful patrol" (in the words of a report by his superior officer) that was publicised by the Admiralty. During this patrol Willmott engaged an enemy destroyer, had to dive deep to escape 43 depth charges from an Italian torpedo boat, took on one enemy submarine at point blank range off Crete probably sinking it, definitely sank a 15,000-ton merchant vessel, and almost certainly sank another U-boat at close quarters. In this latter incident Willmott "had the astonishing experience of looking down his opponent's conning tower and seeing the lights in the control room below" after the German submarine dived directly under *Talisman* to its likely destruction with its conning tower hatches still open. The eminent Commander-in-Chief Mediterranean Fleet, Vice Admiral Sir Andrew Cunningham, added a note to the report on this encounter: "A most successful patrol. Lt Cdr M. Willmott, Royal Navy, displayed a capacity for quick appreciation and action as remarkable as the speed and alertness displayed by his men in executing his orders." On Willmott's sixth war patrol in *Talisman* in September 1942, carrying supplies from Gibraltar to Malta, the submarine disappeared and is thought to have to have hit a mine off Sicily. All 63 crew on board were listed as "missing, presumed dead."

There were other submariner deaths. Twenty-seven-year-old **Frank Gibbs** (28–31) was captaining *H31* – his first command and a boat primarily used to train officers and men – when the Admiralty decided in December 1941 that the German battlecruisers *Scharnhorst* and *Gneisenau* would try to leave their base at Brest with the cruiser *Prinz Eugen* for a sortie into the Atlantic. All available RN vessels were assigned to watch the approaches to Brest and *H31* was one of them, patrolling 250 miles north of Finisterre in the Bay of Biscay. The submarine left Falmouth on December 19 and was scheduled to return there on Christmas Eve. Nothing was ever heard from it again and it was assumed to have been lost after striking a mine. This was to have been Gibb's last patrol in *H31* as he had been given another appointment. He was, notes a file in the RN Submarine Museum archives, "a quiet man and very friendly person (who) had set his heart on becoming a submariner from an early age. A keen sportsman, six foot one inches in height and blue-eyed with fair hair and a fresh complexion, he was also a good swimmer and horse-rider. Service in submarines appealed to him, he said, because 'he would feel more at home knowing every member of the crew personally.'" That was typical of Gibbs' approach to life. "He was greatly respected by all who served with him – always willing to listen and give advice when needed."

Drummond St. Clair-Ford (22–24), younger brother of Aubrey (see Chapter 3) and once regarded as a future Scottish rugby international also lost his life in a submarine. By 1942, he was a Lt. Cdr aged 34 and an experienced officer with a command record going back a dozen years. Taking over HMS *Traveller* at the end of November, he was patrolling in the Gulf of Taranto when the submarine is presumed to have hit a mine and sunk. All 65 of the crew perished. On an earlier patrol while captaining *Sturgeon*, St. Clair-Ford had found one of his "kills" highlighted in a rare and unusual Admiralty press release. **John Haig-Haddow** (33–37) won a DSC commanding the submarine HMS *P42* in 1942 "for gallant and distinguished services in successful patrols" before losing his life right at the end of the war in unexplained circumstances. Another DSC holder was 21-year-old **Roderick Sampson** (35–38), killed in action in the submarine HMS *Tigris* in 1943 off the Gulf of Tunis. Other submariners killed included **John Baker** (27–28) in HMS *Seahorse* and **Lionel Dearden** (33–34) in HMS *H49*.

Three young OPs – **Nigel Adams** (36–40), **Michael Humphrey** (34–36) and **John Scott-Kerr** (32–35) – all died in the battlecruiser HMS *Hood* when it was sunk by the German battleship *Bismarck* in the Denmark Strait in May, 1941. Adams was 18 and had been Chief of the College the year before. Not all the RN casualties occurred in larger ships. Two that did not involve **Anthony Bone** (32–35) and **Maurice Lovell** (35–39), both MTB (Motor Torpedo Boats) commanders. Lovell, only 20 and commanding *MTB 220*, was sunk in an encounter with a German E-boat off Ambleheuse in north eastern France in May 1942 when his craft was part of an RN force trying to prevent the German cruiser *Stier* reaching the Gironde estuary in southwestern France. Bone was killed when his boat, *MTB 710*, hit a mine in an action in Dutch coastal waters in 1945 that earned him a posthumous DSC.

Nigel Adams.

John Scott-Kerr.

Fleet Air Arm losses mounted steadily after the calamitous Norwegian campaign. In the Mediterranean several stand out. **James Coates** (27–30) died flying from HMS *Ark Royal* in November 1940 after the carrier, escorting a convoy from Gibraltar to Alexandria, was recalled to Gibraltar. On the way there, its aircraft were launched prematurely against the shadowing Italian fleet and nine were lost at sea when they ran out of fuel. A month after this incident, **John Medlicott-Vereker** (28–31) was flying from HMS *Illustrious* when his Swordfish was hit by random enemy fire during a raid on a convoy close to the Kerkennah Islands off the east coast of Tunisia. In August 1942 **John Lucas** (35–38) was serving in the new aircraft carrier HMS *Indomitable* and was part of the Operation Pedestal convoy to relieve Malta when the Axis air forces made four raids in one day involving about 120 German and Italian aircraft. The FAA aircraft group never exceeded 24. On August 12 seven FAA aircraft were shot down. "All the pilots (were) up twice and some three times – they responded to every call" reported the captain of *Indomitable* once the fighting stopped. "(We) lost four fighters, two shot down, one missing and one badly wounded in combat who crashed on board on landing." Lucas was one of those killed.

Over the course of the war a dozen other OP FAA officers were killed in places as far flung as Sumatra in Indonesia, Dakar in Senegal and Namsos in Norway, either in operations, or in accidents or, in one case, as a result of being on board an escort carrier when it was sunk. Two young OP contemporaries, **Eric Speakman** (33–36) and **Rodney Rodgers** (33–35), were killed within two days of each other in August 1944 while covering the Allied invasion of southern France. One was flying a Supermarine Seafire from HMS *Hunter*, the other an F6 Hellcat from HMS *Emperor*. Both were Mentioned in Despatches posthumously. Today Rodgers is honoured on a plaque unveiled by the Mayor of Villeneuve-les-Beziers in 2012; a street in the Occitanie town is also named after him.

Rodney Rodgers – a street in Villneueve-les-Beziers.

Rodgers was killed by cross-fire from the ground, something that accounted for **George Carline** (24–25) too. In November 1940 as a member of the Second-Strike Force in HMS *Illustrious*, Carline had taken part in a famous FAA action during the British naval attack on the Italian fleet at Taranto. An account of the battle in *Fleet Air Arm*, a book issued during the war by the Admiralty, gives a vivid account of what these pilots faced: "The Swordfish had to fly through this criss-cross of fire. The air stank with incendiary bullets. Flaming onions seemed to go floating past and burn out. One Observer had a vivid impression of a circle of stabbing flame. He wondered how they were going to get out of it. As the pilot dropped his torpedo, he came down so low that his undercarriage touched the surface, sending up an enormous column of water. But they succeeded in pulling out." Half the Italian battlefleet was disabled or sunk. Carline was awarded a DSC "for outstanding courage and skill in a brilliant and wholly successful night attack." He was to drown in December 1941 when his ship, HMS *Audacity*, was torpedoed by a U-boat 500 miles west of Cape Finisterre.

Deaths among RAF pilots and air crew turned out to be second-only to those recorded in the Royal Navy – 44 by 1946. Generally, detail about these losses, and the personalities and characters involved, is limited to unadorned facts in neutrally-written flight logs detailing aircraft flown, the squadron and airfield and operation involved and, sometimes, what happened. A majority of the OPs were in Bomber Command which suffered 40 per cent losses – worse proportionately than the losses recorded in the trenches in the First World War. **Donald Walker** (28–30), to give one example, was a Squadron Leader in 16 Squadron, a reconnaissance unit flying Lysander aircraft, based at RAF Weston Zoyland in Somerset. Much of the squadron's time was spent flying at dawn and dusk over the Atlantic searching for downed aircrew and survivors of the conflict in the Atlantic. How Walker died in June 1941 is not known. The year before, while a member of 613 Squadron, he had been awarded a DFC for his actions during the Dunkirk evacuation when the squadron had dive-bombed German positions and dropped supplies to Allied troops near Calais.

Alexander Cazalet (27–30) of 107 Squadron Bomber Command was one of many serving in Bomber Command to be "lost without trace." He had been piloting a Blenheim aircraft near Oostende in September 1940. **Keith Falconer** (22–24), a member of 214 Squadron who had been awarded a DFC earlier in 1941, was shot down in unexplained circumstances over Germany having finished his tour of duty. He volunteered to fly one more trip to help familiarise a new commanding officer. A popular member of the squadron, Falconer was married to the well-known actress Freda Morello. What happened to another Bomber Command officer is better known. Wing Commander **Philip Lysaght** (28–31) was leading 295 Squadron on varied missions over occupied Europe in Whitley aircraft. In February 1943 the squadron was tasked with destroying three electricity transformers at Distré, near Saumur in western France. Anti-aircraft fire brought down two of the 14 aircraft taking part. "Lysaght led the raid and his Whitley was the first to leave RAF Netheravon at 2030 hours" according to an eyewitness account in a history of 295 Squadron. "The intention was for him to reach Distré 15 minutes ahead of the others and mark the target." As Lysaght was doing this, his plane was hit by anti-aircraft fire, fell into tree tops, crashed and exploded. It was 2315 hours.

A mission codenamed Operation Gardening to lay mines in coastal waters off Brittany in July 1943 led to the death of **John Owen** (22–26) in a Wellington aircraft– one of two aircraft to be shot down on this mission. An account on a specialist website describes how this happened and what took

John Owen.

place next: "He (Owen) was flying very low at 0130 hours. His aircraft received a direct hit. One body was found next morning lying on a rock, three others were found on the beach (near the village of Lochrist). Next day witnesses identified four bodies that the Germans were summarily burying in the sand on the upper beach Przliogan. Still wearing their flying gear, they showed no apparent injuries. Access to the beach (was restricted) by mines and barbed wire but the Germans directed the witnesses to the scene. The bodies were transported by truck to Magneur Cemetery, Lochrist, and placed inside crude coffins made urgently by M. Cleach, a local carpenter. The burial was preceded by a blessing of the bodies on July 8 in the early afternoon. A salvo was fired by a detachment of German soldiers who provided the Wellington crew with full military honours in the presence of many people who had gathered for a final tribute." Today Owen is buried in Le Conquet cemetery, Finisterre – the most westerly town on mainland France.

Similar determination and leadership were displayed by many other young Pangbournians serving in the RAF. **Wilfrid Harris (30–34),** to give one example, was co-piloting a Wellington bomber on a mission over the Pas de Calais region in northern France in December 1940. The history of 214 Squadron states: "His crew and two others were despatched half an hour ahead of the main force as 'pathfinders' by locating and marking the target, Dusseldorf, with incendiaries. The weather was atrocious and his aircraft lost both engines, falling several thousand

Richard Shuttleworth.

feet before they could be started again." All three 'pathfinder' aircraft were lost. Another occurred in the brutal summer of 1941 when the no-holds-barred air war over the UK was at its peak. **Richard Shuttleworth (34–38)** was a 21-year-old on his first operation as the Squadron Leader of 21 Squadron Bomber Command. Shot down while attacking ships in Rotterdam docks, he was still alive if badly injured when a rescue boat arrived at the location. Taken to a hospital in Amsterdam, he died soon after. He had only just married.

Among the RAF fighter pilots, **Alexander Franks (22–26),** a Squadron Leader known as 'Bonzo,' was flying a Spitfire in 610 Squadron when he died in 1940 in the fierce aerial clashes around Dunkirk. Credited with a number of 'kills' against the Luftwaffe in the March-May period, he was shot down at the end of May by a Me-110 and his body washed up on the Dutch coast. Today he is buried in the Sage war cemetery west of Bremen in Germany. Another was 19-year-old **Sam Sibley**

(34–37) – a Pilot Officer in 504 Squadron. He was flying a Hawker Hurricane alone over France in May 1940 when he was downed in air combat. His body was never found.

The oldest OP to die in World War 2 was **Terence Neill (17–19)**, one of the first 36 cadets to enter the NCP in September 1917. He had been a well-known actor in London and New York before the outbreak of war. By July 1943, when he was 42, he was a Flight Lt. in 296 Squadron and was taking part of the invasion of Sicily when he was killed. His role had been to fly an Albermarle transport aircraft from Malta to the invasion area in south east Sicily carrying paratroopers and towing gliders. Few of the pilots had ever undertaken such a perilous mission, at night over 120 miles of sea to an unknown target, before. Making matters worse, on the evening chosen there were high winds and poor visibility. About 40 of the 189 aircraft involved in Operation Fustian, as the attack was called, were lost or shot down before or as they reached Sicily but exactly what became of Neill is unknown.

One of the gliders that Neill towed might have been piloted by **Astley Cooper (25–29)**, known to his colleagues as Alistair – the Adjutant of the Glider Pilot Regiment (GPR) and a close confidant of George Chatterton (see Chapter 7). With Chatterton, he had played a major part in turning large numbers of raw soldiers into glider pilots ready for action in the air and on the ground. When the GPR was deployed from southwest England to North Africa in June-July 1943, he was awarded an AFC for his role "flying gliders to North Africa. This task, which involved flying both in the face of enemy interception and in adverse weather, (and was) performed with a high degree of courage and determination" in the words of the medal Citation. Cooper, in fact, was captain of one of the first gliders being towed. About 140 miles from land and under attack from German Condor aircraft, Cooper pulled the glider off its tow to allow its tug aircraft to engage the Condors. Somehow, he landed his glider on the sea and launched dinghies with two companions; they were promptly machine-gunned by the Condors. Luckily surviving, the three men were rescued after a day by an RN frigate. Cooper immediately volunteered to undertake another glider tow to Morocco, completing the second operation unscathed. "This officer has been responsible for training all glider pilots engaged on this difficult tow and has set an outstanding example of courage, resourcefulness and devotion to duty."

The botched Allied airborne invasion of Sicily followed, and it was during this operation that Cooper was killed when his Halifax tug aircraft was hit by flak at 500 feet and exploded. In attempting to land his damaged glider, Cooper crashed into a river bed at Lentini. He had had no glider night-flying practice, was piloting an American-made Waco glider he had never flown before and was expected to land without lights, in pitch dark alongside a stone wall. In his book *Wings of Pegasus*, Chatterton describes Cooper in some detail. He was, he wrote, "a small dapper figure…by some stroke of fate he had been in my term at Pangbourne and I remembered him well…For courage and guts, there has not been his equal. I never had an officer who showed such complete loyalty and self-sacrifice." Cooper had come to the GPR from the Cheshire Regiment. "He supplied the inspiration that was needed. The story of Alastair Cooper (is) an epic of courage and determination (and) unlimited patience for he was to see officers, less worthy than he, promoted over his head without grumbling or complaining. He served on faithfully and loyally."

Rodney Watson.

As the Allied military focus shifted from sea to land in 1943, so those serving in the Army began to pay a higher price. The evacuation of the British Expeditionary Force from France in 1940 had already taken a significant toll. An early victim was **Rodney Watson (18–20)**, Acting Lt. Colonel in the 1st Bn Royal Scots, who was awarded a posthumous DSO. Watson had received an MC in 1939 for "distinguished services in Palestine" during the Arab Revolt in 1938 when his battalion lost 15 men in hit-and-run skirmishes with Arab nationalists.

During the retreat to Dunkirk, his battalion was "virtually destroyed" according to a regimental history. Initially based around Waterloo in Belgium, it began to withdraw on May 16. By the 21st, it was south of Tournai and fighting all day. On the 26th the battalion received a fateful order to "fight to the last round and last man." A 'battle of annihilation,' in the words of the Royal Scots official history, followed. Watson took over command on May 27 and was killed at 1000 hours that day when the Battalion HQ was set on fire. By May 30 it had effectively ceased to exist "having held up the Germans for three critical days." Only a handful of Royal Scots returned to the UK, nearly 300 became prisoners-of-war and 500 were killed. About 20 soldiers were massacred by the SS at Le Paradis after they had surrendered. Even regular German soldiers were impressed by their opponents – "They fought like lions" said one.

Four years on, and the boot was on the other foot. While D-Day cost 2,700 British dead – given the huge numbers involved in Operation Overlord a low figure – the 11-week campaign that followed proved hugely expensive in lives lost. **Edward Charlton** (26–31), a Major (Acting Lt. Colonel) in the King's Own Yorkshire Light Infantry, had moved to 9 Parachute Battalion, part of the 6th Airborne Division, and dropped into Normandy the night before D-Day as part of a feint to outflank and capture the powerful Merville battery covering Sword beach. The enemy strength at the battery had been under-estimated and too few paratroopers landed in the vicinity. While the battery was captured, Charlton was among many Allied casualties in the fierce fighting that followed next day.

Frederick Livesey (28–31), a Lt. in the Durham Light Infantry, was killed during the advance towards the Falaise Pocket in August 1944, two months after landing in Normandy. **Geoffrey Lance** (27–31), a Lt. Colonel commanding 7th Bn Somerset Light Infantry, who had been awarded a DSO earlier in the war for "gallant and distinguished services" in the Mideast, came through the actual Normandy landings unscathed but was killed in July 1944 when involved in Operation Jupiter – one of several attempts to surround Caen – after his battalion suffered 556 casualties out of a strength of 845 men.

Geoffrey Lance.

An Army death right at the start of the Normandy invasion was that of **Charles Martin** (30–34), a Major (Acting Lt. Colonel) in the 1st Battalion Hampshire Regiment. Thanks to recently discovered material, much is known about Martin. Originally a member of The Dorsetshires, he had been seconded to the 1st Bn Hampshire Regiment. On D-Day the Hampshires were the first British infantry to get ashore and were making their third assault landing in 11 months. On June 6, 1944, "unsupported by tanks, (they) walked into minefields and a whirlw: of shell, mortar and small arms fire" in the words of historian Christopher Jary. A few days before he embarked for France, Martin had written: "It's incredibly lovely here today…it is very hard to realise that the world is in just about as bloody a mess as it can possibly be." Shortly after landing on Gold Beach, A Company had ceased to exist and the Hampshires' CO was severely wounde "Martin was called forward to take comma As he set off across the beach, he was killed sniper." He is buried in the CWGC joint Bi.

German cemetery at Ryes near Arromanches where the first internments took place just two days after June 6.

Earlier in the war Martin, who was commissioned in 1936 and survived the siege of Malta for three years, had been awarded a DSO related to the Allied invasion of Sicily in 1943 when leading the regiment's C Company. His DSO Citation describes his commitment: "On July 10th 1943 at Marzamemi Captain Martin was in command of the company whose task it was to make the initial landing on the battalion sector and secure a bridgehead. The point selected for this landing was on some rocks with a village just in the rear. An enemy pillbox covered the landing place selected and a wall, approximately eight feet high, had to be scaled before the village could be entered and the main beach to the left be cleared of the enemy. Captain Martin handled his company with such skill that surprise was obtained and it was not until the whole company had been led ashore that the alarm was raised. In the ensuing fighting that took place within the village Captain Martin directed operations with great coolness and he himself led the platoon against an enemy pillbox. Having ensured that the village was cleared, Captain Martin reorganised his company and cleared the enemy defences on the main beach from a flank, thus allowing the main landings to take place. Throughout this operation Captain Martin, by his leadership and utter disregard for his personal safety, gave the greatest inspiration to those under his command. It was to a large extent due to his action that the main landings were carried out so rapidly and successfully."

This Citation recounts a second example of Martin's courage: "On the night of July 22nd 1943, just south of Agira, the company commanded by Captain Martin was ordered to make a night attack on an enemy position. The position was an entrenched one on commanding ground and covered by medium machine guns, mortars and light automatics. As the enemy's main position was being approached and after the artillery covering fire had ceased, an enemy machine-gun post opened fire, pinning one of Captain Martin's platoons to the ground. Captain Martin, having observed this, stalked the enemy post himself over a distance of some sixty yards. He shot one member of the machine gun crew and then rushed in, picked a rifle which was lying on the ground and disposed of the remainder of the by using the butt of the rifle." In a letter home afterwards, Martin explained: istol actually behaved very well but in the heat of battle I'd forgotten how llets there were left and got the most awful shock when the thing went he middle of the fracas. Still – all's well that ends well." In his account, Intelligence Officer described how Martin was found at the bottom of a slit trench grappling with the fourth occupant. "When awarded to Captains, DSOs are usually near-misses for a VC," notes Jary.

Henry Durrell.

In the Royal Navy, **Henry Durrell** (26–30), a Lt. Commander serving in the destroyer HMS *Isis*, was killed when his ship struck a mine and sank off the Western sector of the Normandy beaches with the loss of 154 members of the crew. **Douglas Dawson** (18–19), a Lt Commander RNVR, was killed in late-June 1944 supervising landing craft operations on one of the Normandy beaches. And **R.G.D. Keddie** (31–35), "a first-class officer" and commander of the destroyer HMS *Cattistock*, died off the French coast at around 2235 hours on August 29, 1944 when six shells from a German shore battery two miles away hit the bridge of his ship, killing all four men standing there. The destroyer had inadvertently strayed into an enemy convoy escorted by eight E-boats. It was struck by 39 shells before limping back to Portsmouth. Here a near-riot ensued after

R.G.D. Keddie.

dock workers demanded 'blood money' to clean up the vessel. Repairs in Chatham took seven weeks. Keddie's coffin was covered with *Cattistock's* battle ensign which he had earlier ordered flown on D-Day. Both Dick Keddie's brothers, John and Wallace, had been killed in 1941 and 1942 serving in the RAF.

Derick de Stacpoole (32–37), a Major in the Royal Marines, was killed in action late in the war. At the NCP he had been an outstanding rugby player – "as good as the College has seen for many years whatever position (scrum half, fly half or centre three-quarter) he filled" according to *The Log* which praised his "innate modesty." By 1942 he was a Captain in 103 RM Brigade. When 48 RM Commando was formed in March 1944, he volunteered and was among the first to land in Normandy on Juno beach in June, getting ashore through a heavy swell and a vicious tidal stream. In doing so, however, the Commando suffered "severe losses" which grew worse as it pushed inland to capture coastal villages. De Stacpoole was wounded,

Derick de Stacpoole.

re-joining the unit in August in time to take part in fighting around Douzie. In November 48 RM Commando was tasked with liberating Walcheren Island as part of the Battle of the Scheldt to open up a shipping route to Antwerp. Leading Y Troop, de Stacpoole was killed by heavy machine-gun fire before reaching the enemy. A Royal Marine memorial quotes his commanding officer: "He was a gallant, handsome Irish gentleman and a most admirable soldier. We owed much to the standards he had set." De Stacpoole, a son of the 5th Duke de Stacpoole, came from Co. Meath. His brother was killed fighting in Holland on the same day he died.

Four months after de Stacpoole's death **Tom Symes (29–33)**, was fighting in Burma (now Myanamar) as part of "The Forgotten Army." Another professional soldier pre-war, he had volunteered to serve in the Gold Coast Regiment in 1938 and had already seen action in the Abyssinian Campaign against the Italians in

Tom Symes on right.

1941 and in East Africa in 1942. In 1944 his regiment was sent to Burma as the Japanese retreated. Symes took command of the 2nd Bn as Acting Lt Colonel in February. By March 1945 the battalion was part of the third attempt by Commonwealth forces to retake the coastal Arakan region.

A friend and colleague, Major J.W.M. Ridgway, described in a letter what happened next: "Our Brigade was operating more or less independently of the rest of the Division. We had no Line of Communication and were dependent on air supply in absolutely bloody country, all large hills and thick bamboo jungle. It was impossible to build a light plane airstrip. (Our battalions) had fought a very successful battle but our casualties were mounting heavily and we could not get them out which tied us to the ground owing to lack of men to carry the wounded and fight at the same time. On 15th March Brigade HQ was hit by a Jap [sic] heavy mortar bomb. We remained in occupation of various commanding features until 24th March…On the night of the 25/26th we got all the casualties out by moonlight under the Japs' noses." The plan, in the face of determined Japanese fighting, was to pull back the entire Brigade towards the Arakan coast in stages.

Suddenly a new order was issued to pull out in one day. "Tom carried out a perfect withdrawal. His was the last unit to come out ...and didn't reach its (new) positions until well after dark. No slit trenches were dug and everyone was very weary, not only from the heavy going that day but also from the strain and short rations during the previous two or three weeks." Unexpectedly, someone "started a shooting match" with a couple of Japanese 'jitter' parties (patrols designed to get a reaction). "It was during this time that Tom was killed. I gather that one of his officers was wounded and he went either to assist him or to get the Medical Officer to him. One of the Jap parties concentrated near Tom's battalion area must have spotted him moving. He was killed outright. His death left us very stunned." Symes' was buried "in a peaceful shady spot by the side of the road" but after the war the grave could not be found to be moved to a CWGC cemetery. Today he is commemorated in the CWGC Taukkyan War Cemetery in Yangon (Rangoon), Myanmar.

Throughout the war many OPs, such as Symes, died in unusual circumstances and were involved in anything but routine military situations. Two who were at the College together and, before the war broke out, had worked for British Overseas Airways Corporation (BOAC), were killed in February 1942 off the south coast of England. Flying a BOAC Liberator aircraft from Lisbon for RAF Ferry Command, **Humphrey Page (25–29)** was Captain and his First Officer was **Richard Williamson (24–27)**. On board with them were five passengers including the first US airman (Lt. Colonel Townsend Griffiss) to be killed in Europe in the Second World War. A Court of Enquiry established that the Liberator had been shot down by two trigger-happy Polish RAF pilots who failed to identify it as friendly. No publicity was meant to be given to the incident but, despite wartime censorship, the details were revealed in *The Times* six days after it happened.

On the other side of the world **Francis Moore (23–27)** was killed, presumably by occupying Japanese forces, in Sarawak in March 1943. Pre-war a Colonial Service District Officer in a remote part of Sarawak, he seems to have been inserted into the territory as part of an Australian commando unit attempting to set up a radio-listening post on the north of the island. Another OP commemorated in the Sydney war cemetery is **Hilary Cope (40–43)** who lost his life in September 1945 when serving in HMS *Reaper*, an American escort carrier loaned to the RN and part of the British Pacific Fleet. **Douglas Johnston (30–31)** disappeared on a mystery flying mission in southern France in June 1940 "believed killed on active service." **Richard Howard (30–33)**, a New Zealander, was killed in the London Blitz. A plaque in his memory in St. Mary the Virgin church Luccombe, Somerset, reads: "Beloved by many. Death hides but does not divide." **William Hay (36–38)** lost his life in a motor torpedo boat taking part in the St. Nazaire raid in August 1942. **John Blandy (24–28)** died in captivity as a prisoner-of-war held by the Japanese. He had been a trader in the Far East and volunteered to serve in the 4th Battalion Straits Settlements Volunteer Force in Malaya once war broke out in 1939. The Australian **William Hutton (19–21)**, captured by the Japanese during the fall of Singapore, is buried at the terminus in Thailand of the so-called 'Death Railway' linking Siam and Burma. Another OP to die in captivity was **Roy Elliott (36–39)**. He was just 21 and a Sub. Lt in the submarine HMS *Saracen* when the vessel was scuttled after being forced to the surface by Italian destroyers. Most of the crew of 48 were rescued by the Italians. It is not clear what happened to Elliott in captivity but he is buried in the Rome Protestant cemetery.

For almost 70 years after the end of the Second World War 177 OPs were thought to have died in the conflict. In 2016 a letter arrived at the College from the son of **Colin Felton (23–26)** and added one more name to the melancholy list. Felton had lost contact with the school after going into the Merchant Navy with the Orient Company, joining the Army and being posted to India with the East Surrey Regiment. He remained in India throughout the 1930s, serving in at least three regiments before being seconded from the Duke of Wellington's to the Indian Army Corps of Clerks in Rangoon, Burma. By 1942 Felton was a Sub-Conductor when the Japanese invaded in March and the Allied retreat began. He reached Mytkiyana, more than 700 miles north of Rangoon but at the start of May the airfield there was bombed, rendering it useless for further evacuation flights. Felton and thousands of refugees of all backgrounds and races, soldiers and civilians, had no choice but to walk 600 miles east over the most northern passes between Burma and Assam in appalling monsoon conditions. Many perished on the way, including Felton. "My father was picked up by the trackside but died soon after in a Mission hospital in Gauhati of malaria and exhaustion," his son wrote. Having no known grave, Colin Felton is commemorated in the Taukkayan war cemetery outside Rangoon.

Winston Churchill visits Shoreditch in the East End of London in 1940 to inspect bomb damage days after Jack Easton was badly wounded while defusing a bomb in a neighbouring street. (IWM)

Mike Cumberlege (left) on Escampador *anchored under a cliff in Crete 1941, typing a report. (Cumberlege family collection)*

*Mike Cumberlege in London in 1942 with his wife Nancy
and her sister Nora. (Daily Mail)*

Frank Cox, Chief Officer in ss Strathallan, *died in December 1942 when
the ship was sunk by a German submarine in the Mediterranean while
evacuating Allied troops from North Africa. (www.pandosnco.co.uk)*

Major Alistair Cooper of No. 4 Glider Training School in 1942.
(Paul Pariso; Glider Pilot Regt. Society)

Flight Lieutenant Keith Falconer (third left) in 1941 with the crew of the Wellington bomber aircraft T1784, at RAF Stradishall. (IWM)

*Frank Hopkins (seated centre) with some of the aircrew of FAA 830
Squadron in North Africa, 1942. (www.fleetairarmarchive.net)*

*John Mackenzie (seated centre) and the 2nd Bn Lancashire
Fusiliers following the capture of Monte Cassino in 1944.*

A Toronto newspaper features Wing Cdr Royd Fenwick-Wilson and colleagues of 405 Squadron RCAF on its front page in late-1941. (Toronto Globe)

The crew of HMS Splendid *at Christmas 1942 with the submarine's commanding officer Lt Ian McGeoch grasping the front rope. (McGeoch family collection)*

Jack Slaughter (left) returns to Harwich in Sunfish *after sinking three ships in April 1940* ©NMRN

The cramped mess deck in HMS Graph *captained by Peter Marriott. (IWM)*

The minelaying submarine HMS Rorqual *in Malta with Lt Ian Stoop on board. (Stoop family collection)*

Ian Stoop with his HMS Rorqual *CO Lennox
Napier and another officer having been decorated at
Buckingham Palace in early 1943. (Christopher Napier)*

II

MY DREAMS:
TREMENDOUS AS THE SKY[3]

— ⊡ —

W hen Claude Michael Bulstrode Cumberlege's death could no longer be
denied in 1946, one of his war-time colleagues wrote a heartfelt, revealing
testimonial which appeared in an issue of *The Log* of the Nautical College
Pangbourne. It read: "He knew the risks and what the outcome might be if he
were caught, but loved Greece and the Greeks. The months he spent ashore were
wonderful and made anything that might happen later more than worthwhile. I
know of no other case of such varied qualities combined in one person. He was
truly Elizabethan in character – a combination of gaiety and sensitiveness and
poetry with daring and adventurousness and great courage." That anonymous
correspondent almost certainly was Nicholas Hammond who had accompanied
Mike on several of his clandestine missions in Greece and escaped from Crete
with him in 1941. Hammond went on to have an illustrious post-war career as
a professor of Greek history at Cambridge and Bristol universities, headmaster
of Clifton College and prolific author of books and articles on ancient Greece.

Cumberlege had this sort of impact on all who knew him regardless of nationality,
character, intellect, class or skills throughout his life. Aged 39 when he was shot
by the SS in Sachsenhausen concentration camp in early-1945, the varied qualities
others admired in him continued to be recalled decades after his death. Following
the war, Hammond expanded on his views of Mike in a biography of John
Pendlebury, a renowned pre-war archaeologist and, in 1940, the UK vice-consul
on Crete, who was executed as a partisan by the Germans during the invasion of

---

3 from a poem by Michael Cumberlege 'My Dreams'.

the island. Pendlebury was a good friend of Cumberlege's. "Both were men of vigorous speech and independent ideas, with great force of character and abundant humour; and both possessed that clear-headed audacity which undertakes the apparently more dangerous course after a detached study of the advantages and disadvantages. They possessed, too, the simplicity of motive in facing or inviting danger, something much more spontaneous and automatic than the ordinary man's sense of duty, a rare quality which I only met once again during the war."

The facts surrounding the short life of **Mike Cumberlege (19–22)** can be retold briefly, having been the subject of a full-length biography published in 2018. Born in 1905, he was the son of a maverick Royal Navy officer with a low boredom threshold who craved adventure, volunteered for service in the newly-formed Royal Australian Navy without informing his wife, lived apart from his family for seven years during World War 1, retired as a Rear Admiral and began a peripatetic existence on a converted Belgian trawler. As the Second World War began, he was living with a new wife and a young family in southern France. Mike rarely saw him from 1911 into the mid-1920s and always found the relationship frustrating. So he grew up dependent on his own wits and charm and resources, entering the Nautical College in 1919 with a view to a career at sea. After Pangbourne, he served an apprenticeship in the Merchant Navy while remaining in the RNR before, in the late-1920s, deciding to sail for a living. This he did happily and successfully until war broke out in 1939, skippering ocean-going yachts for wealthy Americans in the Baltic and Mediterranean. Marrying in 1936, he made a base for his wife Nancy and son Marcus in Cap d'Antibes in 1938, remaining there until forced to escape to England following the Italian invasion of France in June 1940.

Called up by the Royal Navy at the start of 1940, he held a variety of intelligence-related posts in Marseilles, London and the Cape Verde islands before being seconded to the Special Operations Executive (SOE) Mideast section at the start of 1941. His brief from Admiral John Godfrey, the Director of Naval Intelligence, was clear: to form a para-naval force of small vessels – mostly caiques (traditional fishing boats) of the type found in the eastern Mediterranean – and run covert operations in the Mediterranean and Aegean seas. In this role, over the next two years he undertook numerous dangerous undercover missions in mainland Greece and Crete in small boats, twice trying to blow up the Corinth Canal, before he was captured by the Germans in the Peloponnese in late-April 1943. For the next two years he survived torture and solitary confinement and inhumane deprivation in Mauthausen and Sachsenhausen concentration camps, despite his prisoner-of-war status, before being killed by a shot through the back of the neck in February-

March 1945 only months before the end of the war in Europe. His courage and bravery were recognised by two DSOs as well as the Greek Medal of Honour.

The essence of Mike Cumberlege the hero was that he was both courageous and brave. Courage generally involves a cause and the presence of fear. That certainly applies to him throughout the Second World War. Bravery is perhaps more innate – a characteristic in the face of danger that is often instinctive and spontaneous and does not necessarily require a prior judgement. Again, the record would suggest that Cumberlege fits the definition. His courage was on display on numerous occasions in wartime – on his pre-determined secret forays into occupied Crete, during his escape from Crete after the German invasion when he was wounded, on his second attempt to blow up the Corinth canal and, most obviously, in his stoic endurance of Nazi brutality while a prisoner of war. Yet his bravery was equally apparent. Early in life, while sailing across the Atlantic, he took on a mutinous crew single-handed in an attempt to uphold the owner's orders. In a gale and thunderstorm off Cape Finisterre, he saved the day when a huge topmast sail broke loose and the boat he was helming headed for the rocks. "Fighting like a tiger, he was able to wrap it (the sail) round and about, having been hoisted up to the topmast head in a boatswain's chair," his sceptical father wrote approvingly after the incident. During the war, before he was captured, he nearly died from paratyphoid; only will-power and determination kept him alive.

Hand-in-hand with courage and bravery was Mike's endless resourcefulness. Lacking any real assets of his own, from the day he left school he made the most of what he had. In the 1930s, still unable to afford the sort of boats he craved, he took to skippering ocean-going yachts for their wealthy owners. "In the 1920s a gentleman's son would not have become a yacht's skipper, but these were the 1930s. An attractive Englishman, with a good background, could take on what was normally regarded as a servant's job with increasing ease, particularly when his master was American," wrote a chronicler of one of Mike's boats. Having rented an unfurnished house in Cap d'Antibes, he set about learning carpentry so the family had some furniture. Stranded in the south of France on the outbreak of war in September 1939, he devised a daring plan to retrieve the yacht he had been skippering from its enforced anchorage in increasingly-hostile Venice and Fascist Italy.

Escaping from Marseilles with his wife and young son in a decrepit tramp steamer, he scoured the port for a lifeboat, found one, had it hauled on board and sat up all night at the ship's telephone as the unseaworthy vessel hugged the enemy-occupied coast to Gibraltar. Ordered to lead a "para-naval force" for SOE, he arrived in Egypt to discover it consisted of just one troublesome vessel. He promptly set about unearthing others by fair means or foul; this was wartime. One of his finds, the tiny *Escampador*, was fitted out for its new role to his personally-supervised specifications. It never let him down. The sea was his life, he understood it like the back of his hand and he never under-estimated it. Ahead of his second operation to block the Corinth Canal, he even set out the precise design requirements for a 45lb mine, visiting the RN's Mining School to see his instructions were followed and calculating to within a few pounds the exact weight of the equipment that his team would need to be flown from England. Others, not for the first or last time, let him down.

Cumberlege was, as the anonymous testimonial indicated, a complex mixture of the practical and romantic. People in every walk of life liked him – from men like John Godfrey, to the Czech steward on one of his yachts, Jan Kotrba, who followed him to Sachsenhausen and execution. He had a great gift for friendship, was prone to inordinate enthusiasms such as his love of the opera singer Enrico Caruso, and always saw life in black-and-white terms – a tendency that got him into trouble more than once. He could be excruciatingly direct to those he did not respect such as "the fine array of utterly useless and brainless ullages (dregs)" who, he claimed, were living in Antibes at the end of 1938. "Nobody, naturally, can understand why Nan (his wife) married me for I have a habit of being shockingly rude to people I don't like," he admitted in a letter.

His boredom threshold, like that of his father, was low. Once, in Croatia just before war began in 1939, he got into a damaging and pointless fist-fight with locals in a restaurant over their treatment of a woman he had never met. It was only resolved by his crew removing him unconscious from the scene as fast as possible. On another occasion, during an interminable journey by plane from Egypt to England via stopovers in West Africa, he took aim at his travel companions – two elderly brigadiers "incredibly British and blimpish and boring." In Cairo and Haifa, he deliberately absented himself from "his" military or naval Mess in favour of more rounded, congenial and cosmopolitan company whenever he could.

Two other Cumberlege characteristics stand out – his leadership qualities; and his magpie-like cultural acquisitiveness. Some people, it is said, are born leaders, some become leaders and some never are 'leadership material.' Mike was a born leader.

Mike Cumberlege in Croatia, 1939.

This first became apparent when he formed and led a multi-national crew on his breakthrough skippering job on *Jolie Brise*, a gaff-rigged cutter that won the Fastnet Race in 1929 and 1930 and was the last boat to carry Royal Mail under sail. Converted by Cumberlege for its new American owner into a comfortable cruising yacht able to carry a dozen passengers, *Jolie Brise* was to sail over 7,000 miles most summers in every sort of weather. To do this, and to keep everyone happy, required a well-trained crew as well as a skilled, inclusive skipper. Mike passed the test.

In *Landfall*, the graceful and expensive yacht which he skippered for the American Paine family for three years to the outbreak of war, the core crew of five men – from Czechoslovakia, Greece, Croatia and France (Brittany) – proved to be intensely loyal, as well as efficient and motivated, and never let him down. In return, he treated them fairly. It was the same story on his forays into German-occupied Crete where his accomplices were mostly Cretans along with his old sailing friend, the Ulsterman John Campbell. And the team he took with him on the ill-fated Operation Locksmith, all of whom were murdered with him in Sachsenhausen, remained staunch to the end by all accounts. Leadership is often a hard-to-define quality. Mike certainly took charge, gave clear instructions, knew what he was doing and planned in meticulous detail. He was charismatic and good-looking, which helps. He could be headstrong, yet he did take advice when necessary. Self-sufficient by nature and upbringing, marriage softened some of his individualistic edges and, throughout his life, he was popular and gregarious among a wide circle.

Mike Cumberlege also was a cultural polymath. In his thirties, his love of Greece and all things Greek assumed a near-obsessional character. If he was close to anything of cultural or historical interest on his sailing trips, he would make a detour to see it, once visiting Cintra "to spend hours in the lovely places where Vasco de Gama, Prince Henry and Juana the Loca rest in peace" as he put it in a letter. Right before Operation Locksmith he spent three days hiking from Haifa to see the Krak des Chevaliers crusader castle on the Lebanese-Syrian border. He read widely; to kill time before Operation Locksmith he learned by heart all 30 verses of his favourite poem *The Loss of Eurydice* by Gerald Manley Hopkins. He consumed classical music and opera avidly. From an early age Mike was a keen photographer, even during huge storms at sea and in wartime on dangerous missions. On his visits to Greek islands, he collected wild flowers and pressed them in books. He had a gift for unlikely friendships; while based in Alexandria one of his close friends was the wealthy Jewish art collector Georges de Menasce. Another was the taciturn owner of *Landfall*, the Boston banker Richie Paine. A third was the British naval attaché and intelligence officer in Stockholm Henry Denham.

In the 1930s, to amuse himself, he began to write poetry, some of which is reproduced in his biography *The Extraordinary Life of Mike Cumberlege SOE*. All his life, from early days at Pangbourne, he wrote prose vividly and fluently. A description of Marseilles in 1940 gives a taste: "*Colourful uniforms and colourful soldiers inside of them – great snaggled-toothed Senegalese, little yellow Annamites, Tonkinoise, Zuoves, Algerians and Moroccans, not to mention British Tommies and sailors of all sorts, Polish Colonels and Czech Generals. Heaven knows what they all are. Binding it all together (is) the good old honest Poilu (French infantryman) with his pack and his naily boots and his pipe and brown burnt face. What a grand people to be fighting with and playing with!*"

That June he showed that he might have been a good war reporter when witnessing an Italian air attack on the city: "*At eleven o'clock I was standing in my window looking over Marseilles, for I had a very good view, and I heard a sinister droning in the sky. I called to Nan (his wife) and said 'Listen, there are bombers somewhere and they are somewhere right over us and the sirens haven't sounded. The noise of the bombers became quite loud and then suddenly the sirens blasted out and Marseilles became like a brown partridge with her chicks when the shadow of a hawk darkens the sun. Everything came to a stop, the trams, the cars. Doors opened above and below, and closed and people hurried past in the stairs. The streets all became very still, a few people running, popping into cellars. And then silence. The shrieking sirens ran down and the silence was all complete. And Marseilles lay there, as quiet as quiet, dreaming in the sun with fleecy clouds overhead. And all the time the loud and angrier growl of aeroplane motors. Nan and I stood in our window and searched the sky but could see nothing – nothing but a summer's morning and a clock ticking and, somewhere very immediately overhead, the sinister hum of engines.*

Suddenly, quick as a flash, bright as a bullet, past on the wind screaming through a white cloud, came the first plane, shining in the sun like an archangel, tilted almost vertically to the ground – a German aeroplane with enemies in it, cool and calculating, people to kill, men who had come across France from a German flying field, and almost on top of the first, a second, and after the second a third, and after the third a fourth and after the fourth a fifth. The first one went whistling past, the wire struts screaming in the wind, followed by the second, the third. Behind a row of houses immediately next to us they'd come, they'd gone. Almost before we could formulate the thought there was the most terrific explosion. Both of us were thrown bodily back into the room. We beat it down the stairs. My knees were knocking together, so were Nan's and nothing we could do would prevent it, although neither of us was frightened. Then it was all over – not a gun was fired, not a single French chaser plane took to the sky. The Commandant in charge had given them Sunday leave because they had been up the night before. The guns weren't manned because someone had given an order. The Commandant was shot the next day. So were one or two others. But it didn't prevent two fine ships, one full of munitions, from being sunk."

In life, though, it is often the controversies rather than the virtues that define the memory and make or break the reputation of an individual. Six episodes in Mike's life tend to underline this axiom. The first, hardly unique to him, centred on his consistently faulty political antennae in the lead-up to the outbreak of war in Europe. He simply was not politically-minded, never read a newspaper if he could avoid it, and insisted on interpreting the deteriorating situation in Europe through rose-tinted spectacles right up to the start of fighting.

There are many examples, mostly rooted in the expatriate, detached lifestyle he led and his patrons encouraged. A few will suffice. In May 1940, as British troops and ships were being extracted from Norway after the ill-fated Norwegian campaign, he wrote to Richie Paine informing him that "everything seems to be going along quite well, thank you, in our war." Only three weeks before the Dunkirk evacuation he praised British generals for having "the courage to move our troops out of a tight spot." He followed this assessment up by passing on a wild rumour that UK forces were shortly to move to Canada to take over protection of the USA – "if it's true, just in time." Fascism, *per se*, never sickened him until some Hitler brownshirts forced him off a pavement and into a gutter in Hamburg in 1938. But on a cruise in the Adriatic in August 1939, he was to refer to "these German swine, led by a madman." His contempt for the Italian dictator and *poseur* Mussolini was deeper-rooted, and for much of the 1930s he was disillusioned by the British Establishment due to its feebleness, defeatism and deeply-rooted class consciousness. Once war began, he reacted conventionally, feeling patriotic and committed, wanting to "get into the fight" as soon as he could and being dismayed by his intelligence posting to the far-away, somnolent Cape Verde islands.

The second episode, rather improbably, involved the Palestine-based paramilitary Jewish Haganah grouping which in time was to become the core of the Israel Defence Forces. When Cumberlege arrived in Cairo in February 1941 he was informed by his boss that a directive received from Prime Minister Churchill required his nascent para-naval force to make use of the Haganah on sabotage missions. Mike's cousin Cle, who had been seconded from the Army to work with him, introduced him to the first half dozen recruits who were being trained in naval operations. Mike mostly came to respect these men, none of whom were sailors, and ensured that they could do useful work in his first caique *Dolphin II*. Reaching Piraeus, Mike took the boat on a week-long "shake-down" tour of the Dodecanese islands to sort out the crew. As the caique arrived back at Piraeus, the port was devastated in a German air raid but *Dolphin II* luckily survived. A two-week reconnaissance tour of Crete with three of the Haganah members still on board followed. All three were to reach a camp in Tel Aviv via Egypt by the end of May as did the other three.

If Mike was concerned by any of this, he never mentioned it and moved on to his first attempt to destroy the Corinth Canal. Years after, in 1989, one of the Jewish members of the crew, Jacob Agayev, claimed in an interview with *Maariv* newspaper that "the English" wanted to "get rid of us Jews and gave us the most daring operations. It seemed (as if) they could not care particularly if we did not return to the land of the living." Another of the Jewish crew members, Yoel Golomb, who had left *Dolphin II* in Athens, went further in 2001, asserting that throughout the period he was on board, relations with the British officers "were not good. They were aristocratic and regarded us as 'natives.' We did all the work on the ship." Both men claimed that they felt abandoned by Cumberlege and only got back to Palestine thanks to their own ingenuity. Mike, of course, was long dead and unable to respond. But at sea he had one consistent philosophy all his life – the safety of the boat was paramount; all crew were treated equally and fairly. The only thing that mattered to him was competence. Given how touchy Palestinian Jewish-British relations were throughout the war years and after, it could well be that he was less sensitive than he might have been to "My three Jew boys" as he labelled the trio insouciantly on the back of a photo of them that he took on the island of Hydra.

During his own escape from Crete in May 1941 – the most dramatic month of Cumberlege's action-packed life – another incident took place which casts him in a different light. All his ingenuity, doggedness, courage, leadership skills and admiration for the Cretans had been on display after he reached the island at the start of the month. The fight to resist the German invasion proved hopeless – a combination of poor leadership, lack of equipment and any air defence, and shifting loyalties on the ground. Cumberlege and his crew moved around seeking action and helping where they could. But in the end, or so it seemed to the other nine men in the caique that he requisitioned, there was no alternative but to try to cross the Mediterranean and reach the North African coast 400 miles to the south. Mike, to the annoyance of the others, disagreed and asked for a vote, losing it. Insisting on a last scouting trip along a remote coast in case he returned one day to a German-occupied Crete, the boat was spotted by 79 German aircraft flying overhead. After that, even Mike thought it prudent to withdraw only to sail straight into an invading Italian amphibious force (he was navigating with a box compass). Two days on, in the middle of the Mediterranean, the little caique was attacked by a Me-110 fighter-bomber. Mike's close cousin, Cle, and one other crew member were killed and Mike was wounded. The boat was to limp in to Mersa Matruh in Egypt, but remorse for the deaths, and for his own stubborn behaviour in delaying the departure from Crete, overcame Cumberlege and it was months before his despondency lifted and he got back on an even keel.

If Mike had a real Achilles Heel it was probably women, as his wife Nancy knew. At the end of his life, locked away in solitary confinement for nearly two years in a dank cell, it was thoughts of Nancy and his baby son Marcus and his cat Birra that seem to have kept him going. But in the long months of absence caused by war, he strayed. He had always been attractive to women and before he married aged 31 in 1936, had had a string of relationships. His wife, Nancy, was ten years younger than him, pretty and free-spirited and shared his love of the outdoors and sailing. Together, they enjoyed a seemingly carefree pre-war existence dogged only by Mike's lack of money. From the start of their marriage, however, Nancy was wary of Mike's easy charm with other women and quick to spot, and stamp on, competition. The war, with its long separations and poor communications, added to her suspicions.

When Mike moved to Alexandria and rented an "absurdly grandiose" flat that quickly became a hotel for all and sundry passing through the city, and followed this up by sharing it with Elizabeth Gwynne (subsequently the well-known food writer Elizabeth David) without informing Nancy (who learned of the arrangement from gossip in England), she went into overdrive and bombarded Mike with furious letters. Gwynne and her lover Charles Gibson-Cowan had been rescued by Mike on Crete and had stayed with the Cumberleges in Cap d'Antibes. Elizabeth ditched Gibson-Cowan on reaching Egypt, but Mike always had an arms-length attitude towards her. But Elizabeth had a beautiful young friend, the flirtatious Renee Catzeflis, and during the summer of 1941 he pursued her relentlessly. Not until the end of October 1941, when he left Egypt on the first of his perilous sorties into occupied Crete, did the relationship fade. It took months for the scars to heal. But heal they did after he spent half a year in London in the second half of 1942 recovering from paratyphoid and planning his second attempt to blow up the Corinth Canal.

With the considerable advantage of hindsight, this mission, known as Operation Locksmith, was flawed from the outset. Avoidable mistakes, bad luck and over-confidence litter the narrative, some of which can only be ascribed to Cumberlege personally. In the first category are decisions made by others that denied Mike both the equipment he carefully calculated he would need and the group of men that he wanted to go with him. None of the four-man team that landed near Cape Skyli in the Peloponnese spoke Greek despite a specific request by Mike that such a person be included in the party, and Mike had not even met one of them prior to the mission. Intelligence on the ground near the canal proved erroneous with the local Arvanite (Hellenised Albanian) population turning out to be German sympathisers. The magnetic mines used to destroy the canal failed to go off, most probably because they floated rather than sinking to the bottom of the waterway. Still, at this point, escape by caique was possible given Mike's sailing skills. Yet he decided to stay in the area and request new supplies from Cairo for another attempt on the canal even after it became apparent that locals knew that a "sabotage group" was somewhere in the vicinity. And throughout the Operation Mike showed an almost reckless disregard for security by signalling Cairo frequently and at length.

None of this chapter of accidents – part self-induced, part not – should detract from the daring, heroism and tenacity of the Locksmith team – Mike Cumberlege, Jumbo Steele who had accompanied Mike on his earlier raids into Crete, Jan Kotrba from *Landfall,* and the radio operator Thomas Handley – in infiltrating behind enemy lines, carrying out a sabotage mission and evading capture for more than three months. "In an age of easy living, where we are seldom asked to choose between ourselves and the greater good, they should be seen as an inspiration to us all," reflected Paddy Ashdown, the former leader of the Liberal Democrat party and member of the Royal Marines Special Boat Squadron, in another context. Even at the time, based on the few messages Cumberlege was able to smuggle out of captivity, he realised that avoidable mistakes had been made. The dividing line between self-confidence and over-confidence is very thin. On this occasion, perhaps, it blurred and snapped.

Finally, there is Cumberlege's period in captivity. From the moment of their capture (in uniform) the Locksmith group were shown no mercy. In theory, following Hitler's infamous *Kommandobefehl* (Commando Order) of October 1942 they should have been shot on the spot despite being in uniform. That they were not probably was due to a show trial the Nazis were preparing in Berlin in 1943 of "saboteurs." To qualify to take part, the Germans needed the members of the team, and especially its commander, to confess that they had been on a sabotage mission. Yet behind-the-line raids such as Operation Locksmith were always considered

legitimate acts of war by the Allies. In Mauthausen extermination camp in Austria
– Cumberlege's first destination – he was tortured for weeks on end; after the war
Nancy received a letter from a woman who had acted as translator during these
sessions and was begging forgiveness. In the end, Mike seems to have agreed that
he was a British agent according to testimony given in 1945 by a fellow inmate in
Sachsenhausen, Mike's second prison, who survived the war. Wing Commander
Harry 'Wings' Day was a five-time escaper from various camps and the only
British prisoner-of-war to be decorated with the DSO and there is no reason to
doubt his account since he managed to correspond with Mike by passing notes
through an intermediary.

Subsequently, Mike endured nearly two years of degrading, humiliating
solitary confinement, fed a diet of wurzels (root vegetables used for cattle fodder),
denied the most basic necessities of life or any of the so-called "privileges" such
as reading material, Red Cross parcels or letters from home accorded to most
Allied prisoners-of-war. By every account, his spirit was undimmed. For some
time, the man in the next cell to him in Sachsenhausen was the Ukrainian
nationalist leader Taras Bulba-Borovets and the pair communicated using
Morse signs tapped on the cell walls. In a memoir published in 1981, the year
he died in Canada, Bulba-Borovets had this to say about Cumberlege: "He was
an extremely good companion in distress. Always cheerful, occupied with new
ideas, very friendly, inventive, honest, modest, steady and resistant to all prison
torments and surprises." Day, too, recalled Mike fondly in a letter he wrote to
Nancy in 1945: "I have the most intense admiration for the indefatigable spirit of
your husband under the most severe mental and very trying physical conditions.
Although the Germans offered to give him more food if he would do some work
for them, he refused. I think, with the help of a little imagination, you can really
appreciate what this refusal meant."

Near the end of *The Extraordinary Life of Mike Cumberlege SOE,* the biography
which I wrote, there is a paragraph that seems apt in the context of this book:
"Mike was a hero of his time – charismatic, imaginative, resourceful, deeply
interested in other cultures and people, anything but a Little Englander. He did
what he saw as his duty and betrayed no one. Those who betrayed him would, in
Nancy's opinion, have been forgiven by him. The sea, the wind, the stars, the tides,
the sails on his boats, the freedom that sailing offered and the way of life it gave
him and Nancy, framed his adult years. So did his great courage and drive and flair
and determination in the face of overwhelming odds. His love of literature and
poetry grew with age and sustained him in his darkest hours. Others admired him

almost without exception and he proved to be a born leader of men whether they were British, Jewish, Arab, Irish, Greek, French, Serbian, Croat or Czechoslovak. He wore his heart on his sleeve, never forgetting the painful death of his cousin or others who fell in battle alongside him. He was human in many ways – never a machine – with a low boredom threshold, little time for those he regarded as fools, often outspoken, poking fun at the pompous and only occasionally diplomatic. War suited his can-do, egalitarian, sometimes belligerent temperament but so did peace with the many opportunities it offered to his adventurous, questing, culturally-acquisitive and more sensitive nature."

One day in 1971 the celebrated writer and traveller Patrick Leigh Fermor, a companion-in-arms of Cumberlege's in Crete, was at a dinner party in Lima in Peru sitting next to "a character that might have stepped out of (Anthony) Powell's novels – an Englishwoman married to a Peruvian and bearing the impressive moniker of Dona Diana de Dibos," he recalled in his subsequent book *Three Letters from the Andes*. "Suddenly I realized who she was: the sister of Mike Cumberlege, that amazing buccaneerish figure." The pair "fell into each other's arms" joyfully remembering a man they both admired and missed greatly even though he had been dead for more than a quarter of a century. In his short life Michael Cumberlege made a lasting and positive impression on all who knew him. As Plato put it in quite another context: "You used to shine, as the morning star among the rising dawns. And now – in death – you shine as the evening star among the shades."

12

THE SPORTING LIFE

— ◉ —

A picture on the front page of the Spring 1927 issue of *The Log* of The Nautical College captures the essence of sporting heroes. Captioned 'Half Term,' it shows an Old Pangbournian who had recently become the youngest player ever to represent England at rugby union, sitting on the steps of a sports pavilion at Iffley Road, Oxford University, surrounded by 30 admiring teenagers, all proudly wearing naval uniforms.

In the past century Pangbourne College, in its various guises, has produced a host of such individuals – heroes both at a small school, with limited sporting facilities set high on a hill above the Thames Valley, and to the wider British and occasionally international community. Placed alongside stories of wartime courage and bravery, such high achievers may seem out of place in a book of this sort. But as Dr. Angie Hobbs, Professor of the Public Understanding of Philosophy at Sheffield University, has written, "Sports heroes act as a replacement for war heroes in time of peace. Sporting achievements provide hope, inspiration and a sense of national identity for a society. If 'heroism' is doing something of outstanding benefit to one's society which most people would find impossible to perform, certain top athletes meet those criteria." She added: "Some argue that this is too casual a use of the term. A sports person cannot be a hero on the same scale as a D-Day veteran. Yet a community's longing for heroes to cheer, motivate and unite will still continue in peacetime. The people a culture selects as its 'heroes' reflect that culture's values, needs and desires."

That youthful rugby international was **H.C.C. Laird (22–25)**, still the youngest player to represent England at rugby union. Joining Harlequins RFC from the College, Colin Laird got into the club's first team when he was 17, making his international debut the next season. His first cap for England was won at the age of

171

18 years and 124 days on January 5, 1927 when he made his debut at fly-half in an 11-9 victory over Wales before 50,000 spectators at Twickenham. Laird went on to gain ten England caps over the next two seasons, scoring five tries, being a member of the 1928 Grand Slam side and losing only twice before a bad injury cut short his career at the top. One of the popular Wills cigarette cards of the time describes him as "a strong, bustling stand-off half...thick-set and powerful. He is a determined runner, and opposing fly-halves can testify to the certainty of his tackling."

At the NCP, as a small 16-year-old weighing less than 11 stone and standing only 5ft 7in tall, Laird had been regarded as one of the best players the young school had ever had. In a review of a fine 1st XV season in 1924, *The Log* noted of him: "His hands were exceptionally good, he was very quick into his stride, and a most determined runner. His tackling was always effective; even though he sometimes showed a tendency to go high, he very rarely failed to bring his man down. He was very successful in actual try-getting – he scored at least once in every match but one – but there was never a suspicion of selfishness about his play, and much of the success of the three-quarter line was due to his assiduous and well-judged feeding. A very powerful and accurate kick, especially with his left foot. Most important of all, he possesses real personality – an invaluable quality in a fly-half." It was a prescient judgement.

Laird had hoped to go into the Royal Navy after the NCP and, in 1925, passed his Admiralty interview board. But a weakness in Mathematics and Science meant that he failed the qualifying examination – "He has no aptitude for this subject" went a dismissive note on his report penned by the rather dour and humourless Director of Studies, C.W. Jude. Armed with a glowing testimonial to his sporting and leadership prowess (he was Captain of the Cricket and Hockey teams and Vice-Captain of Rugby) from the kindlier, more balanced Captain Superintendent, Commander Tracy, Laird instead gravitated into the fast-growing advertising sector and, as was usual at the time, played amateur rugby at weekends. When war broke out in 1939, he joined the RNVR and saw active service in the Atlantic and Pacific, ending up as Assistant Director of the Naval Information Department with the rank of Commander. After the war, he returned to civilian life and in 1963 was working in the advertising department of Granada TV in London. Eight years on, aged only 63, he died prematurely.

Luck and timing undoubtedly play a part in the creation of sporting heroes but so does hard work, a self-centred compulsion to be the best, certain physical attributes, sensible career choices and the kind of innate flair that sets the great apart from the merely good. Through its heroes, sport becomes "the clearest window into human excellence" the writer Alan Tyers has claimed, "because it is more accessible for most people to see why (a footballer like) Pelé is great than it is with a scientist such as Einstein." **Rex Willis (38–42)**, undoubtedly the finest rugby player produced by the College, 21 times a Welsh international and three times a British Lions player, might well have agreed. Like so many of his generation, he was a free spirit who played hard

Rex Willis.

and lived hard. "He was posh, drove fast cars and had long hair and looked an unlikely scrum half," reminisced his fly-half partner for Cardiff RFC and Wales (on 15 occasions), the great Cliff Morgan. "But he also had big shoulders, a strong frame and was prepared to defend you against all opposition." That included fierce local rivals like Neath. "Some of my greatest mates in international rugby were men on the Neath team," Willis once recalled. "But the prospect of them coming through the line-out on their home pitch to flatten you in mid-winter didn't exactly make you want to jump out of bed on a Saturday morning. I particularly remember having to get out of our snowbound team bus to push it up the hill from Culverhouse Cross and getting to the Gnoll (Neath's ground) just in time for another mauling."

Such self-deprecating memories masked a notably strong character who was, in the words of the official history of Cardiff RFC, "the personification of courage." Leaving the NCP in the middle of wartime, Willis joined the Royal Navy and on D-Day commanded a landing craft that conveyed five Sherman tanks and sundry infantry personnel, under fire, to the beaches of Normandy. On being demobilised, he returned to south Wales and entered the family business which at the time consisted of ownership and management of cinemas and theatres. Joining a local rugby club, he was spotted by Cardiff at a time when the club was searching for a replacement for its legendary scrum half Haydn Tanner. Willis progressed so quickly that he got into the Welsh team in 1950 without playing a trial game, excelled on his debut before a large crowd at Twickenham and was ever-present in a season which saw Wales win its first Grand Slam since 1911. On the back of these performances, he was chosen to tour the Antipodes with the 1950 British Lions as third choice scrum half. Selected for the fourth Test against New Zealand, he kept his place for the two Tests in Australia. Typical of the man, he made time in Wellington to board a ship in the harbour to have the "odd noggin" with a school friend, **Graham Bevis (39–43)**. In 1954 he captained the Barbarian XV against the touring All Blacks and remained an automatic Welsh selection until 1956 (captaining the side in 1955). On one occasion he played against Scotland with a broken jaw, before retiring from the first-class game in 1959.

On Willis's death in 2000 an obituary noted: "It was a tribute to Rex's great skill and courage that today he is ranked alongside Tanner, Gareth Edwards and Terry Holmes as the greatest wearers of the coveted Welsh No. 9 jersey." Another obituary recalled his "generosity and flamboyant personality," while a long-time friend and team mate for Cardiff, Wales and the Lions, the centre three-quarter Jack Matthews, remarked: "You could always rely on Rex to take the punishment and never send out hospital passes. We got the headlines; he got the bruises." Most of the time, Rex Willis never took life too seriously. Off the field in the south Wales region, he was a successful and big-hearted entrepreneur and was always regarded by others as someone who cut a dash. Once, arriving in London prior to the Lions' departure for New Zealand, he was informed by a team mate that he had too little luggage for what was a long tour. Undaunted, he raced into the West End and returned to the team hotel replete with piles of shopping "and the very best luggage to carry it in." Somehow, it was typical of the style of the man.

The College's third rugby international, **Daryl Marfo (07–09)**, had what the BBC once termed "a moving climb" from the foothills of the game up to Test rugby – and an equally moving descent in a mercurial ten-year career as a prop forward. His parents separated when he was six and Marfo grew up on a forbidding, gang-plagued tower block council estate in Pimlico, west London. In the holidays, he was sent to Scotland to stay for weeks at a time with his mother's family. Spotted playing pick-up park rugby, he joined Harlequins RFC as a teenager and arrived at Pangbourne on a sports scholarship as a 16-year-old. Over the next two years, he rose to become the first mixed race Chief of the College – an immensely popular leader who earned a standing ovation on Founders' Day 2009.

An up-and-down, peripatetic professional rugby career followed. By the summer of 2017 he was bankrupt and jobless. A chance arose to join Edinburgh Rugby on a one-year deal as fifth-choice prop in the squad. He grabbed it with both hands. By that October, he had leap-frogged into the Scottish XV and played three Tests, turning in an "outstanding" performance against the all-conquering New Zealand All Blacks. Early in 2018, a repetitive back injury flared up and he was never the same player again. But he had reached the top. As he put it himself on his international selection: "When I was told that I had been included in the Scottish squad, it was happiness, pure happiness. The first thing I thought of was how proud I was going to be to be able to tell my mum from Ayr. Then I thought about all the times I'd trained in the local park by myself with my stopwatch, all the times I'd done my fitness drills on my own, all the years of waiting for a chance and it never really coming. It's been a long road for me, mentally and physically. When I got the call, it was just a huge feeling of satisfaction that I'd stuck at it."

Not surprisingly, the sea has always played a central part in Pangbourne life and a number of outstanding yachtsmen have emerged from the College. Four of them are known to have died pursuing their dreams. The first of this quartet was **Peter Parnell (36–41)**, who had been Mentioned in Despatches serving in the minesweeper HMS *Poole* in 1944, and was lost at sea in 1950 when sailing a small yawl (two-masted sailing boat) home from Australia in February. He had left Lorne in Victoria with the intention of calling at King Island but was not heard of again. The second, **Rob James (60–64)**, began sailing in a 'Heron' dinghy from West Wittering before joining the NCP but only occasionally made the College sailing team. After Pangbourne he spent three years in the Merchant Navy with P&O before leaving to read for a Maths & Computer Science degree at Reading University. It was here that he was bitten by the sailing 'bug.'

Rob and Naomi James.

Determined to be involved in the first Whitbread Round The World race in 1973, he wrote to every skipper taking part pleading for a crew berth. He got one – and a demand for £3,000 for a slot on *Second Life*. His father lent him the money. The eight months he spent on this 71ft ocean racer changed his life. Sailing became an all-consuming passion for the next decade before his death at the age of 36 after a freak accident off the South Devon coast in 1983.

During the Whitbread race, James met Chay Blyth, the transatlantic rower, who by then had moved into ocean sailing and was planning to start a yacht charter business. James became a charter skipper, cruising and racing in trimarans such *GB II* and *British Steel* and becoming, with Robin Knox-Johnston and Blyth himself, one of the world's top marathon race yacht skippers. From 1976 he took part in a succession of global challenges such as the Round Britain Race, the Transatlantic Race, the Atlantic Triangle Race (St. Malo>Cape Town> Rio de Janeiro>Portsmouth) and successive Whitbread Round the World races, winning some, setting many records and becoming widely known in the sailing fraternity for his infectious enthusiasm, prudent leadership and outstanding sailing skills. In 1976 he married Naomi. The next year, with just a few months sailing experience behind her, she borrowed one of Blyth's yachts and embarked on a round-the-world solo voyage, completing it in 272 days and becoming the first woman to sail single-handed around the world via Cape Horn. The couple often sailed with, and against, each other and in 1982 joined forces to win the Round Britain Race in a trimaran called *Colt Cars GB*. James's death came as he was sailing this boat from Cowes to Salcombe in March 1983 for an overhaul when he slipped and fell into the sea and could not be saved. "The irony was that, having sailed three times round the world and sailing thousands of miles each year, Rob simply took a step backwards, a rope broke and he lost his life. The rope which broke, and the netting which it supported, were all going to be replaced as part of the forthcoming refit," wrote Nicholas Gray in *Last Voyages*.

Glyn Charles (78–81) was a different sort of yachtsman. His parents never sailed and it was at the College that he discovered his natural affinity with the wind and the water under the tutelage of Michael Atkins. After the College, his progress was meteoric. Within three years of leaving school, penniless and sponsor-less but ultra-determined, he was a member of the British youth sailing squad. By 1985 he was national champion in the single-handed Laser dinghy class, driving around Europe in a beaten-up yellow Ford transit van to take part in international regattas. Soon after, he switched to Solings but twice failed to gain an Olympic place, losing in 1988 and 1992 to his arch rival Lawrie Smith. In 1993 he began offshore racing and got into the GB team for the Admiral's Cup that year – the first of four such appearances. In 1996 he turned the tables on Smith in the two-man Star class, winning selection for the Atlanta Olympic Games. A couple of poor results in the marathon series of eleven races left him disappointed in 11th place.

Charles, a "boyishly handsome" man who was 33 in 1998, was never well off and funded his globe-trotting lifestyle as a 'gun for hire' racing other people's boats. Along the way, he won an enviable reputation as a tactician and helmsman with a well-developed sense of fair play. "He did not have enemies, not least because he was not a political monkey" the Royal Yachting Association's racing manager remarked once. "He was totally honest about his own capabilities, eschewed the mind games of his rivals and was simply a 'good bloke.'" Many noted his rather taut temperament which, it was claimed by some, could let him down. Towards the end of 1998, now back in the Star class, he was in Sydney, scoping out conditions ahead of

Glyn Charles.

the 2000 Olympics. While there he met Rob Kothe, a local entrepreneur who had entered a sleek, state-of-the-art 43-footer for the annual Sydney-Hobart race. At the last moment, after some haggling, Kothe persuaded Charles – who was never keen on ocean racing as he was prone to sea-sickness – to join the crew of *Sword of Orion*. Another OP, **Andrew Roy (61–65)** was also taking part in the race.

A couple of days after Christmas Day 1998, with a fleet of 115 boats underway, a giant storm began to tear down the south coast of New South Wales and into the Bass Strait. Charles was at the wheel an hour after the race began when weather forecasters in Sydney issued a severe storm warning. Next morning, with winds already above 50 knots, Charles and another crewman discussed turning back. That afternoon, with Charles again at the wheel, the decision was taken to make a 180 degree turn and retire. This was achieved, but within 20 minutes an "incredible bang" hit the side of *Sword of Orion*. The boat rolled over, crashed to the bottom of a massive wave, turned upside down but somehow righted itself. But Glyn Charles was overboard, 30 metres upwind, floundering in the huge seas. He attempted to swim but seemed unable to do so, most probably because his legs and ribs had been broken when the boom ripped from its attachments, snapped his safety harness and took him overboard. After five minutes, he disappeared – one of six men to die in the race that year. Only 44 boats – one of them with Roy on board – reached Hobart. Tributes flowed in after Charles's death with an editorial in *The Daily Telegraph* hailing him as "a true sportsman" and *The Guardian* terming him a hero.

That was a term applied, too, to **Andrew 'Bart' Simpson (90–95)** after his death by drowning in May 2013 at the age of 36 while training for the 34th America's Cup races in San Francisco Bay. Simpson's career had many similarities, and some differences, to that of Glyn Charles. Known to one and all as Bart, he began sailing at the age of six. At Pangbourne, he was an integral part of the sailing team for five years – popular, fair-minded, highly respected, intensely competitive. "He never let success go to his head nor lost the common touch," recalled his sailing master, Crispin Read Wilson. Returning to the school several times after he left to lecture and coach aspiring sailors, he became a living hero to the pupils. "He was a huge inspiration to others," the Royal Yachting Association's performance

Andrew Simpson visits Pangbourne.

director said after his death – "a fine role model, humble, lacking any hint of ego and always with a smile on his face for everyone" in the words of an obituary in the *OP Magazine*.

Over the course of a 17-year career sailing professionally, Simpson reached the top of the Laser, Finn and Star classes, won gold and silver medals at successive Olympic Games, became a world champion and twice campaigned in America's Cup challenger boats. In 2009 he was awarded an MBE for his Olympic exploits. During the 1990s he had been one of three 'young musketeers' of British yachting – Ben Ainslie and Iain Percy being the other two – but often seemed destined to be the nearly-man as his rivals were selected for international events ahead of him. In 2007 he teamed up with Percy, a friend and rival from his teenage years, in the Star class, going on to win gold at the 2008 Beijing Games and becoming joint (again with Percy) Yachtsman of the Year. Only a sudden shift of wind robbed the pair of a second gold medal at the London Olympics in 2012 when they led for all but the final one hundred metres of the last race. Bart's tragic end while sailing with the Swedish entry for the America's Cup after the team's catamaran overturned and he was trapped underneath, shocked all who had ever met him.

Unlike those who died pursuing their dreams at sea, **Rodney Pattison (57–61)** lived to tell the tale in his revealing 2019 memoir *Superdocious!* Helming the two-man Flying Dutchman (FD) 20-foot dinghy, he won two gold medals and a silver at successive Olympic Games (1968, 1972, 1976) and was undisputed world champion in the FD class in 1969, 1970 and 1971. No one took this complex, driven character lightly. From his first days at the College in 1957, when he arrived with his own home-built Cadet dinghy, he went his singular way – a largely self-taught, self-funded global superstar in the world of international competitive yachting. Always straight-talking and single-minded – traits which occasionally got him into deep water – many found him hard to understand. An early crewman of his,

Mike Boyce (the future Admiral of the Fleet Baron Boyce), has described his "fastidious attention to detail...not political by nature... compromise is not within his vocabulary... Rodney is one of those people military men describe as 'brilliant in war, bloody awful in peacetime'." But others, such as Ben Ainslie who was to succeed Pattison as the most garlanded British Olympic yachtsman, found him an inspiration – "modest and understated but with a certain aura about him." When he was

Rodney Pattison.

involved in an ultimately unsuccessful UK Admiral's Cup challenge in the early 1980s, he surprised everyone by turning out to be a good team-player, calculating and conscientious. Always racing to win, "focus and commitment are the two words that best describe him" according to one rival. Or, as another competitor, the yachtsman Hugh Cudmore, put it: "Precision is a major part of his personality …There were a lot of people out to get him."

The son of a Fleet Air Arm World War 2 pilot, Pattisson was destined for the Royal Navy from a young age, and was to serve ten years in the Service, mostly in submarines. At the Nautical College he sailed at every opportunity, learning to handle Firefly dinghies on the fickle, shifting winds of the Thames. In the process he sailed with another future Yachtsman of the Year, **Ewen Southby-Tailyour** (55–59), became Public Schools Firefly champion and Cadet Week winner in 1960 and captained an undefeated team for two years "setting an example of both skill and enthusiasm" as described in *The Log*. In the Royal Navy, the intervention of another OP, **Ian McGeoch** (28–31), the senior officer in the Submarine Service, proved vital in allowing him the time off to prepare properly ahead of his first Olympic Games triumph. His easy victory in Acapulco in 1968 had wide repercussions including a raft of rule changes and moves to "professionalise" race management. Ahead of the 1972 Olympics, he realised that he had to resign from the Navy if he was to win a second gold medal.

Pattisson went on sailing competitively well into the 1980s, taking part in many of the blue-ribband offshore races such as the Sydney-Hobart classic, the Fastnet Race, the One-Ton Cup and the original Admiral's Cup while earning a living by importing boats from Spain. Aged 50, he married for the first time. "Boats had always taken precedence over girlfriends," Jane has written. "It took Rodney eight years to get around to sort of proposing." Not surprisingly, it is those who have sailed with and against Pattisson who have the most illuminating things to say about him. One of his Olympic crewman, Chris Davies has remarked: "The angrier he became, the better his performance and he never let any situation get the better of him." Another, fellow submariner Andrew Cooper, has said that Pattisson's "great strength is his ability to focus exclusively on boat speed, something he can do for hours on end. When he gets the bit between his teeth, he bubbles like a volcano and is at his very best." A third, Julian Brooke-Houghton, has described a man "dedicated to sailing for every waking moment…meticulous to the point of distraction, very, very talented (someone who) channels his obsession into making small incremental gains." Always prepared to take on authority, he campaigned for 33 years to get an MBE for Chris Davies and in 2012 took on UK sporting authorities when they barred him from running with the Olympic torch in Dorset prior to the London Games. In his 70s, he began to speak out about the prevalence of cheating in his sport and the way yacht clubs were milking events for their own good. Not one for a quiet life!

Rowing in heavy whaler boats on the river Thames was part of the Nautical College's life from its early days. Rowing in "fine boats" dates from 1955. Subsequently, Pangbourne has won the prestigious Princess Elizabeth Challenge Cup for schools at Henley four times, in the process producing a plethora of male and female youth internationals and several senior internationals. One of these has claims to be the unluckiest well-known OP sportsman – the multiple world championship medal winner (two golds and two silvers), **Toby Garbett (90–95)**, who was forced out of the coxless fours boat for the Athens Olympics in 2004 at the last moment. Selected to row as one of a coxless pair, he was knocked out of the main event by the narrowest of margins before coming first in a nail-biting 'B' final.

In contrast, **Richard Hamilton (87–92)** was a Junior World Champion in the coxless fours in 1991, stroked the College VIII to its third PE Cup win at Henley in 1992, rowed for GB for eight years and stroked the GB VIII at the 1996 Atlanta Olympics before becoming a successful international rowing coach. Exceptional power and aggression, rather than technique, underpinned Hamilton's ascent, but allied to that was a very big heart. Today he runs a large dairy operation in north east Victoria in Australia and sometimes turns back the clock to coach children in the rural rowing community. He credits his time at Pangbourne in various ways for his stellar achievements. "For me, Pangbourne not only taught leadership but, more importantly, how to be part of a team. It taught me to be aggressive and to set a goal and go all out to achieve that goal. And also, the ability to keep getting back up once you have been knocked down and to never give up… The College, through its ability to create leaders, creates very driven, motivated and loyal young men and women who, no matter what the odds, will go on and succeed." In Hamilton's case, the goals were always clear: "For one day in my life I wanted to be the best in the world. I achieved that in 1991. Then I wanted to go to the Olympics and experience the highest level of training and competition in the world. I wanted to test myself against the best and see how I reacted under pressure. Only by putting yourself in competitive situations do you really find out who you are. All this drove me on."

This compulsive, almost obsessive, determination to succeed has resonated with OPs most obviously in endurance activities such as long-distance sailing and ocean rowing, where a number of exceptional performances have been recorded. The most recent was by **George Oliver (94–99)**. He began his heroics as a 16-year-old when he became the youngest person ever selected for a British Schools expedition to the Himalayas. After reaching GB-level youth training camps as a rower in IVs and VIIIs, in 2007 he joined a charity-driven attempt to break the record for a row across the Atlantic. A first effort from the Canary Islands to Barbados failed when one of the six-man crew was injured. After a three-week hiatus, another attempt was launched with only five men aboard. In a 29ft boat called *Oyster Shack* made of carbon fibre and weighing 200 kg, the crew left La Gomera just before Christmas Day 2007.

At first, rowing for 15 hours a day to compensate for the absent oarsman, the crew made excellent progress. Things began to go wrong when the rudder broke and blisters became a problem. At the half way mark *Oyster Shack* was ahead of schedule to break the record achieved in 1992 by a 12-man French Foreign Legion team of 35 days, 8 hours and 30 minutes. Soon after power was lost, meaning no steering lights or radar, sea conditions worsened, the last water-maker broke down and food began to run out. The crew battled on and one day the boat arrived at Nelson's Dockyard in Antigua. The crossing had taken 37 days, 5 hours and 53 minutes – slower than the Foreign Legion team. But as the first five-man crew ever to row the Atlantic *Oyster Shack* chalked up a raft of other records. "I ended up losing two and a half stone and was extremely dehydrated as well as having a very sore bum and scalds on my arm from boiling water," George Oliver messaged the College. "But we didn't have any fallouts at all on board and landed a very happy crew."

Oliver had been preceded across the Atlantic by two other OP rowers. At the time of his achievement in 1997, **Peter Lowe (81–86)** was a 29-year-old London-based chartered surveyor who had spent the previous 18 months trying in vain to find the sponsorship and partner to nail down a seat in the 3,000 miles Tenerife-Barbados rowing marathon. Short of money, he had given up when, five days before the race, an opening arose in a 20ft boat called *The Golden Fleece* and an old rowing friend called Daniel Innes asked him to fill it. After an epic effort lasting 61 days, the pair arrived at their destination, coming 10th out of 19 finishers from a starting line-up of 28 boats. Like Oliver, Lowe lost over 30 lbs in weight. He endured sea-sickness, squalls, and a painful injury as well as "appalling" emotional highs and lows. He had neither trained in the boat nor seen it before the race. Yet "this was the chance of a lifetime, the biggest challenge of my life, the biggest challenge ever," he felt. Rowing hour-long shifts round-the-clock, the maximum sleep either of the pair got was 75 minutes. The uncertainty and loneliness spurred them on. "It was always dangerous – you never knew what was going to happen next," Lowe admitted once it was all over. Passing the finishing line early one morning "was the best feeling I ever had. I was elated, absolutely elated." Withing three weeks, Peter Lowe was back at his desk in an office in London's West End.

After this epic effort, Lowe gave many talks and "even bearded John Ridgway in his lair at Ardmore." This was **John Ridgway (51–55)**. At the time a Captain in the Parachute Regiment, Ridgway and Sergeant Chay Blyth in 1966 became the first

John Ridgway.

pair to row the North Atlantic in the 20th century, taking 92 days to complete the feat. The two men had no shelter on the boat, no communications at all, and two other competitors died. When he reached Aran Island off the west coast of Ireland in a gale, Ridgway sat by the boat "to sort things out… Why had I survived?" he wondered. He decided to make the most of his life – to try everything, not just boating. It was the start of a hazardous existence of extreme adventuring and courage and bravery sustained over many years based on three principles: self-reliance; positive thinking; and leaving people and things better than he found them. By the time he hung up his paddle, Ridgway had rowed across the North Atlantic, sailed thrice around the world (once, aged 63, to highlight the plight of albatrosses – see Chapter 15), trekked through the Amazon basin, climbed mountains in Patagonia, kayaked around Cape Horn with his daughter, made half a dozen television films and written 13 well-received books. In tandem, he had run a successful adventure school that he and his wife founded in 1969 on the rugged, inhospitable north west coast of Scotland on the very western rim of Europe. By doing so, he underlined one of his core beliefs: "Life is colourless without physical struggle." Never a boastful man, Ridgway's unique record inevitably attracted worldwide attention even as his instinct was to shun the limelight.

Exactly why he chose such a dangerous and perilous, yet paradoxical, lifestyle is a complicated matter. Early on in a solitary childhood, Ridgway was adopted – "a severe setback (but) a spur for achievement" he has written. He "began to find himself in those early days on the near-empty Thames fly-fishing alone, in my small rowing boat below Windsor." He always wanted "to feel alive" and sought new challenges well into late-middle age. "A convinced rebel against authority," he spent 17 years in uniforms. At the age of 30 he became self-employed and a risk-taker, constantly on the look-out for new opportunities. Initially, his motivation was straightforward – "to get forward, you must first climb out of the trench…I was trying to make my name" he admitted once about his trans-Atlantic row with his Platoon Sergeant. At the time he had no financial backing or even a suitable boat. But he had sailed in small boats from a young age. Blyth, in contrast, had barely seen the sea. Both men had done long-distance canoeing together – and they were young, fit, determined, skilled in survival techniques and undaunted by the elements. Three months after leaving Cape Cod, having survived two hurricanes, 3,000 miles of back-breaking rowing and lack of food and water, the pair stepped ashore rather the wiser. Overnight, they became global media sensations. Both saw an opportunity to make a living.

For Ridgway, this first experience of a severe, non-military endurance test left him with a determination to make a difference to other people's lives as well as to his own. Three years after reaching Aran, he opened his adventure school in Sutherland with his wife Marie Christine. When a Peruvian friend was killed in a terrorist attack on his remote jungle farm, leaving a young child living in poverty, the Ridgway's adopted her as a sister to their daughter Rebecca – "a tricky thing to do, but we felt we had to help her," John informed Scotland's *Daily Record* newspaper in a rare interview when he turned 70. In a note in 2020 he felt that his motivation in life had been "*Joie de Vivre* – the moments of exultation in far-away places, the struggle, competition. Anything but the dreaded 'ennui." Throughout, one of the "rocks of my life" had been his driven, ever-determined housemaster at the Nautical College, the New Zealander D.M. Holland. "It was Don Holland who helped me to understand that leadership is not a popularity contest... And (Don Holland who) helped me realise that from those to whom much is given – a long time before the end of the day – much will be expected, not least from themselves" he has written. And it was a Don Holland quote taken from *Lavington*, a classic of 19th century English literature which, seared into Ridgway's mind, set the tone for the School of Adventure – and defined the parameters of his life: "Follow your calling... Bound along if you can; if not, on hands and knees follow it, perish in it, if needful. But ye need not fear that."

No such inspiration from schooldays buttressed the stellar record of motor cyclist **Mike Hailwood** (**54-56**). His definitive biography, *Mike Hailwood: The Fan's Favourite* by Mick Walker, tiptoes around his time at Pangbourne. "Mike's schooling was not an easy experience although, in retrospect, it served to toughen him up for his future life ... He hated

Mike Hailwood.

Pangbourne as soon as he arrived." At the age of 16 he asked his father if he could leave and (his father; a wealthy garage owner) agreed. Another biography adds: "Michael went to his room, packed and simply got in the car. He didn't look back. The future, whatever it was, would not be cold showers, iron discipline and at least one beating he would remember all his days." As he aged, Hailwood mellowed and acknowledged that the school had bred in him a feeling of independence. He represented the NCP in boxing, winning 13 of his 14 bouts, and was "never fitter in my life." And, most crucially, it was at Pangbourne that his phenomenal will to win emerged and grew.

The statistics of Hailwood's motor cycling career, impressive as they are, do little justice to the man or to his impact. In 22 years at the top from 1957–79 he won 76 Grand Prix races, ten world titles and 14 Isle of Man TT races. He rode everything from a 49cc two-stroke bike to a 1000cc superbike. "A modest, even shy man, never motivated by money or glamour, he shied away from the massive publicity he attracted," according to Walker. This down-to-earth quality brought him immense popularity from fans worldwide who knew him as 'Mike the Bike' and knew that he would never give less than his best. With nothing left to prove on two wheels, he turned to four-wheel racing in a less stellar 50-race career for some of the smaller teams in Formula 1. In 1973 he hit the headlines when he plunged through flames to rescue another driver, an unconscious Clay Regazzoni, from a crumpled, burning car after a four-car pile-up in the South African Grand Prix. When Mike Hailwood got back to the pits after the incident, he said nothing; it was only next morning that his wife Pauline read the newspapers and discovered that he had saved a man's life at the potential cost of his own. "That's the symbol of a brave man, a great man" observed the F1 legend Jackie Stewart who won that race. Hailwood always maintained that his selfless action was 'something anyone would have done.' Few were fooled. The next year his bravery was acknowledged with a George Medal to go with the MBE he had received earlier for his motor cycling exploits.

Mike Hailwood was to die prematurely in 1981, aged 40, two years after he retired from racing, in a "banal" road accident outside Birmingham after a truck made an illegal U-turn on a dual carriageway, killing him and his nine-year old daughter. The truck driver was fined £100. Since his death, Hailwood's popularity has only grown and by the 21st century he had become a "true legend" in Mick Walker's words. "Besides his will to win there was Mike's great ability to ride any bike" often switching capacity sizes and makes at the same meeting and doing as well in wet or dry conditions. Like John Ridgway and others featured in this chapter, he lived for new challenges. An obituary mentioned his "boyish grin, wide as the back of an Isle of Man ferry" and his "marvellous sense of humour and barbed wit, often deployed to deflate paddock poseurs." Motorsport in the 1950s and 1960s was a dangerous "here today, gone tomorrow" game – and Hailwood, ever the party animal, revelled in that devil-may-care ambience; "he was a little bit wild" acknowledged his wife. Yet, after a race he wanted space and time to himself and always hated being recognised away from the racing circuit. What endures today is the memory of his driven committed personality, his racing record and his popularity, not least with rival riders. Buried alongside his daughter in the churchyard of St. Mary Magdalene, Tamworth-in-Arden, the inscription on his gravestone reads: "Too good in life to be forgotten in death." He has not been.

13

THE TROUBLED
POST-WAR WORLD

— ◉ —

After two global wars in little more than a generation, the desire for lasting peace in the world was palpable in 1945 amongst almost all sections of populations, East and West, except for the one that mattered most – that making policy. Within weeks of the war ending in August, British troops were again involved in armed clashes – a pattern that was to be repeated for the next 75 years. Outright war, rebellions, ideologically-driven confrontations, nationalistic uprisings, dissent and terrorism occupied UK, NATO and UN forces with barely a pause through this period. As recently as 2018 an OP serving in the Royal Navy, Hugh Botterill (89–95), was decorated for his work conducting board-and-search operations off the Libyan coast. In only two years, 1968 and 2016, were there no British deaths in military operations. A total of 7,187 UK servicemen died in medal-earning theatres. The worst year was 1951 when 829 men and women lost their lives in three separate conflicts in Malaya, Korea and the Suez Canal. Nor was the UK alone. Similar grim reckonings can be made in countries as diverse as France, USA and Russia/Soviet Union.

Large numbers of Old Pangbournians remained in Allied armed forces in 1945. One, **Campbell Cooke (18–19)**, on being demobilised in late-1945, joined the UK Prison Service. Shortly after, he witnessed the hanging of the traitor William Joyce (Lord Haw Haw) at Wandsworth jail. Others soon found themselves thrown into a no-win, police-type security deployment in Palestine that was to become all-too familiar in the decades ahead. Administered by the UK under a League of Nations mandate dating from 1920, the struggle between Arab and Jew over the future of Palestine ultimately drew in more than 100,000 UK servicemen. Around 750 were killed in the three years to mid-1948 as protests, riots and terrorism escalated. When the last British troops sailed away, it was with a deep sense of relief.

All sorts of demanding responsibilities were involved. **Tom Baillie-Grohman** (30–34), to give one example, was a regular Royal Navy officer who had had a lively Second World War, including commanding the escort destroyer HMS *Whitshed* in actions against German forces and taking part in the Normandy Landings. In 1944 he had been awarded a DSC "for courage and skill" in three times driving off single-handedly nine German E-boats by clever ship handling and quick thinking as they sought to attack an Allied coastal convoy. By 1948 he was King's Harbourmaster at Haifa and was in post during the tense final weeks of the British Mandate. "His sound judgement, restraint and consistent disregard for his own safety under difficult and provoking conditions were important factors in maintaining the essential services of the port at a critical time" ran the Citation for the OBE he was awarded. Baillie-Grohman retired from the RN in 1956 and, no doubt seeking a quieter life, established a vineyard near Godalming in Surrey. The venture was to be cruelly dubbed "TP Barely-Growing such was the state of his vineyard" in a dismissive review in *Wines of Great Britain*.

Four Army officers – **Andrew Hacket-Pain** (17–18), a member of the first term entry to the Nautical College, with the 1/6 Queen's Royal Regiment; **Tony Savory** (32–35) in the Duke of Wellington's Regiment; **Richard Hewitt** (27–31), commanding officer of the 2nd Bn East Yorkshire Regiment (see Chapter 7); and **Gordon Higginbotham** (38–40) of the Sherwood Foresters – all had to carry out controversial and highly dangerous internal security duties as terrorist activity in Palestine worsened. In effect, this meant enforcing curfews, establishing cordons, carrying out house searches, handling riots, and guarding convoys and key installations. Hacket-Pain's obituary in 1987 referred to "numerous near-death situations which, due to his innate modesty, he was reluctant to discuss." He received a military MBE, as did Savory for "gallant and distinguished service." Higginbotham was awarded a Military Cross for "gallantry in action" when commanding a unit consisting of two platoons and two tanks. An extract from the Citation stated: "Had it not been for the prompt, skilful and determined use of this Force, there is no doubt that the I.Z.L (a Zionist paramilitary organisation) would have penetrated deeply into Jaffa."

Several OPs had police roles. **Patrick Bisley** (41–44) served in the Palestine Police Force as a member of the Inspector General's Escort. Bored by lack of action, he volunteered to drive armoured cars when fighting broke out, and had "a very exciting time." In a letter to Pangbourne in 1948 he wrote: "I was ambushed one day and arrived back at the Police Post with a truck that looked more like a pepperpot on wheels than anything else. Luckily no one was seriously hurt, but as a mine was detonated within five feet of the truck it was a long time before I could hear properly. My last job was minesweeping between the Jewish and Arab lines – driving an armoured car along the road first thing each morning and machine-gunning anything that looked as if it might go off." From time to time, he ran into **Ian Ranken** (27–31) who was trying to enforce law and order in the marine section of the police. Another at sea was **J.E. O'Leary** (36–40), a Lt RN, who was Mentioned in Despatches and served in a police patrol vessel intercepting illegal immigrant ships.

More ambiguously, the celebrated Second World War Special Operations Executive officer, **David Smiley** (30–34; see Chapter 8), given the chance to return to active service, took part in Operation Embarrass. This was a desperate plot by the Atlee government, run by MI6 and the Foreign Office, to thwart illegal Jewish emigration to Palestine. With three companions, Smiley sailed around Italian ports in 1947–48 in a yacht called *Valfrere*. Its cover story was that the group was dealing in contraband cigarettes. In truth, it was looking for empty cargo ships likely to be used by underground Jewish groups to smuggle Jews into Palestine. Having spotted such vessels, Smiley's task was to destroy them by placing limpet mines on the ships' sides, so deterring, it was hoped, other ships' captains from engaging in the traffic. Five vessels were mined, one destroyed totally and two others damaged badly. No one was killed and the operation went undetected. Sailings declined somewhat before events in Palestine made the mission superfluous.

Four days before British forces finally left Palestine on June 30 1948, the US Air Force, the RAF and the French air force had begun the Berlin Airlift. This lasted for 15 months to the end of September 1949, after the Russians closed all surface routes to the Western-held part of the city, and marked the physical start of what became known as the Cold War. During the months of the airlift, more than 100 RAF cargo aircraft ferried nearly 400,000 tons of food, fuel and equipment to the besieged community. One OP, Group Captain **M.C. Collins** (19–21), served at Airlift HQ in Germany in 1949 and received a CBE for his work. Another, Flight Lieutenant **P.E.H. Thomas** (33–37), was awarded an AFC as one of the pilots who, as a group, spent more than 200,000 hours flying down three tight, narrowly-defined air corridors into West Berlin from West Germany. Ferrying in supplies, too, was **Pat Hornidge** (27–31). Between 1941–47 Hornidge had been a test pilot with Bristol Aeroplane Company. In 1948 he switched direction joining a firm called Flight Refuelling Ltd and flew over 140 sorties in Lancaster aircraft delivering petrol to Berlin, sometimes accompanied by **George Stone** (34–37). After the airlift, he went on to become one of the world's leading exponents of air-to-air refuelling operations.

Half a world away in China a protracted civil war was reaching a climax as communist forces closed on the nationalist capital of Nanking in April 1949. A British warship, HMS *Amethyst,* was sent up the Yangtse river to guard the UK embassy in the city and came under sustained fire from communist troops positioned along the river bank, was grounded and suffered heavy casualties. Three RN ships, including a frigate HMS *Black Swan,* were sent to re-float *Amethyst* and escort it to safety, but came under sustained fire and had to retreat. Second-in-command of *Black Swan* was **Miles Chapman (35–38).** He described what happened in a letter home: "Our casualties were light (12 wounded) and the damage, although fairly extensive, was fortunately placed…It was really the extreme shortness of range and width of the channel (which) precluded avoiding action. That was the deciding factor. We were so completely a sitting target. It was uncanny the way they (Chinese communists) went for the bridge of every ship involved. I was extremely angry that my cabin got a direct hit from a 75-millimetre shell, thereby wrecking it." *Amethyst* was to escape down river at the end of July after months of face-saving stalemate. In 1957 the ship was the subject of a famous post-war British film *Yangtse Incident.*

Hard on the heels of this minor East-West confrontation, and the successful end of the Berlin Airlift, North Korea and China invaded South Korea in June 1950. For the next three years several dozen OPs were involved in the first truly 'hot' war of the Cold War era. Under the auspices of a United Nations Security Council decision, 21 countries, led by the United States and including the U.K., contributed to a U.N. force created to resist the communist invasion. All told, more than two million people were to die in this largely-overlooked conflict including 1,129 British service personnel. Mercifully, none were OPs. This was largely because the great majority of those involved served in the Royal Navy which was confined to offshore actions including bombarding enemy forces and supporting operations on land, often north of 38th Parallel dividing South and North Korea.

Several were decorated including **Arthur Rowell (22–25),** commanding officer of the frigate HMS *Whitesand Bay,* who was awarded two DSCs, **Michael Craig-Waller (25–28)** and **Aubrey St. Clair Ford (17–18).** Both the latter, after considerable Whitehall wrangling, received US Legion of Merit medals. Craig-Waller was awarded a DSC. St. Clair Ford (see Chapter 3) commanded the cruiser HMS *Belfast.* According to his Citation, St. Clair Ford was "an inspiring and aggressive leader…(He) skilfully maintained a close blockade of the Korean coast with limited forces, harassing the enemy between the Taedong and Han estuaries, closely supporting covert and para-military operations North of the 38th parallel and providing effective protection for vital military installations on the West coast islands. By his outstanding professional skill, initiative and inspiring devotion to duty (he) contributed materially to the success of the naval campaign."

Much the same might be written of **Ben Bolt** (21–22) and **Frank Hopkins** (24–27). Bolt commanded the small aircraft carrier HMS *Theseus* – one of only two left in service in the RN by 1950 – and Hopkins had charge of the 44 aircraft on board. Under Bolt, the carrier deployed for five months in Korean waters and was in almost continuous action, most notably in support of 15,000 American and British Marines hemmed in around the port of Hungnam in North East Korea. Over 86 days, in bitter weather, aircraft from *Theseus* flew 4,446 sorties and the ship's guns expended more than half a million rounds of shells – "a sustained rate of intensity probably unsurpassed anywhere" according to an Admiralty press release issued when the carrier returned to Portsmouth to a rapturous reception in late-May 1951. Bolt was awarded a DSO, Hopkins was Mentioned in Despatches and the *Theseus* air group won the Boyd trophy, awarded annually for the best feat of naval airmanship. *Theseus* was replaced in Korean waters by HMS *Glory* in April 1951. Two of the FAA flyers in *Glory* were **Peter Stuart** (34–38) and **John 'Bill' Bailey** (31–35), both of whom won DSCs for their efforts. In the Second World War Bailey had taken part in operations against Kirkenes in northern Norway, against the *Bismarck* in 1941, and 1942 against the Japanese and Italian fleets in as well as being involved in Operation Pedestal to Malta in the carrier *Indomitable*. After *Glory* left Korean waters, Bailey was attached to the US Air Force and flew 20 sorties in F-86 Sabre aircraft, in the process becoming the first and, so far only, British pilot to fly a jet aircraft in combat with a Soviet aircraft (the MiG 15). Between 1940–55 he set a world record of 2,282 deck landings. He died in a road accident in 1967. Another flying operational sorties with the USAF in Korea was the future Air Commodore **Dennis Mitchell** (33–36; see Chapter 9) who took advantage of a secondment to USAF to volunteer, without informing his wife in far-away Belgium.

Robert Furze.

The most extraordinary example of RAF-USAF cooperation during the Cold War lay ahead. **Robert Furze** (42–46) had entered RAF Cranwell in 1947. Over the next seven years, 'Mac' Furze, as he was known, won RAF bombing competitions and became one of the Service's best long-range, high altitude pilots, usually flying the speedy Canberra jet bomber which could operate at heights around 50,000 feet but had a relatively short range. In 1953 he took part in a Canberra in what has become known as the "last great air race" over a 12,300 miles course from London to New Zealand. He landed in 24 hours 35 minutes and came third just 44 minutes behind the winner. Soon after, in the words of a report in *The Times*, Furze found "himself participating in one of the most remarkable, but least publicized, aerial intelligence-gathering operations of the early years of the Cold War in which British aircrews flew American reconnaissance bombers (with RAF markings) in deep penetration sorties, at high altitude, into Soviet air space over western Russia."

This highly-risky mission had been triggered by an American desire to obtain good-quality images of Soviet air bases, factories and missile sites. The snag was that in 1951 the USAF had been forbidden by President Harry Truman from overflying the USSR. The pugnacious head of USAF, General Curtis LeMay, decided to circumvent this ban by asking the British to stand in for the USAF, using a US aircraft (a version of the B45 Tornado) with RAF markings. The subterfuge went ahead, and the first of these flights (not involving Furze) took place in 1952 and evaded Soviet air defences, to the fury of Russian commanders. After two years, more sorties were deemed necessary. Furze was selected to fly one of the planes with Squadron Leader John Crampton. Three aircraft took off late on the evening of April 28, 1954 refuelling off Denmark.

Furze, Crampton and their navigator took on the longest of the three routes, penetrating 1,000 miles into southern Russia to gather intelligence on 30 targets. This time Soviet air defences were ready even if it was doubtful that Soviet MiG fighters could reach the 36,000 feet at which the B45s were flying. An obituary of Furze, published by *The Times* when he died in 2011, recounted the events that followed: "As they neared Kiev, the RB45Cs aircraft ran into a barrage of well-predicted (accurate) anti-aircraft shell burst exploding just ahead of them. Diving under the flak, the RAF crews turned and headed for the safety of West German air space, a thousand miles away, at full throttle. They kept their eyes peeled for Soviet fighters which, as they learned subsequently, had been ordered to ram them on sight rather than risking their escaping in a cannon engagement." Unable to refuel in flight and very short of fuel, all three aircraft limped in to West German airfields in one piece. Furze was awarded an Air Force Cross. A tall, handsome, modest man with "a quiet and gentle nature," in the words of an obituary in *The Daily Telegraph*, Furze went on to command a low-level tactical nuclear strike squadron in West Germany. Before that, he had done a stint as an instructor at Cranwell. Here his AFC, granted for "an act or acts of exemplary gallantry while flying, though not in active operations against the enemy" intrigued young officers who could never discover exactly what this "gallantry" in peacetime might have been.

Kenneth Dyer.

In 1962 another Old Pangbournian, the Canadian **Kenneth Dyer** (29–30), was to play an even more dramatic and central role in the Cold War during the Cuban missile crisis – the closest the world has come to a nuclear exchange. At the time Dyer, who had won a DSC in the Second World War after sinking a German submarine in the North Atlantic, was a Rear Admiral commanding Canada's East Coast fleet. In mid-October the US moved to its highest military state of alert, Defcon 3, after aerial photos showed that Soviet guided missile bases were being constructed on Cuba. On October 22 the American President, John F. Kennedy, demanded unconditional withdrawal of all Soviet missiles on the island and set up a naval blockade to prevent any further shipments of military equipment. Five days earlier, Dyer had met unofficially with his American opposite number. That same night the Canadian Navy – primarily an anti-submarine force – made contact with a Soviet submarine 300 miles off the Canadian east coast. Eleven more contacts soon followed.

In Ottawa the government of John Diefenbaker dithered, misreading the seriousness of the situation. Dyer decided, on his own initiative, that he had no option but to prepare for the worst. So he ordered the dispersal of those ships at his disposal – 22 destroyers, an aircraft carrier with 28 planes, two submarines and 22 patrol aircraft – in order to pursue Soviet submarines in a wide section of the North Atlantic off Nova Scotia and the approaches to New York. Before long, he was asked by the US Navy to extend the deployment further south. Still receiving no firm direction from Ottawa, he signalled his intentions and went ahead when there was no political reaction. The immediate crisis was resolved on October 28 but, unbeknown to most, the Soviet submarine menace remained. Dyer kept his ships at sea. The peak of the Canadian deployment occurred on November 5 at which point eleven Soviet submarines were being tracked by Dyer's force. Altogether, from October 23 to November 15, 1962, 136 submarine "contacts" were made in the Atlantic in or near the Canadian "zone" according to *The Sea is at our Gate*, a book about the incident. The author, Tony German, concluded that Dyer was "a courageous leader who had done what had to be done when Canada's political leadership had so shockingly failed the test." For years after, RCN officers recalled the episode with pride. Dyer, much respected in the Canadian Navy, was soon promoted to Vice Admiral.

Many of the tectonic plates around post-war British defence and security policy were shifting by that time. The process had begun in 1947 with the independence of India in 1947, but the first real Cold War manifestation was in Malaya where a communist insurgency rooted in the large Chinese minority population raged for a dozen years to 1960, involving scores of Old Pangbournians in operational roles. Much of this conflict took place in the jungle from where Maoist fighters launched attacks on rubber plantations and tin mines run by colonial-era owners, and used assassinations, ambushes and sabotage as part of a terror campaign. In response, the UK developed counter-terrorism tactics that became widespread in the decades that followed – forcibly resettling villagers, deploying helicopters on sudden punitive raids, and trying to marginalise and isolate the rebels in their remote camps. Much of the military manpower, especially in the Army, was provided by conscripts. Yet the backbone was forged around career professionals, such as Royal Marine commandos, deployed across the Malay peninsula on tough, relentless seek-and-destroy missions. **Peter Hellings (30–34)**, to give one example, was Brigade Major of 3 Commando, **David Roberts (30–35)** was a Troop Commander in 40 Commando and was Mentioned in Despatches, and **Robert Carter (34–37)** of 45 Commando was awarded a Military Cross and Mentioned in Despatches. Carter – "very much a Marine's Marine" according to a relative – was awarded an OBE for his role in suppressing a rebellion in Tanganyika (Tanzania). On the 300th anniversary of the Royal Marines, he had the honour of leading the march through London to parade before the Queen at Buckingham Palace. In the Army, **C.P. O'Bree (34–36)**, a Major in the 6th Gurkha Rifles, "chased bandits in Johore State with a fair degree of success" in 1951–52, while **Bryan Parker (43–47)** served with the Worcestershire Regiment 1950–52. He died of an unspecified illness aged 27 in 1956 during his second operational tour in Malaya.

Working in tandem with these men was **Tim Hatton (39–43)** who was awarded a Colonial Police Medal and an OBE for his efforts. Hatton had been commissioned into the Gurkha Rifles in 1945 and, aged 20, had fought at the end of the Second World War in West Java in 1945–46 when communists and nationalists attempted to prevent Dutch colonialists returning as the Japanese occupation ended. Next, aged 23, he led a Gurkha company that escorted 100,000 non-militant Muslims 250 miles by foot and cart out of India on a three-week trek to the new Pakistan border in 1947 during the partition crisis. Demobilised in 1948, he spurned a place at Oxford University and joined the Malayan Police Service. Specialising in intelligence work and making use of his language facility, the all-consuming focus of his life for the next 12 years was the 'Emergency.' In a police service riven with division, and weakened by uncertain leadership until the arrival in 1952 of Gerald Templer, the 'Tiger of Malaya,' Hatton proved his worth time and again in dangerous undercover operations. In 1958–59 he cooperated with two decorated World War 2 officers, **Anthony Innes** (30–34) and **James Acland** (33–37), both of whom were serving in military intelligence. The Emergency over, Hatton helped to establish a Malaysian constitution. In 1967 the Malaysian government appointed him at the age of 42 to head the Malaysian Police Service Intelligence branch. The Citation for his OBE praised his "abundant energy, unselfish approach…and outstanding moral courage."

No sooner had stability returned to the Malayan peninsula after more than 20 years, followed soon after by independence, than an armed 'Confrontation' began with Indonesia over the future of Sarawak and Sabah – located on the disputed island of Borneo but part of the new Federation of Malaysia. By 1964, more than a dozen OPs were serving in UK military roles in Sarawak including **Richard Holworthy** (50–55) in the Army, **Mike Callaghan** (54–59) with the Border Scouts, **Digby Lickfold** (46–49) and **Martin Banks** (52–56) as RN helicopter pilots, **Ian Shuttleworth** (57–62) in charge of a commandeered fishing vessel patrolling offshore, and **Sandy Lade** (57–61) in 42 Commando Royal Marines. Lade led a team of 30 men that was based in dense jungle at a heavily defended and isolated border post which could only be supplied by air drops. From here the unit patrolled continuously, specialising in night ambushes.

Lickfold, a Lt Cdr in the FAA, was awarded an MBE. His citation stated: "In September 1963, while he was senior pilot in 845 Wessex Squadron of the Fleet

Digby Lickfold in 1957 (front left).

Air Arm in Sarawak, a platoon of the Gurkha Rifles made contact with the enemy in the jungle and as a result several terrorists were killed and one Rifleman was seriously wounded. Arrangements were made to evacuate the wounded Rifleman by boat, but because of deteriorating weather Lickfold took off for a prearranged rendezvous, taking with him the Regimental Medical Officer. On arrival, it was found that an evacuation party had not reached the position, so being unable to wait because of shortage of fuel and the worsening weather he returned to base, leaving the M.O. behind. Having refuelled, Lickfold decided to make a further attempt to evacuate the wounded man, whose condition was reported to be critical. He arrived at the rendezvous in conditions of poor light, pouring rain and low cloud and picked up the casualty and the Medical Officer. Having returned safely to base, he subsequently took off again in appalling conditions in order to take the Rifleman to hospital…Lt Cdr Lickfold, by his personal courage and determination in the most adverse conditions, was undoubtedly responsible for saving the life of the wounded soldier. He flew in conditions totally unacceptable in any normal circumstance."

It was three years afterwards, in this unforgiving, very distant relic of empire, that the last known death in combat of an Old Pangbournian took place. The military essence of 'Confrontation' was covert surveillance, pre-emptive strikes, lethal firepower and surprise. **Ian Clark (50–53)** also served in 42 Commando Royal Marines and was particularly skilled at this type or warfare. His colleagues knew him as "a very professional soldier with a quiet personality and an unusual hobby – collecting battle dress shoulder tallies." Already a veteran of active commando deployments in Cyprus, Aden and Borneo (1963), Clark volunteered to return to Borneo for a second spell in 1966. At the time of his death, he was taking part in Operation Cricket – a clandestine mission to destroy an Indonesian military camp near Sebedang, inside Indonesia, before the imminent end of 'Confrontation.' Having carried out a "textbook recce" of the site, he was asked to lead two Marine companies into action. The incursion succeeded and the camp was destroyed, but while withdrawing through thick jungle under random enemy fire, he was killed by a single bullet.

Ian Clark was buried in a Commonwealth military cemetery in Singapore that became a housing estate. Subsequently, his remains were repatriated to his native Scotland and re-interred

Ian Clark.

in Edinburgh. Posthumously Mentioned in Despatches, Royal Marine veterans continue to feel that Clark should have been awarded a Military Cross. A posting on an RM website reads: "It was my privilege to serve under this cracking Officer in 45 Commando RM. He inspired total confidence, screamed competence, and had that air about him. It was a pleasure to be with him…I think he was destined for High Office. What a loss! Salute!"

The security challenges in Malaya and Malaysia from 1948–66 formed part of a pattern facing the increasingly-stretched UK military establishment as the end-of-empire era dragged on. Newly-independent countries emerged across the globe, the East-West ideological stand-off got a grip, the Vietnam War began, global trade patterns altered and post-war reconstruction preoccupied many governments and especially those in straightened, if recovering, Britain. One "Emergency" followed another – in Cyprus 1955–59, Kenya 1952–60, Aden 1963–67 and Northern Ireland 1969–98 to name four. In addition, UK troops often found themselves "volunteered" for United Nations duty. Today the colonial era, and the way it ended, is often characterised as a moral stain on western and British society. Yet as Ben MacIntyre, a well-known historian, wrote in *The Times* in 2020, "If we simply assess the past through the prism of contemporary mores, we miss the nuance and complexity of history…The empire can never be understood if we cling to adulation or condemnation. The truth lies in the shades of grey between those extremes."

The post-war military career of Brigadier **John Mackenzie** (29–33; see Chapter 7) epitomises such nuances. Having experienced more armed conflict in Greece, Korea and Jordan, he was transferred to Kaduna, Nigeria in February 1961 to command of 1 Nigerian Brigade. In a letter home, he described what happened next: "After a week's notice I took over command of No. 3 Nigerian Brigade Group in the Congo in December 1961. It is quite like old times as my command is composed of different nationalities – Nigerians, Indians, Pakistanis, Danes, Swedes and Liberians. My 'parish' is a large one consisting of Kasai Province, the size of France, with a population of four million, split into 24 tribes who dislike each other. Their repertoire in crime includes massacre, arson, looting and cannibalism with the modern touch – the human carcase has been found in refrigerators (as) the family 'chop.' Quite recently…two of my officers carried out a brilliant exploit, evacuating missionaries and nuns from the area Kongolo-Kasongo-Mbulula in Katanga, where 22 Belgium missionaries had been taken from their schools, stripped and shot. We managed to get back one missionary who had escaped into the bush. Both officers were beaten up, but came through all right.

"I have nine aircraft under my operational command, including helicopters. These are absolutely invaluable and we fly every day all over Kasai keeping a firm grip on the situation and maintaining some law and order. There are a great many problems to be solved, the most urgent requirement (being a) drastic reduction of the indisciplined forces of the Armée Nationale Congolese and the Gendarmerie. Next comes the complete lack of transport for the circulation of food, people and money. Money itself is a major problem. (There is) none in the banks, and salaried workers have not been paid for periods varying from 3–18 months. Hospitals lack doctors, equipment and medical supplies; education is only carried on in the missionary schools with reduced staffs. And so, the awful tale goes on."

Two other Old Pangbournians were dragged in to similar no-win conflicts and quickly found themselves facing the complexities, drawbacks and ambiguities involved in international peace-keeping. Both would likely agree with MacIntyre's equivocal analysis. Both rose to become Commandant General of the Royal Marines. **Norman Tailyour (28–32)** held the position from 1965–68. He joined the Marines in 1933 and throughout his career followed the dictum 'If you don't take risks (with a smile), you will never achieve anything.' Direct, honest and unafraid to court controversy, everyone knew how they stood with Tailyour. During the Second World War he specialised in landing craft operations. Twice Mentioned in Despatches, he was awarded the DSO as commanding officer of 27th Battalion RM in North West Europe in 1945 "for gallant and distinguished services." Post-war, he won his second DSO in Cyprus when commanding 45 Commando RM – known as the 'Cocktail Commando' because of its social gatherings. The following year he was wounded by 'friendly' fire when landing a helicopter in Port Said during the 1956 Suez Crisis – claimed to be the first helicopter-borne opposed assault from the sea in history. Absolutely loyal to the Royal Marines and much admired by officers and men alike, he was knighted in 1966, retiring after two years. Appointed Captain of Deal Castle, he did much to rejuvenate the old fortress. Like his son Ewen (see Chapter 14), he was a keen yachtsman. He died in 1979.

Peter Hellings (30–34) followed Tailyour as the Marines' Commandant General from 1968–71. He had seen active service from 1939–45 in Italy and North West Europe (see Chapter 7) and during post-war insurgencies in Malaya and Cyprus. In effect, he lived on a war footing for 30 years until his retirement in 1971. Probably the only man to have won both the DSC and the MC, Hellings was additionally Mentioned in Despatches twice. During the Second World War he won his DSC as a member of a special Marine unit formed to carry out rear guard actions at Boulogne as France fell in 1940. He survived, and in 1942 took part in the disastrous Allied raid on Dieppe, arriving at a beach still in enemy hands. His landing craft was hit by a storm of fire and broke down, but escaped under the cover of smoke. The next year Hellings participated in the invasion of Sicily and was awarded his Military Cross for gallantry in Operation Devon at the port of Termoli as Allied forces slowly pushed north up the Italian peninsula. Returning to England, he took part in operations in North West Europe in 1945 and was Mentioned in Despatches for the first time. After the war, in the words of an obituary, he "became a kind of stormy petrel, serving wherever there was trouble." This included stints of varying intensity in Hong Kong, Malaya, and Cyprus where, in operations against Eoka fighters, he was Mentioned in Despatches for a second time. Despite his record, the last thing Hellings would have described himself as was 'heroic.' He had a relaxed, easy-going manner, was very approachable yet always rose to the occasion, even, according to the *Daily Telegraph*, practising with bows and arrows in case they might come in handy. All manner of honours and awards were showered on him, including a knighthood in 1970.

Another OP intimately involved in the Cyprus Emergency was **John Willoughby** (28–31) who, in 1955–56, commanded the Middlesex Regiment in the Larnaca area. The 1st Bn Notes for 1956 give a flavour of what this involved: "During the remainder of the month (September), EOKA activities intensified…A bomb was thrown at Lefkara Police Station, guarded by a detachment of 'S' Company, and on the 24th a Sergeant and his wife were shot while returning from church in Larnaca. The Sergeant was wounded fatally and his wife slightly. Three ambushes were reported in the area during this period…The increase in EOKA activities brought about a period of intensive patrolling, snap checks and searches of vehicles, cyclists and places of entertainment in the town and rural areas. During the past year the Battalion has played a part in developing the new technique of internal security operations. The baton, shield and dye-sprayer have become commonplace. Riot drill, snap

checks, cordons, curfews and ambush drills are part of the daily routine…These demands have placed great strain on the officers and men alike. Weeks of continual guard (duty) and patrolling interspersed with cordons, curfews and searches, with little sleep and no recreation, during the hottest summer for years, have been borne with great cheerfulness by all ranks." A decade on, the Wilson government sent John Willoughby to oversee the UK's withdrawal from Aden 1965–67 where, in the words of an

John Willoughby.

obituary, "his rugged personality and able leadership skills helped to maintain security as terrorism against British troops reached a peak." Willoughby defined these conflicts as "half-war." He was promoted to Major General in 1965 and knighted in 1967.

Throughout the 1950s and early 1960s compulsory National Service in the U.K. provided much of the manpower for these kinds of deployments. **Jeremy Hodgson (51–54)** saw active service with the Marines in Cyprus. **Peter Gould (46–50)**, while doing his 18-months tour with the Gordon Highlanders in Malaya, attracted publicity in 1952 when he killed "a bandit who had been menacing rubber planters for three years." **Robin Montgomery (46–49)** did two years in the King's African Rifles 5th Regiment which acquired a fearsome reputation in anti-Mau Mau operations in Kenya, earning him an MBE and leading to a career in the Army. The ill-fated Suez intervention in 1956 involved **Jeremy Collingwood (50–55)** in the carrier HMS *Eagle,* and regulars such as **Pat Crosbie (43–48)** of the Parachute Field Regiment who was dropped onto an airfield west of Port Said.

Many of these operations have already disappeared into the mists of time. The Radfan Campaign in 1964, to give an example, is barely known today. A succession of fire-fighting sweeps through mountainous country, it was linked to the Aden Emergency and centred on a rebellious region near the border with Yemen where tribesmen were raiding and attacking isolated government facilities. In April of that year UK forces were deployed to seize the main rebel stronghold. **Christopher Ledger (57–61)**, serving in 45 Commando R.M., was subsequently commended by The Queen for "brave conduct." A report in *The Surrey Advertiser* stated: "In three days of heavy fighting against determined attacks by the enemy, Lieut. Ledger's patrol was subjected to heavy and sustained fire. Despite considerable communication difficulties, his conduct and military skill were of a high order and his determined efforts to ensure the successful air evacuation of his seriously wounded Marines to hospital in this critical situation almost certainly saved their lives." Aged 21 at the time, Ledger has recalled that "the conflict was fought in floppy hats, a belt with ammo and water bottles, on foot and in a hostile environment. It was exciting, demanding and very much a subalterns' war." His immediate reward, notwithstanding his age, was to be made Military Governor of Perim Island at the foot of the Red Sea in 1965, charged with suppressing piracy, slaving, and drug and weapons trafficking.

A similar tribal-based clash coloured the communist-inspired Dhofar Rebellion in Oman. Officially, the UK military was never involved in this war which lasted throughout the first half of the 1970s. But many British officers, including **Colin Howard (61–66)**, **Ewen Southby-Tailyour (55–59)** and **Charlie Daniel (63–68)**

Ewen Southby-Tailyour in Aden, 1969.

from the Royal Marines and **Nick Knollys (62–67)** from the Scots Guards, were. Howard wrote about his time in the Jebel Akhdar mountains in 1971 in an issue of the *OP Magazine* when he was one of a battalion of 200 troops, mostly Omani and Baluch, who destroyed a Chinese training base with accurate mortar fire after a perilous march through the night in difficult terrain. "For me, for the first time in my military life, the feeling was sharp reality" he recalled. A 2006 book by Ian Gardiner, the commanding officer of Knollys and Daniel, described the tough and dangerous role these two took on a bit after Howard's deployment. For six months Knollys commanded an isolated, exposed post called Ashawq in one of the defensive lines set up by the Sultan's forces stretching from coast to mountain to prevent rebel incursions. He insisted on flying an Omani flag at the top of a long pole – an act of defiance in what previously had been rebel-held territory and one that was designed to boost the morale of his soldiers (all Omani). "The courage required to sit still and stay sane under artillery fire is not to be under-estimated," wrote Gardiner in his book *In The Service of the Sultan*. "Being mortared or shelled is an experience which, once endured, remains branded on the memory for life." Daniel, who served in the Omani Army for three years and was decorated for bravery by the Sultan, as was Southby-Tailyour, took part in a number of high-risk operations including evacuating casualties by helicopter in the dark. All these young men, in Gardiner's estimation, had volunteered to "prove themselves." As Daniel put it in a letter, echoing David Smiley (see Chapter 8) a decade earlier: "There was an opportunity to prove one's metal against a common enemy, communism... We had to do what we had to do and report back that the job was done."

Another who seized the chance, and was to remain in Oman for nearly ten years flying helicopters in the Sultan's air force and the Royal Oman Police, was **M.H.S. (Bill) Bailey (58–62)**. He had served in the Royal Marines and gained a civil pilot's licence in the UK before being encouraged by RM friends in Oman to join them. For three years from 1971 he flew helicopters resupplying isolated units led by men like Howard and Knollys and evacuating casualties from the Jebel region. The helicopters were unarmed for load-carrying reasons but the pilots did carry a sidearm – in Bailey's case, a 7.62 FN which "he knew and trusted." Two months after arriving, carrying drinking water to resupply a company, his Bell 205 aircraft came under small arms fire from the ground, its radio was shot up and it was leaking fuel from the belly "like a colander" when it landed. "The first entry bullet hole was about a foot behind my head. We had taken eight hits," Bailey has written. The conundrum of how to evade ground fire when descending in a helicopter proved to be a concern throughout his decade in Oman, although a "spiral" technique he used did make a difference. Twice in this period he took time off to experience the soldier's life on the Jebel in order to improve liaison between the "flyboys and the grunts." The Sultan awarded him a medal for bravery. Bailey moved on to found, and command for six years, the Oman Police Airwing. His duties included accompanying rebel sympathisers to prison. As he put it: "They were dealt with in a typically salutary fashion." Such an edgy life is not for everyone, but he had no qualms. In his words: "Without doubt, the most fulfilling period of my 45-year flying career was spent in Dhofar."

The end of empire was to bring little relief from these "half-wars." In the 1970s seemingly endless hit-and-run firefights against insurgents, usually termed terrorists, followed even as Britain's reach in the world shrank – in Northern Ireland where 1,441 UK troops were to die from 1969–2007, in Iraq 1991–2011 where 178 died serving in Coalition or UN forces, and in Afghanistan from 2001 to the present day where the British death toll has exceeded 450. In none of these "medal-earning theatres" could the fighting be termed conventional warfare, but it was often, especially in Afghanistan, intense and bloody. Equally, military men and women were frequently called on to play the part of aid workers, offering humanitarian relief, building and opening roads, helping to rebuild shattered communities and brokering ceasefires.

Nothing illustrates this dichotomy better than a 1991 image of an OP in northern Iraq. **Rory Copinger-Symes (79–83)**, a Lieutenant aged 26, had been serving with 45 Commando Royal Marines for six months, commanding an anti-tank missile troop in South Armagh, Northern Ireland. When the deployment ended early in 1991, his unit was given five weeks' leave. An account he has written continues: "I had no idea what was going on in the world when I was suddenly recalled as I'd been skiing in the Alps for three weeks. Unbeknownst to most of us, after the war in Kuwait in 1991 Saddam's forces had started persecuting the Kurds in the north and most of them ran away into the mountains on the border with Turkey. Within days I was inside Northern Iraq near a place called Zakho where the Commando HQ had been established. The CO grabbed me almost as soon as I arrived and told me to jump in a helicopter to find one of the company commanders, who was out on patrol but had lost touch and, if we had enough fuel, to fly up into the mountains to see where the Kurds were.

"We stayed around Zakho for about a week and occupied the town, pushing out the remnants of the Iraqi military and secret police. My company, Support Company, was ordered to move east to secure Batifa as this was a key choke point on the route into the mountains. With Iraqi troops still occupying it, the Kurds could not come down from the mountains. So, we moved east and secured Batifa to set up a base there. We then patrolled the local area from Batifa to find out where the Kurds were and what other Iraqi forces remained in the area. I was tasked with conducting an aerial reconnaissance further east and specifically of a place that all the locals told us was the provincial or regional capital, Al Amadiya. This town was an ancient place, perched on top of a striking flat hilltop that dominated the surrounding area. From the helicopter, I could see a football field in the centre, but few people or troops in the town. I was ordered to move to Amadiya and lead the first wave in an airborne 'assault.' So off we went and landed on the football field…much to the excitement of the few kids still in the town.

"The local English teacher had remained there and I persuaded him to be my translator. Very quickly we set about finding the few remaining Iraqi troops in Amadiya and sent them packing as well as a small team of secret police that we were told about. The next challenge was to get the town ready to receive the Kurds when they returned; it was filthy. By this stage I had, effectively, been tasked to 'run' Amadiya with my troop. So we secured the town, and set up check points at the two main entrances, while I persuaded the locals to start cleaning the rubbish and we established a food distribution site using the fire station. Gradually the Kurds started to trickle in, and we set up a rationing system to feed them.

"Word evidently got out about what we were doing and the media appeared. A journalist and photographer working for the London *Evening Standard* asked if they could follow me for a few days and do a piece on our activities. So they did exactly that. On the first night I was told that a woman with a small baby had just arrived, in poor condition. I trundled off to see what we could do, journalist and photographer in tow, and realised the baby needed milk. But baby milk was not something we had! Luckily there was a small Medicine Sans Frontier team in town so I set off to find it and that was when the picture was taken. The rest, as they say, is history. The photo was syndicated worldwide, with several articles, and I ended up giving a host of media interviews." Soon after, Copinger-Symes joined HMS *Polar Circle,* as officer commanding the RM detachment on board, and spent time in Antarctica. By 2006, with Baghdad again in turmoil, he was back in Iraq, heavily armed and this time wearing body armour. Managing to fly to Zakho, he was delighted to discover the town safe and prospering, and was able to walk around without his helmet and armour and go to a local restaurant for a meal.

The prolonged Allied and NATO intervention in Afghanistan since 2001, following the 9/11 Twin Towers attack in New York by Islamic extremists, drew in a number of Old Pangbournians serving in the Army and Royal Marines and liaising with Afghan government forces. At one time, the senior UN diplomat in Kabul was an OP – **Andrew Tesoriere (64–68)**, an Afghan specialist for 30 years and future UK Ambassador to Latvia and Algeria. Most of the UK military focus, however, was not on the capital but on huge, arid Helmand province in the south of the country covering 20,000 square miles. In 2008–09 **Daniel Holloway (94–99)** was a young Captain serving in a UK Operational Mentoring and Liaison Team alongside soldiers of the Afghan National Army. Sent to "an austere and remote patrol base in the Garmsir District in southern Helmand," he was Mentioned in Despatches. His Citation gives a graphic taste of the complexity of his lonely role: "Holloway took to the mentoring role superbly, immediately fostering an excellent relationship with his counterpart ANA (Afghan National Army) commander... On delicate combat operations, he was fearless, determined and an inspirational commander. During an offensive operation in December 2008, he led his team robustly. In a similar offensive operation in January 2009 Holloway again led from the front, impressing upon his ANA colleagues the requirement for offensive spirit, inspiring an assault into the heart of a well-prepared and heavily armed enemy position, and leaving the enemy forces in disarray and on the retreat. (His) mental strength, physical courage and inspirational leadership peaked in adversity" – as in a deployment on 16 February 2009 when the unit he was with ran into an enemy ambush and his 'front man' was shot in the head. "Holloway dashed forward under enemy fire and recovered the casualty...(his) commitment, determination and leadership have been outstanding."

Tough soldiering facing a well-entrenched, motivated enemy in unforgiving and unfamiliar territory surrounded by a suspicious and wary population, typified many British military experiences in Afghanistan. **Angus Fair (83–88)**, who had already been awarded a DSO in 2006 as a Major in the SAS in Iraq, commanded the spearhead force in one of the most celebrated British offensives in Helmand – Operation Panther's Claw in June-July 2009. This was intended to drive hardcore Taliban fighters out of an area they had controlled for the previous two years, and to stabilise Helmand province ahead of a Presidential election. Fair, at that time a Lt Col, and the men and women of the Light Dragoons battle group ran into a dense network of IEDs (Improvised Explosive Devices) that made caution the watchword – while trying to cope with the extreme physical conditions.

Temperatures soared way above 40 degrees Centigrade and each soldier needed to drink six litres of water a day simply to keep functioning.

Ten days' arduous combat ensued – "the most intense fighting over a protracted period I have experienced in my 20 years in the Army" Fair remembered, looking back at three major tours in Afghanistan. Taliban forces did subsequently retreat from the wider Babaji area and two-thirds of its local strength was "eliminated." Against that, eight British soldiers were killed in one day during the operation and five times that number were wounded. "It was a highly attritional summer. But it was the start of consolidation and the ownership of the ground (in Helmand province). It made a big difference to our operations and to the people living there," Fair argued in an interview in 2009. He was awarded a Bar to his DSO. In part the citation reads: "(He) has dealt with extraordinary levels of tactical complexity and danger…His tactical understanding and his ability to motivate and cajole his men in the very harshest of operational environments proved decisive. His leadership during this phase of the operation was nothing short of inspirational."

After the operation, Fair put on record that any past generation would have been proud of his soldiers' commitment and spirit. In subsequent by-lined articles that year in *The Times* and *The Daily Telegraph*, he continued to emphasise the success of Operation Panther's Claw, stressing the hearts-and-minds progress being made on the ground. "I am convinced that true achievement in a campaign such as Afghanistan cannot be measured in weeks or months but must instead be gauged over years…Probably the most significant demonstration of progress (made in Helmand) was the distribution of wheat seed to farmers. In the face of Taliban attacks on the distribution sites, and on locals queuing for seed, some 2,000 farmers received wheat, with more to follow." Citing also the growing preparedness at the time of local and vulnerable villagers to engage with British troops, the improving capabilities of Afghan security forces and police, and increasing disillusion in Helmand's towns and villages with the Taliban's indiscriminate violence, he argued that the Allies were at a "tipping point" with popular opinion and consent moving "irreversibly in our favour."

By 2014 all British combat operations in Afghanistan had ceased on the orders of the Cameron government. Terrorism, IEDs and random bomb attacks resumed in Helmand. Babaji was held by Taliban forces for three years to 2018, and even in 2020 sporadic fighting continued in the province. Yet the local context had changed. Fair returned to Afghanistan for a high-level advisory role in Kabul in 2014–15. He was "pleasantly reassured" by what he found – less corrupt working institutions, and more competent and motivated individuals taking charge. As a result, the Taliban was finding it harder to "pull the wool over the population's eyes." If there was one incident that gave Fair long-term grounds for optimism it had been when the Taliban fired on that queue of thousands of farmers lining up to receive grain seed in 2009. Eleven years later he reflected: "That laid bare to the local population the real dynamic at work and cut through their (Taliban) false narrative...Today the population in Helmand is better informed and not as isolated as it was. It is much less easy for the Taliban to pull the blanket bluff it did – and therefore easier to mould a compromise."

14

FIGHTING IN
THE FALKLANDS

— ◎ —

The short, but hard-fought, Falklands War in April-June 1982 involved almost 50 Old Pangbournians, most of whom were part of a South Atlantic Task Force, including more than 100 ships and some 6,000 troops, despatched to the islands by the Thatcher government after double that number of Argentinian troops had launched an unprovoked invasion of the sparsely-populated British colony. Thirteen OPs were subsequently decorated. None was killed. Four were serving in vessels that were sunk by enemy action. Around 30 were officers of the Royal Navy, six were in the Royal Marines, four in the Merchant Navy and two in the Army. Eight were involved in behind-the-scenes military coordinating roles in the UK. Seven of the OPs in the Royal Navy went on to achieve flag rank.

These bald facts and figures give little indication of the variety or scope or intensity of the involvement. Several of those concerned have subsequently remarked that they never worked harder in their lives, or felt more fatigued. More than one still feels ambivalent about the whole conflict. Almost, but not quite, out of the blue a war blew up 8,200 miles from the UK at a time when British defence spending was contracting, the focus of the armed forces remained firmly on the Cold War and the UK role in the North Atlantic and continental Europe, and complex combined sea-land-air operations of the type required to invade and recapture the distant Falklands had never been practised in the islands. When the call to arms came, few of those involved, including the commanders, had any idea of conditions on the Falklands or knew anything about the capabilities of the enemy, or grasped the complexities of the mission, or had been briefed on their likely roles. Even fewer had been involved in a shooting war and almost none realised how hard-fought this conflict would prove to be.

Roger Lane-Nott.

One OP was at sea tracking a Soviet submarine in the Atlantic as captain of a nuclear submarine when he received a rare personal order from the First Sea Lord to "proceed with all dispatch" back to the naval base at Faslane in Scotland in strict radio silence, and "store for war." **Roger Lane-Nott (58–63)** had never received such an order before, had been at sea in strict isolation in HMS *Splendid* for the previous three months, and could not begin to imagine what grave crisis awaited him. Many years after the event, he wrote about his Falklands role in a book published privately *Now You See Us...* Aged 36 when he set off for the South Atlantic in *Splendid* on April 1 in a "spearhead" role with his crew of 98, none of whom had been to war before, he consulted *Jane's Fighting Ships* on the journey south to discover more about the enemy and listened to the *BBC World Service* for news and context. Many questions he sent to Northwood, near London, where the overall RN Command was based, about the Argentinians' capabilities went unanswered. Throughout, the Rules of Engagement changed almost from day to day. "This was an exceptional situation and we were all going into the unknown... Diplomatic options are running out and the only option is to fight and kick the Argentinians out of British territory," he confided in his diary on April 7.

When Lane-Nott and his weary men finally got back to Devonport on June 12 after a 73-day deployment, the daily calorie intake for each man had been cut by a fifth and the crew was auctioning tea bags for £50 and a sausage for £60 so low had supplies on the submarine become. In between Lane-Nott and *Splendid* had played a dangerous cat-and-mouse game with those parts of the Argentinian Navy that dared to take to sea, and succeeded in bottling most of it up in its home ports. All the while, Lane-Nott and his crew had declining faith in the sketchy and conflicting intelligence they received from Northwood. One result was that the submarine went to Action Stations more than once while circling the Falklands or patrolling off the Argentinian coast – yet the nearest *Splendid* came to actual engagement with the enemy was when it found the escorts protecting the carrier *25th May.* After following them for 24 hours convinced that they would bring *Splendid* to the carrier, Lane-Nott was diverted by another intelligence report. News of the attack on the Argentinian cruiser *Belgrano* outside the 200-mile Exclusion Zone by HMS *Conqueror* – the first time a nuclear submarine had sunk anything in anger – left Lane-Nott "professionally envious." By 2015, he was not so sure. In the background, but always there, the successive sinkings of RN ships in San Carlos Water proved distressing to all in *Splendid*. "Very depressed …we did not seem to have any luck at all," Lane-Nott noted on May 25. Ordered back to the UK the next day, as the re-capture of the Falklands proceeded, all the crew felt the submarine, despite performing well mechanically, had been pulled out too early. "It was disappointing not to have been allowed to sink something," Lane-Nott reflected on the long voyage home, not helped when the submarine's first mail drop for months from an RAF Nimrod hit the water and sank.

Such a seemingly sparse return from a unique deployment suggests that *Splendid* was wasted in the South Atlantic. Nothing could be further from the truth as Lane-Nott assessed the matter. Above all, the mere presence of a Royal Navy nuclear submarine, and two others like it, off the Argentinian coast deterred the enemy from trying to reinforce its garrison on the Falklands by sea. And it was widely accepted that national honour was at stake and had to be upheld. "There is no doubt in my mind that we had to react in 1982" despite warning signs going back at least five years before the invasion took place, Lane-Nott wrote in 2015. "It was a close-run thing, with many mistakes made and a certain amount of luck on our side. (Yet) I am clear it was a just cause and my Ship's Company agreed." By 1992, he was Flag Officer Submarines, Head of the Submarine Service.

Lane-Nott's view of the Falklands conflict was echoed by another RN officer who did see action, was sunk, but survived to tell the tale. **Michael Layard (49– 53)** was a Captain in the Royal Navy and went on to become a full Admiral and Second Sea Lord. He had made his naval career in the Fleet Air Arm. Like many of those selected to be Senior Naval Officer on board one of the 46 merchant vessels requisitioned by the Ministry of Defence, he was between appointments when the Falklands crisis flared up. Deceptively low key, he said little but thought a lot, was decisive and was widely trusted. Sent to the laid-up Cunard-owned 14,950 tons roll-on, roll-off container ship ss *Atlantic Conveyor*, his job was to liaise with RN Task Force commanders and with Ian North, the captain of the merchant ship – a lifelong seaman in his sixties, with a snowy white beard and probably the only person in the entire Task Force operation who knew what to expect if a bomb or torpedo or missile hit. Layard got on famously with North – in his words "a man in a million…a remarkable old sea dog" – and the pair "made just about a perfect team" according to the 'Battle Group' Task Force Commander, Rear Admiral Sandy Woodward.

Layard's first challenge was to oversee nine days' conversion work to prepare *Atlantic Conveyor* for its war role in the Falklands – modifying the ship with steel plates, creating a helicopter pad aft, making shelters for stores, installing containers on deck to hold extra fresh water and oxygen, finding space for a vast quantity of spares for the ships of the Task Force and working out how to disembark the cargo – on the high seas if necessary. It turned into "a remarkable team effort" and *Atlantic Conveyor* left Devonport on April 25. Late on, a decision was made to add weaponry – 600 cluster bombs, missiles, grenades and small arms – all stored in unreinforced containers in open-plan holds. Crucially, the ship was not armed and did not have a defence system; a legal argument in Whitehall prevented this. Departing the UK on April 25 with 125 military and 35 crew on board, as well as eight Sea Harriers and 16 helicopters, *Atlantic Conveyor* reached Ascension Island on May 5 and the 200-mile Maritime Exclusion Zone around the Falklands on May 19. Here the Harriers were offloaded to two Task Force aircraft carriers. After four days *Atlantic Conveyor* was instructed to move with all speed under cover of darkness to San Carlos Water on the night of May 25, to disembark its precious helicopter cargo and to begin transferring its stores ashore. That evening, at 7:40pm as darkness neared, with virtually no warning, the ship was hit by two Exocet missiles on the port quarter eight to ten feet above the water line.

In a book published in 1995, *Signals From The Falklands*, Layard recounted what happened next. "Air Raid Warning Red – emergency stations, emergency stations.' I heard the broadcast on my way to the bridge and took the stairs three at a time as I pulled my lifejacket over my head...On the bridge we started to try to establish the extent of the damage and casualty list...A mere ten minutes later the aft Damage Control Party was being beaten back by fierce and spreading fires as the piles of stores and equipment between decks went up in flames." Layard informed the Task Force about the situation and two destroyers edged nearer. Only 20 minutes after being hit, "it was clear that our ship was doomed." The stores on board, including bombs and solid rocket fuel, could blow up at any minute and the whole upper deck had become too hot to stand on. North and Layard together decided to abandon ship. Efforts to retrieve some of the helicopters from the fire failed; eleven on board were lost. As a result, British troops were forced to 'yomp' (fast walk carrying a 100lb load) the 50 miles over boggy terrain from San Carlos to Port Stanley to recapture the Falklands.

Layard and North were the last men to drop into the icy sea, at which point they realised *Atlantic Conveyor* "might take us to the bottom with her" such was the force of the swell as the ship's rounded stern section rose and fell around them. After a couple of duckings, with Layard holding the bulky North up, both were still alive and trying to reach a nearby life raft. On a third swell, Layard went down for "what seemed like a lifetime" but eventually broke surface. North did not. When Layard was plucked from his life raft by the crew of the frigate *Alacrity* holding a dead body (not North's), he passed out. "When he did regain consciousness," wrote Woodward in 1992, "he could only see the bright orange glow of the burning Cunarder and he sat with his head in his hands and wept for his friend, Captain Ian North." Layard was to author the Citation for North's posthumous DSC. "When the ship was hit on 25th May Captain North was a tower of strength…He left the ship last, with enormous dignity and calm…A brilliant seaman, brave in war, immensely revered (he) loved his contribution to the campaign and epitomised the great spirit of the Merchant Service." Layard himself was awarded a CBE. He mourned Ian North 30 years after the conflict: "Many features (of the campaign) have stuck in my mind but two have left an indelible mark. Firstly, how brilliant the people were, in thought, strength of character and deed. Secondly, given willing hearts and when the need is imperative, there is no limit to what can be achieved. We astonished ourselves."

Jeremy Sanders (56–60) must be one of those surprised individuals. He was Staff Officer Operations to the commander of the 'Battle Group.' A communications specialist who had commanded his own frigate, he proved to have the right qualities – tact, persistence and a keen eye for detail – to work alongside the often-irascible Woodward. Accommodated in a small rabbit hutch of a space under the flight deck of HMS *Hermes*, he and his team of four received more than 500 signals a day in the pre-email era. They rained in 24/7 from multiple sources. It was Sanders job to decide which signals Woodward had to see, which should be assigned to appropriate other officers and which must be dealt with immediately. "The days were long starting at 0630 and ending 20 odd hours later," he has recalled. "One of my better decisions had been to keep the Task Force on GMT time." This meant that in *Hermes* it was simpler to liaise with Northwood and allow ample time to prepare for the Argentinian air force's regular early morning raids. Another of his decisions was to cut through red tape during HMS *Conqueror's* pursuit of the *Belgrano* to get the Rules of Engagement changed. "No matter how great the harassment factor, Jeremy would somehow handle it. Every couple of minutes of the day he dealt with sudden needs, obscure commands, implicit suggestions… translating my wishes into clear and precise written instruction…And his duties did not stop there…He was the man to check that the orders did indeed happen," Woodward wrote in his account of the war *One Hundred Days*.

Two OPs commanded RN ships of the Task Force – **Hugo White (53–57)** in the frigate HMS *Avenger* who was Captain of the 4th Frigate Squadron; and **Mike Harris (54–59)** in the guided missile destroyer HMS *Cardiff*. Harris's First Lieutenant in *Cardiff* was **Michael Johnson (59–63)**. Both ships were involved in